Need or Greed
OUR PRACTICAL CHOICES FOR THE EARTH

Need or Greed

OUR PRACTICAL CHOICES FOR THE EARTH

by

Judith Hoad

Newleaf

Newleaf
an imprint of
Gill & Macmillan Ltd
Goldenbridge
Dublin 8
with associated companies throughout the world
www.gillmacmillan.ie

© Judith Hoad 1999

0 7171 2596 3

Index compiled by Helen Litton
Print origination by
Carrigboy Typesetting Services, County Cork
Printed by ColourBooks Ltd, Dublin.

I dedicate this book to

three heroes of my lifetime,
Nelson Mandela
Mordechai Vanunu
Aung San Suu Kyi
in recognition and gratitude for their suffering,
for upholding honesty and the equal value of every
   human life
and as representatives of those many unknown
   people who have done, or who are prepared to
   do the same.

CONTENTS

The world has enough for everyone's need,
but not for everyone's greed.

Mahatma Gandhi

INTRODUCTION

When I was a little girl during the Second World War, I thought doctors, teachers, lawyers, bankers, businessmen and politicians got their jobs by virtue of excellence and because they were honest and thoughtful of the needs of others. I admit to a sheltered childhood, war, or no war. My father had broken the mould of his artisan family by taking an extra-mural degree in Social Science and had become a Probation Officer. Every morning, before he went to work, he played Bach, Scarlatti, Lizst and Chopin on his piano, even after its case was lacerated by imploding windows on the night of a London 'doodle-bug' raid. Jazz was called 'boop-a-doop' and not allowed in our house. I never heard it until I left home at the age of eighteen. I made up for lost time after that, although I also sang Handel, Bach, Kodaly, Lully and Verdi in a university choir.

Most of my parents' friends were, like them, Quakers among whom pacifism was a way of life. Forbidden to listen to the radio news, read comics, or adult newspapers, I knew the evils of war only by direct experience: air-raid warnings — the 'moaning minny' of the siren; nights spent in the air-raid shelter in our garden and days in those in the playing fields of my primary school.

Our teachers were all women, gentle, but strict. I was astonished by their claims that builders no longer knew the recipe for the hard concrete used by the Romans, or how the ancient people who once lived in what we now call Peru had raised large stones high in their houses and temples so skilfully that not even a sheet of paper can be inserted into the joints. I thought how careless artists had been to have lost the knowledge of how to make the blues of medieval glass or text illumination. I was an adult before I discovered that professional people, businessmen and politicians are as muddled and distorted by their birth and upbringing as the rest of us, but that their power and authority sometimes allow them to act out their problems on a larger platform than the rest of us. Loss of information, or skill, is often due to prejudice, or fashion among such people.

I had hopes of women, only to discover that to get to the top in their chosen career they had to use the same tactics and practices as the men, but even more toughly, in order to compete with men. But I was never really aware of feminism as something that impinged on me. I had grown up with no sense of being inferior because I was female. My mother taught me to knit and cook; my father took me to chamber music concerts, gave me books of poetry and discussed classical literature with me. I was an only child until I was six years old, when my brother was born. I did feel aggrieved that he was allowed the *Eagle* comic, while I was still permitted only the *Children's Newspaper*, but by then the rules that governed my infancy had been modified by my mother for her son — and I was both too old to be affected by the change and too young to realise there was one.

By the time I was thirty, when bra-burning became the rage, I hung onto mine, because I found it more comfortable than going without and I thought the basic justice of equal pay for equal work was so evident that the inequality would be done away with as soon as it was recognised. My husband and I treated one another as equals. We did different jobs about our home, but our mutual efforts achieved our mutual comfort and we shared the rearing of our children.

So I was a slow learner of the inequalities, injustices and irrationalities that constitute human society. I learned by determinedly speaking up when I found injustice, or inequality. One of these lessons occurred in 1970, when we joined an 'anti-nuke' group. The all-too-predictable problems of how the national Electricity Board was going to dispose of the mounting and dangerous nuclear waste accumulating at Windscale, Trawsfynydd and Yr Wylfa occupied us. We wouldn't allow them to bury it in 'our' Welsh mountains and we should prevent them from dumping any of it at sea. We went on marches wearing skull masks with which we inadvertently antagonised the workers and their families at a power station town. The real lesson lay with another group, too distant from our home for us to join, but near enough for us to have friends who were members. Someone, or several people, wiser than any of us, saw the negativity inherent in creating anti-anything, so the Newport and Nevern Energy Group began. It lasted longer than any other anti-nuke group, partly because it didn't say that that was what it was, but mainly because it taught coppicing and how to make logs out of used newspapers. Some members made a contract with the education authority and insulated the roofs of the primary schools in the area. Wind and water generation of electricity was demonstrated at the group's annual open days and many other positive ideas grew and developed. It was a tiny effort if one looked at the UK as a whole, but for those who lived in or near the area it was major and life-enhancing.

When Chernobyl blew, I felt an anger I'd never known before. My gut churned with rage against 'them' (whoever 'they' were), and with an impotent frustration that what had happened couldn't be reversed, or cleaned up for as long as it was possible to imagine into the future. I wrote a poem about it that still brings back that sensation whenever I read it.

Never before in the known history of mankind has so much changed so rapidly. Technology and its inventors have swept us along with the vision of 'progress'. Never before has so much damage been wrought to our environment in so short a time. Doomsday has hovered over the last three generations, my own, my children's and my grandchildren's, like a pall. In some parts of the world, 'development' has taken whole populations in less than a generation from a state of sufficiency and contentment to one of phrenetic anxiety about 'enough' and to compromised air, water and food. I shall explore a lot of these events and situations in the book.

I shall also look at other things, which I call 'New-day' events and situations that are anything but doomsday. For example, it is no longer possible for national governments to bamboozle their populations with propaganda about other nation states, because the same technology that has brought us international travel and the threat of annihilation has also brought us the telephone, the fax, Citizen's Band radio and the Internet, so people can contact others and tell their own stories at grass-roots level. The mass media, which brings us tales of death and devastation in newsprint and in news programmes that have become a spectator sport, also bring a view of communities in other parts of the world, thus giving us greater knowledge than we would have without it. In other words, some fairly amazing things are happening in our world — all over it, not just in the wealthy-wastrel West — and they are not by any means all doomsday.

I think it was in *Supernature* by Lyall Watson that I first read of the 'Hundredth Monkey Syndrome'. If I remember correctly, the example goes something like this. On an archipelago of islands, uninhabited by humans, live many types of wild life, including monkeys. The islands are too far apart for the monkeys to swim from one to another. On one island a monkey licks a banana and pulls at the stalk, which comes away with part of the skin. The monkey pulls at another part of the skin and peels the banana. No monkey has ever done this before. Soon, lots of monkeys have learned to do it. There comes a time when many monkeys on the island are peeling bananas on a daily basis and their numbers are increasing all the time, until a point is reached that has been defined as the 'Hundredth Monkey'. At this stage other monkeys on other islands start to peel bananas, apparently spontaneously.

This seems to me to be a meaningful allegory to explain many events in our known history and I am confident it can be applied to the major dilemmas of our own time. Once enough people start doing environmentally and socially acceptable and enhancing things on a daily basis, the Hundredth Monkey Syndrome will come into play and the route to Doom will be diverted. Our grandchildren's grandchildren may then inherit a world almost as beautiful and as peaceful as some of us can still remember existing before Hiroshima and Nagasaki, Bhopal and Chernobyl, Bosnia, Burundi and Northern Ireland and before the General Agreement on Tariffs and Trade (GATT). Perhaps this book will do something to bring us closer to that day. I hope so.

Part One

AIR

One

CREATING AN ATMOSPHERE

Is not the Sky the Father and the Earth a Mother?
And are not all living things with feet or wings or roots
their children?

Black Elk

M y private workplace is a room at the end of our house that I call my office. Next to it is an open barn where we store our winter fuel and beyond that stand two poles. On one is a radio aerial and on the other a small windvane that burrs and hums as the wind spins it. It provides an almost constant background sound to remind us of the fresh Atlantic air we're blessed with. Its purpose is to generate power for our radio-phone. Some years ago, when we applied for a telephone, the engineers decided we live too far from the road for the wires to be brought to us on poles and that the ground is too difficult for the wires to be laid underground, so we would have to have a radio-phone, plugged into the mains.

The engineers then found another set-back, for we have no mains! By choice we have lived in electricity-free houses, two in all, for the past thirty years. Hence the wind generator. It was only the second installation of its type in the Republic of Ireland at the time. We were therefore in the unusual position of being both at the forefront of technology while living in the simple way so many generations had lived in our traditional Irish house, before the mains were offered in 1953.

The Atlantic coast of Ireland is the western edge of Europe, a place whose character is slow to change. It is rural and sparsely populated. It has few industries, those that do exist are mostly recent and small (not 'heavy' industry) and, therefore, relatively non-pollutant. The prevailing winds are westerlies — fresh washed from the ocean, carrying the smells of the countryside, seasonal flowers and foliage, turf (peat) smoke from a neighbour's chimney, all of which we sense on this clean air we breathe.

Our air on the west coast of Ireland, is formed from a mixture of gasses, of which oxygen is the one most important to human life. These natural gases of earth's multi-layered atmosphere have always performed a dance of changing partners, up and down and in and out of its many layers. This happens on a global scale, a local scale and in each breathing creature. Carbon dioxide is exchanged for oxygen in the tiny alveoli that line the sacs of our lungs; it is the exhaust from the energy created by our bodies using the oxygen we breathe in and the food we eat.

Carbon dioxide and oxygen are the two most widely used gasses in our planet's atmosphere: all living creatures make use of one of these gasses. Animals, birds, insects, fish and reptiles, like us, extract oxygen from the air and expel carbon dioxide into it. The trees, grasses, shrubs, ferns and bushes all extract carbon dioxide and expel oxygen, thus maintaining a balance, so that the gaseous renewal is taking place *between* living creatures as well as *within* each living organism. At some time, the air we breathe in has been the breath of all other creatures on the planet. When you absorb yourself in considering this fundamental state of being, it is wondrously beautiful in its simple synchronicity.

Most of us never learn the basic information about the atmospheric envelope we live in and as oxygen and carbon dioxide are so important to our very survival, we would do well to know more about them. Before exploring the life-cycle of oxygen, some simple facts are useful:

- 'O' represents an oxygen atom, a basic element
- 'O_2' represents the compound made by two oxygen atoms combining to form a molecule of the gas we call 'oxygen'
- 'CO_2' represents a molecule of the gas, carbon dioxide, which is one atom of carbon attached to two atoms of oxygen

- 'H$_2$O' represents a molecule of water, which is two atoms of hydrogen attached to one of oxygen (we have to talk about water because oxygen passes some of its life-cycle as part of water).

The life-cycle of oxygen is an endless one, but, for the sake of argument, let's look at it from the point at which rain falls on a plain in a thunderstorm. The plain has little or no tree cover. Some of the water will seep into the earth, a lot of it will rush away into existing water courses, or those created during the storm, while the rest of it will evaporate back into the atmosphere. The enormous up-thrust of energy in such a storm carries the water vapour higher into the atmosphere than normal. (It is calculated that at any moment, 1800 thunderstorms are taking place around the surface of the earth.) There are two characteristics of water we need to know at this point: 1. of all fluids, water absorbs more heat than any other, but it does this very slowly and it retains it longest, because it releases it very slowly; 2. it is the presence of water vapour — the humidity of the air — that prevents the air near the surface of the earth from growing instantly cold at the setting of the sun. In the Sahara and similar large desert areas, where the ground is barren of plant life, the air is much drier than the oasis, where the plant life holds moisture. Night-time temperatures in such deserts can consequently be dramatically lower than the day-time temperature. The drop in temperature in the oasis, however, is far less, owing to the humidity.

The thickness of the atmosphere above the earth's surface varies from thinnest at the two poles to thickest at the equator. In general terms, its outer 'skin' is plus or minus 500 kilometres above our heads. Like an onion, within this skin, the atmosphere is composed of many layers. These have variable temperatures, different densities and a range of components, with a constant interchange going on within and between them. The outer skin is called the exosphere and gravity there is so weak that there is nothing to stop molecules without an electrical charge from slipping off into space, lost to the earth's atmosphere forever. This becomes important because of the rising water vapour that has evaporated from the surface of the earth.

In the innermost skin, from the surface of the earth up to between six and eight kilometres above it, water in the air is heated by infra-red rays from the sun, but remains unaffected by ultra-violet rays, which pass through it (resulting in sunburn even on a hazy or cloudy summer's day). However, from being heated, the water vapour becomes less dense, so as it rises, it is less affected by gravity but more affected by much stronger ultra-violet rays and gamma-rays than it was within the inner skin.

These two forces of radiation split the water molecule, at which point the two hydrogen atoms — lighter than oxygen — rise further, while the oxygen atom begins to fall back towards earth. The single oxygen atom is now exposed to more incoming ionising radiation (the same force that we refer to as 'radiation' when we discuss the hazards of exposure to uranium or plutonium). This radiation drives the single oxygen atom to combine with its close relation, the O_2 that our bodies recognise as the gas we breathe. Together these produce O_3, which is ozone.

Ozone forms a protective shield — one of the many layers of the atmosphere — that prevents the penetration of excess ultra-violet rays to the earth's surface. But there is no great gain without some small loss: ozone created this way costs the earth water that cannot be replaced, ever, owing to the escaping hydrogen.

Denuding forested areas is the essential background to what I have described, the Half Hydrological Cycle, as it is called by Callum Coats in his book, *Living Energies*. When rain falls on forests, however, it is trapped in the foliage, so its descent to earth is slowed and will not cease until some time after the shower or the storm is over. The roots of the trees, which absorb some of the water, also slow its movement both into the soil and over its surface. But, in the absence of trees, the water has no impediment and may fall too fast — or, if it falls as snow, thaw too fast — for the earth to absorb it. It will flow then toward ever lower channels, taking soil and soluble nutrients with it.

The deforestation of the Tibetan plateau by the Chinese represents a profound illustration of another disastrous aspect of the

Half Hydrological Cycle: in the highlands of Tibet are the sources and headwaters of all the major rivers of Asia. With the removal of hundreds of square miles of forest, these rivers, formerly rising and falling seasonally in a predictable and controllable way, now prove to be an annual dangerous flood hazard, due to the speed with which rainfall and thaw now flow, without the trees to slow them.

In the past twenty years, we have become accustomed to news reports of deaths and devastation, crops swept away and homes destroyed by flooding in the Ganges river valley and delta, the river valleys of Nepal and Bangladesh and the Yangtse in China itself. No doubt 'lesser' devastation takes place along other rivers; their size is all that prevents them from reaching international news headlines. For the individuals whose lives or livelihoods are destroyed, however, the loss is total, regardless of who knows it.

The Full Hydrological Cycle, therefore, takes place where the rainfall drops onto trees where they grow as forests and the net loss of hydrogen either doesn't happen or is less critical. Trees draw groundwater to the surface as well as slowing rainfall as it sinks. Without tree cover, the rainfall can only follow the groundwater as it sinks down, until it is below the reach even of the deepest rooted trees and will never rise again. There is, therefore, not only loss in the upper atmosphere of water the earth needs to live, but also into the earth itself; both are due to the drastic deforestation that has taken place in recent decades — and continues to take place — not only in Tibet, but in the Amazon Basin of South America and in Indonesia, Canada, Australia as well as elsewhere on a lesser scale. So, we could be breathing oxygenated air from an ever-diminishing layer, rather like a goldfish living in a pond that is evaporating, until only a trickle of water is left at the bottom, leaving the fish floundering and starved of accessible oxygen.

Just as we exhale water vapour with every breath, so trees 'exhale' water too, by a process called transpiration. In rain forests mature trees are estimated to transpire up to 600 litres of water every day. If such transpired water were to fall like rain entirely beneath the tree's canopy of leaves, every square metre of ground underneath the tree would receive twelve millilitres of water each day. Trees that grow in semi-arid areas transpire rather less, but a fourteen-metre eucalypt transpires 375 litres daily.

In 1977, the Australian Forestry Report revealed, to that date, an annual harvest of 9,212,667 trees. A précis of Callum Coats' calculations in his discussion of the water lost to the atmosphere by trees that have been felled is as follows. If the felling rate had remained constant for twenty-two years, not counting any replanting — because the discussion involves mature trees — the overall loss could be assessed as that of a lake of water, 1,000 kilometres long, 13.9 kilometres wide and one metre deep.

This loss of transpired water from trees that have been felled causes desertification. The increase in desertification and the loss of atmospheric oxygen are preventable. Indiscriminate deforestation could be stopped immediately and the planned planting of millions of tree seeds and saplings begun at once to replace the mature trees already lost. This has already begun in Kenya, where women have formed co-operatives dedicated to planting trees in their members' villages.

Professor Wangari Maathai is a Kenyan academic who taught anatomy in Nairobi university and whose abiding concern is environmentalism. The National Council of Women asked her to lead them in an effort to reduce poverty in Kenya. She saw environmental degradation as the cause of the problem and tree planting as the single activity that solved most facets of that problem. As trees grow, they provide increasing shade and moisture retention; as they become mature enough to be harvested, they provide food and firewood.

By 1994, Professor Maathai's initiative, that had developed during the previous twenty years into Kenya's Green Belt Movement, resulted in over 15 million trees being planted. The fee paid for every tree that survived has helped this women's movement to provide an income for even the poorest among the tree growers. Professor Maathai has said, 'The most important tool that we have given to the people is the knowledge of how to collect seeds, plant them and nurture the trees.' In many parts of Kenya, the Green Belt Movement's tree planting has reversed the present or imminent desertification resulting from inappropriate land use — monoculture cash crops demanding the use of expensive chemicals and machinery — so that now the trees are retaining both soil and moisture.

Professor Maathai's qualities that have made her an articulate activist have cost her her marriage — her husband of ten years was granted a divorce on the grounds that she was 'too educated, too strong, too successful, too stubborn and too hard to control' — and the opprobrium of Kenya's President Moi. In 1992, she maintained that the President was frustrating the development of the country toward democracy, after which she endured a year of police harassment that included both hospitalisation and imprisonment for herself and other women as they demonstrated peacefully against government policy. Yet the Green Belt Movement continues as one of the growing number of similar initiatives to resist desertification and to restore a better quality of life.

However, globally, movements such as Green Belt are not yet planting as fast as mature trees are being felled, nor are they making any marked impression on the increase in carbon dioxide in the atmosphere. The latter occurs due to the volume of fuels burned by motor vehicles, electricity generating stations and heating in buildings. In addition, carbon dioxide is being produced faster than ozone is being created. Carbon dioxide is one of the principal gasses implicated in the destruction of that all-important protective shield, the ozone layer in the upper atmosphere. Along with other gasses, it pits and finally creates holes in the ozone layer, through which damaging amounts of ultra-violet rays can penetrate to the earth's surface. The increasing incidence of melanoma, a rapid-growing skin cancer, in many parts of the world, is a painful reminder that people have to do something at once to prevent it getting worse. Another gas involved is methane, which makes another connection between ozone depletion and deforestation. The extensive and rapid deforestation in South America has been to create grazing for beef cattle. The fashion of eating beefburgers, led and encouraged by a few multinational companies, has led to a huge increase in the world population of beef cattle. An area of grass the size of an average kitchen floor has been calculated to be needed for every beefburger eaten. A fart from a ruminant — beef cattle are among the larger ruminants — is mostly methane. The combined farts of the world population of beef cattle have made a definable increase in the amount of methane rising into the upper atmosphere.

Methane has other qualities, apart from those that damage the ozone layer. It can be burned to provide heat and power. The processes that take place in the bovine gut can be mimicked chemically and continued on the muck those same bovines excrete. The *Journal of Anaerobic Digestion and Associated Technology* is called *Methene Gen;* it covers the use of methane and other waste materials as fuel for power and heat. The burning of methane also results in more carbon dioxide.

As I write, a gale is blowing from the south west. It is conceivable that some of the air I am breathing at this moment was once exhaled by a methane-farting cow grazing on clear-felled land that until recently was ancient rain forest in Colombia, or Brazil, or some other part of South America, while the oxygen I need may have come from the vestiges of the forests on the same continent. Trees have been described as the lungs of the planet and their use of carbon dioxide and their 'exhalation' of oxygen show how fitting this description is. Trees are far more than lungs, however: they are home, food and shelter to a myriad other species in their branches, trunks and roots; they provide shade and moisture to creatures living below them as well as maintaining the soil that feeds them.

By the same token, it is impossible to talk about air without including water, trees and the multiplicity of life forms, including human, that influence and are influenced by air. With trees as the focus, a slogan of the *Chipko* movement in the Himalayas of North India emphasises this by asking a question and answering it in the same slogan, 'What are the benefits of the forest: soil, water, pure air, the essence of life.'

Chipko is a Hindi word that means 'tree-hugger' and has been used by another women's movement which had the inspiration to use tree-hugging as a way of protecting the forests from being felled. Like most natural forests — as distinct from the slave-tree forests planted by people in arbitrary rows — the forests of the Himalayas include a self-seeding selection of trees traditionally cherished by the indigenous population. The pattern following colonialisation in the Himalayas was the pattern that followed colonialisation on every continent: landscapes cherished by the indigenous inhabitants were exploited by the colonisers for the natural resources that grew there. The colonists on all continents in the last 500 years have been European and Christian. From Sunderial Bahuguna, a forest protection activist in Bhageerathi Valley of North India to Malidoma Patrice Somé, the African philosopher, indigenous people are voicing their conviction that the combination of science and technology, informed by the Christian teaching that humanity has mastery over all of Nature, is responsible for the destruction of their environments (and, I would add, of the environments of the peoples descended from the colonists). Forests, waterways, agricultural practices, cultural and community values have been either exploited, debased, polluted or ignored as meaningless by the colonists.

In the Himalayas, where women embrace trees, according to religious, folk and oral tradition, the forests have always been protected by 'rings of love' as an anonymous writer has described it. As in other cultures, hilltops were dedicated to one or more deities and on these forested hilltops in North India, the trees were treated with great respect.

Many varieties of trees from virgin forest have been harvested for their beauty and their durability over the last two centuries, but predominantly in the second half of the twentieth century. Most of these are hardwood trees, ebony, mahogany, or cedar. Their close grain takes a glowing polish showing a range of beautiful colours when they are worked. Hardwoods take a long time to grow. A hardwood could grow to a mere sapling in the twenty years it would take the average softwood to mature to a size suitable for cutting into planks for floors. Paradoxically, hard-woods are often transported thousands of miles to be used for furniture making, from countries where people's houses are *not* furnished with many tables, chairs, bedsteads, clothes closets, bookshelves, desks or stair banisters. Whole forests of these trees have been clear felled as cash crop, with no thought of retaining younger trees to grow on.

When Jan Alexander came to live in Ireland in the late 1970s, she was surprised to find that the island had only four per cent forestation, the lowest in Europe. She was also very distressed by the amount of timber that Ireland imported. Her concern resulted in her founding *Crann*, Irish for 'tree', an organisation dedicated to planting deciduous native trees, reviving coppice skills and tree nurture. On land donated through lease to Crann, by Lord Longford, she and her co-workers began a tree nursery. The group's public relations, combined with genuine success in the projects it had undertaken, brought official recognition and invitations to participate in forestry planning for the whole of Ireland in partnership with government agencies. No-one pretends that Crann's tree-friendly policy has permeated all forest work in Ireland, but it has caused a significant change in attitude toward further public education about forestry, associated skills and appropriate uses for timber.

Softwoods grow relatively quickly and are used for paper making, as roofing frames, or floorboards, or for pallets. For these two reasons they are being planted under government-funded schemes in several European countries, quite often in relatively good agricultural land. Generous grant schemes, paid out annually for several years, are the incentive to farmers to surrender their land to this use. And it is surrender, because, once the land has been planted, the deep drainage channels that are cut between the rows of saplings ensure that the land cannot be restored for grazing or arable use. This scheme is proving a non-contested way to clear the land of small farmers, long a bane to government.

Using softwoods, hardwoods, or combinations in mixed plant-ings, several groups are at work overthrowing accepted ideological and political paradigms. In the Earthstewards Network publicity literature, the organisation claims that their 'underlying strength is our global community of caring members'. This group combines tree planting with the growth of acquaintanceship and love among people who would normally never have a chance to mingle. For example, since 1990, American groups which have included Jews have gone to the Palestinian areas of Israel to plant trees and to enjoy the hospitality of their Palestinian host families. In 1996, members of Peacetrees, as this initiative is called, went on phase one of a series of visits to Qyang Tri Province in Vietnam to clear, with expert guidance, the landmines that still litter the land and cripple the population when one is accidentally triggered. Phase two will be a visit to plant trees where the landmines once lay, in order to re-create the forests that existed before the Vietnam War.

All the projects undertaken by Earthstewards are primarily concerned with communication and understanding where it has not previously existed or has been difficult: between men and women, between Jew and Moslem, between different Christian denominations, as in Northern Ireland; between people of different coloured skins and cultural backgrounds. As each tiny island of communication is created, so the ocean of hatred and misunderstanding is diminished. People who have the primary experience of communicating with the previously unknowable, return home and spread their news to others, thus extending an archipelago of islands and evaporating more of the ocean of hatred and misunderstanding.

It may be a surprise, but Ireland is the country of least afforestation in Europe. Irish people customarily go abroad to work for charities or voluntary service NGOs (non-governmental organisations), but in Ireland itself there are lesser known initiatives that don't have secretariats, or offices, or even much publicity. One of these is the Tree Walk, which for the years 1996 and 1997, spent the four tree-planting months of February to May walking and camping around the country with the sole intention of planting trees. The group consisted of predominantly young people of several nationalities, including Irish. Six formed the main core, with other people joining for various lengths of time. The Tree Walk was the inspiration of John Crossan, whom I first met

in 1993 when he was supervising the recording of the twelve
conference speakers at the Earth Wisdom Camp in Co.
Roscommon. Having felt unwell one day, John went to lie down
beneath some trees where he realised that, if he needed help, he
could call out to passersby, but that trees can't do this. As the idea
of the Tree Walk grew, he explored tree nurseries for the availability of native species of oak, ash, birch and hazel and the cost
of saplings. From 1993 to 1995, with the help of friends, he
collected over $1/4$ of a million used aluminium drinks cans, the
sale of which for recycling raised £300. John used this money to
buy saplings from Future Forests, a small, independent tree
nursery in Co. Cork and to buy basic foods for the core group.
Several busking sessions in Dublin raised more money and kept
the resources flowing into the second year's Walk. Using a couple
of horse-drawn wagons and also pushing hand-carts and a bicycle,
the group set off in 1996 from Galway and in 1997 from Cork.

With no prior publicity, no training in community relations, no
one to give them guidance in the group dynamic and only one,
Dublin-based friend to phone in emergencies, their bonding was
their passionate desire to plant trees around Ireland. Their clothing
was the warmest and most waterproof they could find. Boots or
wellingtons were a basic necessity and some of them wore their
hair in dreadlocks. Understandably, many of the people they met
assumed that they were undesirables about to settle into a
parasitic ghetto in their neighbourhood. The Tree Walkers had to
learn to state their intentions clearly and immediately on any first
encounter. They made a point of visiting schools at every opportunity on the focalising, sun-wise spiral route north and east that
ended, in 1997, in the Slieve Bloom mountains of Co. Offaly.

In the many classrooms where they were welcomed, they
explained to the children that they were selling nothing, but they
thought that Ireland needed more trees and that they were happy
to plant them for anyone who would promise to look after them.
After a few questions, they would play an impromptu concert on,
mainly, instruments they had made for themselves. Popular among
these was Gareth's didgeridoo that he played in 1997, after

spending the previous winter making it from a fallen oak branch he found on the first Tree Walk.

The walkers planted trees in school yards, housing estates, town squares, parks and in private gardens. They played music in pubs as well as schools, so having played to the children during the day, they often found themselves playing to the parents in the evenings. They visited homes for the elderly and the handicapped and wherever they went, they made friends amongst whom was discovered a mutual demystification of their respective ways of living, as well as a common bonding around the trees that were planted.

It is hard to resist calling the Tree Walk a 'grass-roots' organisation and equally hard not to make comparisons with other events that have an apparently strong experiential element. One is the Esso National Tree Week, almost a quarter of a century in being, that is organised in the UK by the Tree Council to encourage good management and care of trees and woodlands. But there the comparison ends. Esso undoubtedly use a tree-oriented project to give an acceptable face to their main operation, the sourcing, extracting, processing and marketing of pollutant fossil fuels. There is also no doubt that their tree project provides employment to environmentalists, foresters and others, as well as information and experiences for the general public. But, for me, the totality of self-funding, self-commitment and spontaneity that is the Tree Walk, small scale as it is when compared with the Esso venture, has an integrity about it that Esso's never will.

Kevin Hayes is the key man who provided contact, ferry services and emergency cover for the Tree Walkers. He was an initiator and is now a trustee of the Earth Wisdom Foundation that grew out of the Earth Wisdom Camp of 1993. The Foundation's express intention is to 'present information and knowledge of beneficial technologies, discoveries, traditions and beliefs not generally available in our culture, to as wide an audience as possible'. It is not surprising that Kevin also initiated a group called Round Table, out of which has grown the Guerrilla Gardeners who have moved into sites around Dublin which are decayed and derelict. With the co-operation of Dublin Corporation, who supply machines with drivers, when they are available, the Guerrilla Gardeners have cleared rubbish from these mostly small sites, delivered top soil and planted shrubs and flowers. Their friendliness and their commitment have brought forth donations of more plants and cuttings from local residents who often leave them anonymously overnight.

A sub-group has grown out of this activity, alert for any developments where existing gardens or woodland are at risk of destruction. When any is found, in go the Guerrillas to rescue and recycle whatever is growing. A man with access to city maps and records has calculated that there are 168 acres of derelict land between Dublin's Grand Canal and the Royal Canal — years of work for Guerrilla Gardeners! Like the Tree Walkers, these gardeners work for love, not money and their spontaneous activity and beautifying handiwork is calling forth more of the same from residents who are the first beneficiaries — and their work is not being vandalised.

Science has shown us how the gasses that form the air interact with plant life, animal life and the distribution of water over the surface of the planet. Technology has shown us alternative energy sources from those it formerly found for us, which science has shown are destroying our environment. It is taking ordinary men and women from many parts of the world to show us how to find time and energy to rescue and revitalise our environment with love. They recognise the interaction between all things that live on Mother Earth, often with the same spirituality that the Christian colonists denigrated and swept aside in their God-given, greedy rush to exploit what they had taken by force. For more millennia than we know, the balance of nature and human respect allowed enough for all creatures. In mere centuries, a lack of respect has resulted in an imbalance that may prove, literally, breathtaking, unless more of us engage in local ventures to restore the balance and the respect, as the women of Kenya, the Chipko activists, Crann, the Tree Walkers and the Guerrilla Gardeners have done and are doing.

Two

A HAZE IN THE AIR

Your friend is your needs answered.
He is your field which you sow with love
and reap with thanksgiving.
And he is your board and your fireside.
For you come to him with your hunger
and you seek him for peace.

Kahlil Gibran

———————

Some years ago, I travelled from my home in Donegal to Dublin, a journey of four and a half hours, using the national bus company. In those days the anti-smoking lobby had effected a small, inefficient, but socially significant change: the back of the buses had seats for non-smokers, while smokers retained the right to be so in the front part of the bus. Although I had been a non-smoker for many years, I sat in the smokers' section because I had to alight quickly for the connection I needed to make when we would arrive in Dublin.

After the halfway mark in Cavan town, I found myself choking in smoke pouring over my face from above. When I looked up, I realised the person in the seat behind mine was holding a lighted cigarette on the top of my seat back. I turned round and asked the man, politely, to move his hand, because smoke was both blinding me and choking me. My request was met with verbal abuse and the command to move to the back of the bus if I didn't like the smoke. I remained silent for a few minutes before — as nothing changed — turning again to the man and, using a quiet, but distinct tone, I asked him, 'Shall I tell you how

I feel when you hold your hand over my head so that the smoke from your cigarette chokes me?'

'I don't care how you feel,' he said, helpfully.

'Well,' I replied, 'I'll tell you anyway. I feel' — and I said this deliberately and distinctly — 'I feel as you would feel if I pissed on you.' The effect was shock, horror and disgust and changed not a wit of the man's behaviour, but a woman, who had lit up on the other side of the aisle during this altercation, quietly extinguished her cigarette.

Maybe my melodrama contributed to the eventual decision to ban smoking altogether from Irish buses — I like to hope so.

Sooner or later people have always had to stand up and demand change when they experienced suffering, or perceived injustice. Populations have rioted against food shortages, more specifically, groups such as the Luddites organised themselves to take action against a particular perceived injustice, in their case, the introduction of mechanised forms of weaving machine. The industrialisation which caused the Luddites to organise brought many situations in its wake that gave factory workers problems. Workers organised themselves into trades unions in an attempt to solve these problems. Strikes are not like riots and personal injury is a less probable result. There is a wealth of areas to explore in the history of human protest, but this is not the place to go into detail. However, even a cursory examination of history shows that riots, ancient or modern, are usually put down either by police or the military arm of government. The Luddites took action in destroying the power looms they saw as threatening their livelihoods. They were tried, convicted and severely punished. But, in a way, they could be said to be the precursors of the trades union movement in which workers have not only organised but funded themselves, set up secretariats and achieved improvements for workers by negotiation. Trades unionists' successes in achieving changes to benefit fellow workers could be regarded as the precursor to the protest groups of the last quarter of the twentieth century.

There are today more aids to organisation than in earlier times. There is a communications system that affords enormous amounts of information for and about protest and pressure groups. Telephones, fax machines, Citizen's Band Radio and the Internet are outside the constraints of government censorship and, on the whole, of the propaganda machines of governments. No longer is a slow evolution of techniques for protest necessary, for there is a fund of ideas and encouragement to tap.

Non-violent direct action, such as the tree squats at Twyford Down, or Oxleas Woods in England, or the Glen of the Downs in Ireland, or the underground squat on the site of the extension to Manchester Airport, have the merit of aiming at the only place where the political, industrial and commercial bullies are really vulnerable: their profits. Protesters have become competent at creating barriers in the form of temporary homes and connecting paths or tunnels that become expensive for the developers to remove. The longer the delay to the project, the more damaged is the budget for it. There is still the risk of physical injury, but the protesters of today are imaginative and willing to communicate in the hope that those against whom they protest may eventually understand the reason and change their ways.

Living conditions in many of the countries where protests take place are far more complex than they were prior to the Industrial Revolution, although people live with the same range of needs: shelter, warmth, food, a means to attain these things and human relationships. It is the enormous range of choices that industrial- isation has brought that has created difficulties. A new sort of propaganda, no longer the solely political one, but the propaganda of sales advertising, is now used to manipulate our choices by creating a constantly renewed hunger for 'improvements' to our lives. There has probably been no time in history when people have had such large shelters, such varied and luxuriant artefacts with which to adorn them — or clothes and ornaments with which to adorn themselves — nor so many efficient ways to heat them, nor such amounts and varieties of food as exist today in the industrially developed countries. But the advertising propaganda that is designed to titillate the appetite for more is also vulnerable to protest; renamed 'subvertisement', an example is a parody on the advertisement for Marlborough cigarettes in which one mounted man turns in his saddle to speak to his mounted companion and the caption reads, 'Tom, I've got emphysema.'

The nomadic cultures of which we are aware, those of Africa, North and South America and Australia had few personal possessions and mostly impermanent shelters. Anyone who was likely to up sticks and move every few months would naturally not encumber themselves with property. But the feudal cultures of Europe were settled communities. The overlord's dwelling was built, furnished and maintained by members of the general population. It was out of this culture that industrialisation emerged, but paradoxically, it is members of the Europeanised and industrialised cultures of the world who are among the most articulate in recognising and protesting the price this development has cost and continues to cost in exponential increments that have nothing to do with finance.

Protesting that you do not wish to share a space with smokers because of the health risks has won the day in public transport and in public places in many parts of the world. It represents an enormous change in attitude, because it shows that we are at last cherishing the health of others, whether we smoke or not.

Of all the recognised physical addictions, smoking is the one which non-smokers are obliged to share. But humanity has other addictions that are not so readily accepted as such. I call these the 'gimme' addictions. They are fed by the advertiser/pusher who creates desire and envy out of which is born acquisitiveness. It is the desire for heated homes and buildings, for powered gadgetry, for out-of-season and exotic foods and other goods, for holidays in distant places and a motor car that is causing the damage. Like the physical addictions of smoking, some of these addictions also have physical effects which are being visited on all life on Earth.

Science long ago discovered the power that can be harnessed from burning combustible materials. It took technology longer to invent a huge variety of artefacts that could be motivated by that power. The explosive energy created by fire is the energy that motivates the turbines that provide the electricity for the gadgetry around the home, the office, the factory, the public buildings.

Some twenty-five years ago, my husband and I met a woman who learned in conversation that we lived in a house without electricity,

'But it's essential!' she exclaimed.

'No, it isn't,' Jerry said. 'We manage very well without it.'

'But it's essential,' she repeated.

'How can it be when all the generations of your ancestors managed without it?'

I suppose gadgets such as automatic doors, vacuum cleaners, computers, hedge trimmers, photocopiers, kettles, conveyor belts, cash registers, escalators, traffic lights and x-ray machines would all come under the heading of 'essential' to this unimaginative woman. Twenty-five years later we are still refining our electricity-free lifestyle and find it very comfortable.

The electricity that motivates the gadgets is derived from burning coal, peat, oil, wastes or uranium rods. That charter flight to Barbados, or Bangkok, Bali or Budapest, gets there by burning oil and the car you wear does the same. I claim that people 'wear' their cars because the car has become like a fashion accessory that many drivers cast off at regular intervals, not because the car has ceased to function as a mode of transport, but because a 'new and improved model' has been shaped to take its place.

Explosive power is dirty. When it is used to make electricity, it is also very wasteful. The source material is changed forever into ash, gasses and heat. Only about a third of this released energy is converted into electricity. The remaining two thirds of the heat and all the gasses ascend into the atmosphere. Planes, trucks, vans, cars and motor bikes are similarly wasteful, releasing enormous amounts of gasses, water vapour and elements such as sulphur and lead into the atmosphere. Some of this effluent falls quickly to the ground, where it poisons plants and other creatures. Condensation trails from aircraft create cloud and haze. Power stations, factories and house chimneys do the same. The gasses emitted, along with those from other sources, such as methane, have earned the group name 'greenhouse gasses', because they are heating the earth's atmosphere in much the same way as a nurseryman heats his greenhouse. But we don't have riots about such issues. The results are not so pressingly evident to most people as the haze in a room full of smokers, although they are potentially just as dangerous. No doubt that was one of the reasons why it took a long succession of scientific and ecological press releases and a considerable amount of lobbying before governments began to take notice.

In 1992, the first international conference on climate change was held in Rio de Janeiro. In fact, the conference was two conferences. At the official one, politicians and leaders of a number of governments made speeches in which they said they recognised the problems and announced their good intentions to change the situation, while at the same time being guarded and non-specific, as they bore in mind their symbiotic relationship with commerce and industry. No-one among these speakers was really prepared to grasp the nettle. At the other, unofficial conference, the so-called 'fringe' of non-government organisation, it was different. The speakers from the NGOs had no need to placate commerce and industry. They could talk freely about what had resulted from the indiscriminate use of explosive power, what was predicted to happen if it continued and also about what changes could be made and what was predicted to happen if the changes came about. The unofficial conference also drafted treaties about topics and for communities neither of which previously had ever been considered by governments. It was like a People's Union of Nations.

Both conferences were brave and new, but the result was a timid acknowledgement by the official conference of a need for change with no treaties drafted or entered into by governments, while the treaties drafted by the NGOs merely constitute an historical souvenir of peoples' hopes. Media reports on the speeches spanned the globe. Chats between delegates to both aspects of the conference brought together people who would not otherwise have met. These contacts are another, subtler way to spread information that spans the globe. I remember a tangible sense that, disappointing as the official outcome seemed on the surface, somehow we were all ready to move forward to a cleansing of humanity's dirty habits.

Such movement as resulted has been slow, with now only a very small proportion of all electricity being generated by wind or solar power. There has been much talk of the financial cost of making changes, but precious little talk of the real, non-financial costs of not making changes — at least by those in a position to make changes. And the spin doctors have advised playing down the effects the greenhouse gasses are having on the global climate. When the second conference on global climate change took place in Kyoto in December 1997, it ended with little sense of hope or movement, despite the formulation of a treaty. The terms of the treaty were scarcely significant and the loopholes through which governments could squeeze to abdicate their responsibilities were numerous. Even if, as the spin doctors suggest, the warming of the global climate is as a result of a natural, cyclic swing from warm to cold and back to warm again, what is being burned around the globe has, by its very volume, to be a factor.

Planning for transport has been the primary preoccupation for urban planners for the past half century. In the UK, two men were out in front in the early stages of this planning focus. One was Beeching, who axed all the railways that didn't run to ferry ports, thereby depriving much of the population of cheap and reliable passenger and freight services. This action gave government funds a huge boost with the increase in taxes from heavy goods vehicles and buses as well as the tax on the fuels they use. The other was Buchanan, whose preoccupation with the circulation of traffic was directly responsible for the destruction of many beautiful and hitherto functional town and city centres throughout Britain.

Planners stopped seeing towns as organic, integrated places for human occupation, where the people who lived in them could do so with ease and comfort and on a human scale. Instead, they have tried — and succeeded in an unfortunately large number of instances — to create a series of linked 'theme parks'. A residential theme park, houses; an industrial theme park, places to work; a commercial theme park, shops; a play theme park, sports areas. And they gave these places emotive, posh-sounding names, like industrial estates, housing complexes, shopping malls, sports arenas, or leisure centres. Many districts at the edges of large cities are referred to as 'dormitory' areas, showing at once that the inhabitants have to travel so far to work, to shop or to play, that the only time they can spend in their homes is the time they need to sleep! These are not *homes*, they are hutches for performing humans to be popped into when they are not wanted. And most of this travelling from one theme park to another is done by car, creating traffic effluent.

Some traffic authorities, recognising that the production of motor cars has far outstripped the speed with which city roads can be altered to make space for them, have found ingenious ways to limit the numbers of cars on city streets. In San Francisco, for example, a toll is charged on drivers entering the city limits without a person occupying every seat in the vehicle. Even limited traffic clogs city centres at speeds slower than in the days of horse-drawn vehicles, which has led to the introduction of park-and-ride schemes in some towns.

Some governments are investing in major inner city transport schemes that include surface or underground railways. Attention is also beginning to be given to the need for transport that is free of effluent and cyclists are at last being taken seriously. In this area, it appears that NGOs and local groups are achieving far more through knowledge of local needs than most traffic authorities seem willing to, or capable of. Sustrans in the UK, for example has researched and mapped a nationwide series of routes for cyclists. For the leisure cyclist they cover holiday routes through scenic areas, but an important aspect of their work is the establishment of cycle routes in cities where cycle paths are free of motorised traffic. They also research, establish and map traffic-free footpaths in towns and cities for commuters, shoppers and school students. They publish and sell a number of handbooks and offer some free information sheets, among which is one designed for disabled people, to explain how they can access the cyclists' network.

The Women's Environmental Network (WEN) has also brought traffic and pollution problems to the fore in the UK. In clear language, their campaign notes explain the connection between the transportation of food, traffic emissions and the increase in respiratory disorders such as asthma. They point out that the Trans-European Network, TENS, is planned by the EU to enable the free flow of goods throughout Europe. The 140 road schemes entailed to complete the system has been estimated by WEN to lead to an increase of 128 million tonnes of carbon dioxide entering the atmosphere by 2010. WEN also makes the connection between the purchasing practices of supermarket chains and the traffic effluent emissions of the food transporters. Standardised foods with long shelf lives (chemically reared and preserved by chemicals or by irradiation) required by the EU's Common Agricultural Policy are bought in bulk by the supermarkets from large-scale producers — usually using chemical-dependent monoculture techniques — from all over Europe. This is at the expense of fresh, possibly organically grown, more varied local produce which has not been carried vast distances to a central distribution point, before arriving at an individual retail outlet.

This problem is severe, given that approximately one quarter of all transport in the UK is food related and tonnes of foodstuffs are exported while the same commodities are also imported.

WEN also points out why the out-of-town hypermarket is a planners' mistake: all shoppers need motorised transport to get there and back. The many small, local shops that were put out of business by the ability of supermarkets to buy in bulk at reduced cost, were far more appropriate for daily shopping in quantities that were portable on foot or bicycle. In the suggestions list for individual action, WEN encourages the establishment of new branches of WEN; joining Local Agenda 21 groups, which concentrate on sustainable futures relevant to local conditions and needs; and walking or cycling for short journeys. They also advocate joining Freewheelers, a nationwide, lift-sharing organisation and using local public transport whenever possible.

Only through the chosen actions of NGOs and individuals can progress be made to reduce vehicle emissions because the petrochemical industry and car manufacturers continue to practise protectionism. More than twenty years ago I read of the invention of a car engine that ran on hydrogen and emitted water vapour as its exhaust: its patent was bought up by an oil company and suppressed. Recently, I read of an Australian who had invented a car that ran on air and had no dangerous emissions. The work of other experimenters, including an eighteen-year-old girl motor cyclist, have also come to light. She worked on a hydrogen-powered car in USA, was denied a patent when she applied and forbidden to manufacture the engine she had developed.

Because of these restrictions enthusiasts for non-pollutant transport have taken another route. Instead of manufacturing the engines they have invented, they have made available plans which show how any petrol or diesel-engined car can be adapted to run on hydrogen. Currently such a conversion has been estimated to cost £1000–£2000 per car. The more people who do this and let others know how it can be done, the less resistance the petro-chemical and car manufacturing industries will be able to exert and the sooner beneficial change will come about.

In some countries, the symbiotic relationship between government, commerce and industry is more overt than in others. In those countries, vehicle emissions are far less important to the inhabitants than more serious environmental degradation all around them and the persecution suffered by any who dare to complain. This has been the situation in the Ogoniland region of the Niger delta for nearly forty years. The relationship which brings this about is between a totalitarian, military regime, the government of Nigeria and Shell, the multi-national petro-chemical company.

Shell discovered oil on the Ogoni plain in 1958. Ogoniland, like most delta lands, is agriculturally rich and the Ogoni people had an enviable lifestyle with plentiful food. Strangely, mineral rights almost always take precedence over farming rights and this is what happened in Ogoniland. Oil extraction upset farming in many ways. Oil pipelines were erected to take the shortest route between the point of extraction and the point of storage. Brackets carrying the pipes were installed about eighteen inches above the ground over anybody's land. The gas discovered along with oil deposits is often burned off on site. The flame is large and burns twenty-four hours a day for months, sometimes years, on end. The heat is intense, so there is no question of crops surviving for a considerable distance radiating from it. It was not uncommon in the 1950s, 60s and 70s for white engineers to regard black women farmers as inferior and to ignore them.

While that attitude may or may not prevail in the 1990s, Shell came to depend more and more on the military government to deal with protests as they arose. As the depredations grew, so did the organisation of the protesters. Shell ignored them, the government oppressed them. It was not in the government's interest to allow any interference with Shell's production, because eighty per cent of the Nigerian government's income is from the royalties paid by Shell for the oil it extracts. The royalties are paid in Lagos, not in Ogoniland. The Ogoni people receive neither royalties, nor compensation — not even a fair hearing for their legitimate complaints about the oil company's methods.

Instead, the national government's soldiers harass them, arrest them, destroy their homes, hold special tribunals, not recognised by law and against whose decisions there is no appeal and execute them after finding them guilty of trumped up charges. This is what happened to the peaceful protest leader, poet and visionary, Ken Saro Wiwa and eight other Ogoni protesters who were summarily executed after such a tribunal, despite appeals from governments around the world. They died on 10 November 1995 by hanging. Their families have not been allowed to take their bodies home for burial. The authorities have disposed of the bodies and refuse to say where or how.

Many other Ogoni have been killed, either by state-directed murder, or as a result of violent harassment and many others are herded into jails such as Port Harcourt Prison in the Rivers State of Nigeria. Amnesty International has tried to bring pressure on the Nigerian government to safeguard these people from torture and other ill-treatment and to guarantee that they are fed properly and receive medical treatment, but to no avail.

During the mid-1990s, documentary films were shown in Britain and in Ireland on national television, highlighting the activities of

Shell and the effects on the Ogoni and their land, after nearly two generations of increasing environmental degradation and persecution. Ogoni Solidarity Ireland is one group that works full time to encourage Irish people to boycott Shell products and to inform Shell employees and Shell franchise holders, such as petrol filling stations, why they are doing so.

Shell is not alone among oil companies in its mal-treatment of the inhabitants of land where they extract oil, but it is one of the largest with a very poor history of relationships in the localities where it works. If enough of us choose not to use Shell products and say why, eventually Shell will have to take action to put right the terrible wrongs they have perpetrated. How can any of us tolerate the inhuman way in which the Ogoni people and their land have been treated and continue to be treated, simply so that we can have oil?

It is very easy to shrug off what Shell is doing in what may be, to us, an obscure part of Nigeria. But while it is not, at the moment, in our own back yard, it is in theirs and as more parts of the planet are affected by apparently far-away activities, it is rapidly becoming clear that Ogoniland *is* our backyard. What has happened there since 1958 could start to happen within sight of our own front doors tomorrow. The truth is that it need happen in no-one's backyard, because petroleum is unnecessary. There are other, far less pollutant ways to make products equivalent to those derived from petroleum. The real problem is the wealth that it and its by-products generate for the handful of controlling corporations involved. Perhaps an attempt to convert the directors of these corporations would have results more positively far reaching than we expect? If, as individuals, we wrote to the ministers for Foreign Affairs, for the Environment, for Trade and Industry in our own governments and also to the United Nations Commission for Human Rights, to express our concern about what continues to take place in Ogoniland and, perhaps, our sense of vulnerability that something similar might some time affect ourselves, the shower of letters would start that process of conversion. Our needs, fears, wishes, only become known when we express them and, when enough of us express them, changes begin.

Three

INVISIBLE DANGERS

*Behold, My Brothers, the Spring has come; the Earth
has received the embraces of the Sun and we
shall soon see the results of that love!
Every seed is awakened and so has all animal life.
It is through this mysterious power that we too have
our being and we therefore yield to our neighbours,
even our animal neighbours, the same right
as ourselves, to inhabit this land.*

Sitting Bull

If you shut your eyes and concentrate on your childhood, what is the most evocative sense that comes to you? Many people find it to be the sense of smell. The first thing a child does when it picks up its favourite comforter is to smell it. My comforter was a scrap of silk cloth that I used to rub between finger and thumb. Gentleness was the key to keeping a rolly crease moving and to sense the abrasion of one surface across the other as it moved. Always, the smell of silk makes me, involuntarily, want to reach out to 'phmeer' it — my name for my childhood habit — and for the comforter itself.

What about Germolene? Or Dettol, or sawdust, or certain sorts of woodsmoke, or lavender water, or . . . ? We can all make our own list. This important sense, the sense of smell, plays a part in the liturgy of all the world's great religions. The First People of Turtle Island, North America, use smouldering desert sage smoke in a purification ceremony; Christian churches (not the Protestant, non-conformist ones, though, who virtually deny the bodily senses altogether) use frankincense smoke to purify the mind and instil a sense of reverence; Hindu and Buddhist temples are redolent with incense for the same reason. In every instance this practice is to do with cleansing and purification, as though the residual scent leaves no space for negativity or grossness of any kind. All the ingredients for incense are natural — saps, gums, leaves, barks, flowers and fruit, bound together by dried cattle dung.

As we breathe in, the air and whatever particles are suspended in it passes over a complex of nerve endings in the nostrils, the olfactory nerve sensors that translate the particles to register in our brains as smells. Activating our sense of smell is an involuntary result of breathing. Centuries ago everything humanity smelled came from a natural source. Modern humanity's nostrils, however, are assailed by many scents, few of which are of natural origin. An ancestor, smelling incense, the smoke of a campfire, or the scent of a predatory animal, would register the odour and act upon it, if necessary. There would have been no debilitating side-effects from the act of breathing. Today, most of the odours we come across derive from inorganic sources, such as exhaust fumes from vehicles, the result of burning a fossil fuel. Other odours, also derived from unnatural sources, have the disarming prefix 'organo', which simply means that a particular element has been bonded to an organic radical. The resulting compound is, however, of unnatural origin. Particles from some of these substances, when they are inhaled, are having seriously debilitating effects on an increasing number of susceptible people.

In the early winter of 1996, I answered the phone to a man who told me, 'My wife has multiple allergies, she's even allergic to perfumes. Can you help her?'

I suggested that she appeared to be experiencing Multiple Chemical Sensitivity (MCS).

'What's that?' he asked.

One whiff of exhaust fumes, petrol, diesel, paraffin, most deodorants, aftershave lotions, scented washing-powders — or the clothes bearing that scent — scented disinfectants, floor washes, washing-up liquids, pressed paper trees advertised as 'air fresheners', hair spray, fly spray, other insecticides, herbicides, fungicides, household paints (which often include fungicide), pot-pourri and many cosmetic perfumes start a painful series of sensations in the woman's nose. The throat and tongue rapidly become exceptionally dry, the bridge of the nose tight, creating within a matter of seconds of registering the smell a headache that can last from many hours to several days.

All the substances to which this woman was allergic are the air-borne particles from compounds the base of which is petro-chemical. In identifying her disorder, I broke a frustrating chain of fourteen years' experience with orthodox medical practitioners, all of which ended with either — the kindest — 'I can find nothing to treat,' to 'It's all in your mind, I'll send you to a psychiatrist'.

In 1985, when she was studying medicine, Cindy Duering's apartment was treated for a flea infestation with a routinely used pesticide. Cindy's body reacted as though severely poisoned and she quickly developed an extreme form of asthma, peripheral nerve damage and an inability, induced by the pesticide poisoning, to metabolise porphyrin. Porphyrin is a synthetic, aromatic com-pound, containing methylene and derived from coal-tar and other fossilised substances. This inability causes seizures even at low exposure to many chemicals, including synthetic perfumes.

Although she was forced to give up her medical studies owing to this irreversible illness, Cindy, now living in a sealed and filtered house in North Dakota which she can never leave, founded the Environmental Research Network (EARN) in 1986. In 1994, EARN merged with Chemical Injury Information Network (CIIN) which has 5000 members in thirty-two countries. Since 1986, Cindy has researched and written about many aspects of the causes, experi-ences of and alleviation of Multiple Chemical Sensitivity. She has become a world authority on the subject and her address can be obtained from the Right Livelihood Award Foundation.

When the Industrial Revolution began, no-one intended that harm should come from any aspect of scientific or technological development. Only during the last fifty years or so has there grown increasing doubts about the benefits to be derived from using some of the inventions to which science and technology have given us access. Fifty years ago, penicillin was regarded as a 'magic bullet' that could kill all undesirable bacteria. An allergic reaction to this wonder drug was not recognised, but for the last ten years or so, all patients on admission to hospital are asked if they have an allergy not only to penicillin, but to any other substance, medicinal or otherwise.

Medication administered by a doctor is for an individual and a record of its use is usually available afterwards. Vehicle exhaust, on the other hand, is so ubiquitous that no-one can trace a specific source. Petro-chemicals have been developed as by-products of the vehicle fuel industry to the point where there is hardly any area of life from which they are absent, as can be seen from the list of substances that affected the woman who consulted me.

Scientific study has explored the components of our diet. Phosphorus is a non-metallic element available in most foods, and the recommended daily allowance is 800 milligrammes for the average adult, half as much again for a pregnant woman. This element is important for the development and maintenance of all body tissue and a deficiency can result in physical weakness, with aches and pains — including bone pains — in neurological and respiratory disorders; the same range of problems encountered by someone experiencing organo-phosphate poisoning, a major contributor to MCS.

Organo compounds are used in many thousands of varied products. The only way for a susceptible person to avoid inhaling the particles from any of them is to stay in a clean-air environment from which such things are excluded. How is it possible to do this? Imagine being denied a ride in a car, dry-cleaned clothes, scented washing powder, deodorant, pot-pourri and the host of other implicated products, not only for yourself, but for everyone with whom you come into contact. It's a depressing prospect for susceptible people.

From the absence of harmful intention at the outset of scientific and technological development, a time arrived when effects such as MCS were being at best ignored, at worst suppressed. In the UK, following an article that appeared in July 1988 in the *Independent* newspaper concerning three people who were compensated, after suffering from adverse reactions to using pesticides, a group was formed called PEGS: Pesticide Exposure Group of Sufferers. The acronym was to give a hint to enquirers that here was something to hang on to in often very distressing circumstances. The four-fold aims of this group are to give counselling to those affected, collate information about the incidences and effects of exposure, record symptoms and treatment and spread awareness that 'whilst in a perfect world chemicals might be used safely, in real life incidents do happen and there can be dire results'. In Ireland, PAIN — Pesticide Action and Information Network — has been founded with the same purpose. People whose first allergic reaction has been to pesticides often find that their sensitivity then extends to a multitude of other products and that any exposure can result in hospitalisation. Some elected officials in PAIN, themselves affected by organophosphates, were driven to resign by anonymous threats to themselves and their families. The threats are thought to have come from people with a vested interest in not allowing public revelations to appear about the adverse effects of pesticides.

An intricate and complex problem becomes evident here. Not everyone is susceptible to the same substances. Failure to recognise allergic reaction to medically prescribed penicillin fifty years ago is being repeated now with failure to recognise allergic reactions to a wide range of substances far more difficult to identify. Doctors have no precedents for recognising allergic phenomena, especially when they are atypical. Only the size of the problem and the courageous demands by organisations such as PEGS and PAIN have convinced a small number of medical experts that a real problem exists. Palliative treatment — and little more is possible, because of the constant likelihood of further exposure — is all that can be offered, but a change by manufacturers from harmful to benign formulae is a matter of urgency. It is with the manufacturers that the nub of the problem lies. At one level we, the buying public, have expectations that we can travel in any vehicle, wash our clothes, disinfect lavatories, perfume our bodies and our boudoirs, delouse our pets and more, with no threat to our health. At another level, the structure of the companies that manufacture the harmful products makes change extraordinarily difficult. We are not even dealing with companies that are owned, funded and sell within any one country's borders; they are the few and enormous multinational petro-chemical companies. The complexities of manufacture and sale of organo-compound by-products from petroleum to subsidiary companies would daunt the most competent economist. Therefore, the impregnation with toxic substances of our atmosphere and the air we breathe becomes an issue of the moral culpability of many businesses, the primary manufacturers and also their subsidiaries. Their record to date for protecting vulnerable sections of the world community is, to say the least, abysmal.

In the 1980s, a very small number of medical people in the UK and USA recognised that a problem existed. Their field of research came to be known as clinical ecology. As non-conformist practitioners, many of whom succeeded in alleviating symptoms, they were vulnerable not only to favourable newspaper and media reporting, but adverse reporting and comment as well, when some of them were maligned for unsubstantiated reasons. Most of these practitioners kept on working, although some were forced to move, or temporarily to close down their treatment centres until the pressure was lifted. Sadly, this sometimes had the effect of denying therapies to needy patients.

Vitamin and mineral supplements figured high among the remedies clinical ecologists discovered to be helpful in treating the multitude of allergic reactions to common products. Germanium is a rare metal but it is found in abundance in garlic, ginseng, comfrey, aloe vera, chlorella and pot barley. The benefits to be derived from germanium are broad, but it is especially valued for its enhancement of the immune system, when it is given as a food supplement, usually in tablet form. A book by Sandra Goodman, *Germanium; the Health and Life Enhancer*, was published in

1988. The timing was unfortunate for the author and for others who had been involved in the research and promotion of this rare metal as a possible remedy for people with AIDS or HIV. This was because the pharmaceutical company, Wellcome, were at the same time introducing a chemical compound known as AZT for the same disorders. Wellcome had an arrangement with the British National Health Service (NHS) to do clinical trials on AIDS and HIV sufferers using the hospital facilities and the government-paid doctors of the NHS to perform the leg work. Books such as Sandra Goodman's, research papers, sales promotions for probiotics (lactic acid milk derivatives), or germanium as immunity enhancing food supplements (such as that by Monica Bryant's firm, Symbiogenesis) represented an unwelcome alternative to AZT. This was especially the case given that the sources of germanium are natural and products derived from it inexpensive (and, at that time, readily available). AZT had been withdrawn from the treatment of cancer patients in the 1960s because of its toxicity and serious side-effects, but Wellcome brought pressure to bear on the British government to ban the use of germanium and have products made from it withdrawn from sale in preference to the use of AZT for HIV and AIDS patients.

Pharmaceutical companies are multinational, like the petro-chemical companies with which they have close ties. Wellcome is one of the largest. Martin J. Walker, in researching his book, *Dirty Medicine*, explored numerous company records — all of which are readily available to public scrutiny — to learn the names and affiliations of the members of a range of government committees and commissions associated with Wellcome and the AZT programme, from which that company earned millions of pounds. About these bodies and each of the members Walker asked these questions:

- What are the individuals' areas of expertise?
- Did they go to university? If so, who taught them?
- If they did scholarly research, e.g. for a PhD, where did their funding come from?

- On the boards of what companies do they serve?
- If they are employed, who pays their salaries?
- Who are their spouses, live-in partners, closest friends? (Apply the same questions to them.)

The discoveries Walker made of the interconnectedness between bodies set up by government (presumably to foster the interests of the public) and Wellcome and its subsidiaries were many and frequent. The advice given to government by these bodies was exclusively in the interests of the pharmaceutical company. Is it any wonder that there has grown a commonly held belief that politicians are furthering their own ends and that Big Business is intent on ripping us off?

Another example is the nuclear power industry. As far as I know, no-one can smell radioactive fall-out, but when the reactor burned out at Chernobyl in April 1986, the radioactive particles that arose from the fire went air-borne around the globe. Like exhaust fumes, radioactivity is ubiquitous, but unlike exhaust fumes, none of our senses can detect it. However, our bodily systems can. The numerous official denials that clusters of childhood leukaemias or thyroid cancers at areas of high exposure to radioactive emissions or fall-out, such as at Chernobyl or Windscale/Sellafield, cut no ice with most people. Commonsense tells us that these illnesses are only to be expected in such places and the fact that they occur more frequently in these places is only confirmation that industrial and military radioactivity is dangerous.

It is common knowledge, from many media sources, that the population around Chernobyl has lost not only its homes, but access to all the land in the area which is now too radioactive to be used safely to grow food. If that were not tragedy enough, children have been born dead or deformed and many who survive birth are unhealthy and very likely to become part of the high numbers of cancer patients — and may not reach maturity. Despite this, there are still people who claim that nuclear power for electricity generation is 'clean'. That it is very unclean can be shown in a variety of other ways.

First, the plant at Windscale/Sellafield was established to reprocess spent fuel rods from nuclear powered electricity generating stations. The product from reprocessing is bomb-quality plutonium, in demand throughout the world for making nuclear bombs. As few places in the world have been set up to produce such a commodity, Windscale/Sellafield is, therefore, the UK's most important industrial site to the British government.

Secondly, the by-product from reprocessing at Windscale/Sellafield is a waste, most of which will remain radioactive for thousands of years. Even so-called low-grade radioactive waste will remain dangerous for tens or hundreds of years and satisfactory ways of storing it have not yet been found. Furthermore, how many generations of humanity will it take to monitor all this waste until it can be deemed safe? The irresponsibility toward future generations is incomprehensible.

The same irresponsibility is being shown to present generations as a result of EU legislation passed in the autumn of 1997. The EU announced that it would permit, without licence and therefore without record, the use of some of this 'low-grade' waste in the production of household goods, notably plastics, glass and metals. This surely carries recycling a Bequerel too far.

Thirdly, on 11 July 1985, the Greenpeace ship, *Rainbow Warrior* was anchored in Auckland Harbour, New Zealand before completing its intended journey to blockade the French nuclear-bomb test site on Mururoa Atoll in French Polynesia. On board was the Portuguese photographer, Fernando Pereira. The French government, who had already refused to respond to appeals from people who live on islands likely to be affected by the explosion of a 'test' bomb, sent agents to blow up the *Rainbow Warrior*. Pereira, there because he was concerned about the environmental pollution such a nuclear test would cause, was killed. If these activities were not carried out by government decree or with government approval, they would be termed acts of terrorism. Terrorism is unclean.

Fourthly, local fishermen tell us that diseased and deformed fish are netted daily in the Irish Sea — a stretch of ocean recognised worldwide as the most radioactive. Twenty years ago, a man used to bring a van carrying fish from the small fishing port of New Quay, on the Cardigan shore of the Irish Sea, to Lampeter, the market town where we did our shopping. He used to call his wares, and my children were convinced that what he was shouting was 'nuclear mackerel'. We never bought fish from the Irish Sea from him or anyone else. The radioactive pollution that prevented us from doing so could equally prevent others from buying Louth lamb or Cumbrian cattle.

Ireland is a declared nuclear-free country. This only means that the anti-nuclear lobby was strong enough to prevent a nuclear-powered electricity generating station from being built in Carnsore Point. Being 'nuclear-free' doesn't make Ireland, or anywhere else on the planet inviolable to radioactive pollution. This is recognised by Constance Short, Mary Kavanagh, Mark Dearey and Ollan Herr, who reside in the Dundalk area of Co. Louth, the Irish county whose shores face those on the other side of the Irish Sea where Windscale/Sellafield stands.

These four people came together in March 1994 to contest the addition of the THORP plant to facilities at this site, as it represents such a direct health hazard to the population of Co. Louth. The Dundalk residents and their neighbours can be equated to the residents of Kiev. The only difference is that a major accident took place at nearby Chernobyl and, so far, relatively less serious accidents have taken place at Windscale/Sellafield. A major accident at Windscale/Sellafield would, like that at Chernobyl, affect all life on the planet to a greater or lesser degree. The people of Co. Louth, however, like the people of Cumbria, are those living nearest and therefore in the greatest potential danger. The 'lesser' accidents at Windscale/Sellafield are, in any case, cumulative in their effect.

In October 1996, the Dundalk group was granted permission by the High Court in Dublin to take a case against British Nuclear Fuels Ltd (BNLF), who operate all aspects of the processing at Windscale/Sellafield and also a case against the British government. A few months later, in a general election campaign, Fianna Fáil — then the main opposition party — published the statement:

'In government, Fianna Fáil will ensure that the case taken by the Dundalk residents is fully funded.'

In November 1997, Fianna Fáil, by then in government, reneged on this promise, offering instead an ex-gratia payment of £200,000 toward the cost of the action, an offer the residents have refused. The four are prepared to mortgage their homes in support of their intention to prove BNFL and the British government culpable in allowing this hazardous industry to continue. It is improbable that the mortgages raised will realise much more than the sum turned down and, although local fund-raising is going well, the four will need far more than £200,000 if they are to follow their legal challenge right through. If they lose the case, they also expect to lose their homes. I admire them for their courageous independence. Those of us who care that radioactive fallout is already causing genetic and health damage to livestock, fish and people, would do well to support this and similar campaigns.

One day in 1986, Adi Roche was in the Cork office of the *Campaign for Nuclear Disarmament* (CND), when a fax came through. 'For God's sake, help us to help the children.' It was signed by a group of doctors in Chernobyl. That was the cue for Adi to commit her life to helping those children and their families. She takes medicines and clothing to Ukraine and brings large groups of children from the Ukraine each year to spend a month with Irish families. Each such stay in our relatively unpolluted atmosphere is reckoned to add two years to their lives. Adi has had to comfort distressed parents and relatives of the children as well as stand up to obstructive officials, but she continues to follow a life of single-minded independence, dedicated to her work. The public are more likely to listen to observations and statements from Adi, or the Dundalk residents, than we are to scientific disclaimers — no-one would commit so much to a cause that has no foundation. Such people are an example to us all. When enough of us commit ourselves, changes will take place: Chernobyl and Windscale/Sellafield will close.

On the Shannon estuary is Aughinish, the site of an Alumina factory, where one million tonnes of bauxite is converted into aluminium metal every year. In addition, there are two conventional electricity generating stations — Moneypoint and Tarbert — a pharmaceutical factory (once run by Syntex, but now run by Roche), the Wyeth baby-food factory, Koala smokeless fuel factory and Southern Chemical, where polystyrene is made. All in close proximity to one another and on one or the other shore of the Shannon estuary, these factories sprout, like mushrooms, in agricultural land — *good* agricultural land.

In May 1994, owing to several years of serious animal health problems in the area, a public meeting was called in Askeaton. Attended by about seventy people, the problems described included infertility, spontaneous abortions, calves born with impaired breathing who died shortly after birth and stunting and deaths among adult animals. Liam Somers was the farmer whose experiences at that time appeared to have been the most severe, but another man had found a white deposit covering about one third of the area of a fifteen-acre field to which he attributed the start of his animals' ill-health. Others spoke of choking being experienced when a vapour, often invisible, would drift across their land.

At the end of this meeting the Askeaton/Ballysteen Animal Health Committee was formed from members of the local community. The committee started with two objectives: to support affected farmers and to try to identify the source of the problems. Members met with local politicians, the Minister for Agriculture, Food and Forestry, Ivan Yates; the Irish Farmers' Association; Teagasc (Government Agricultural Advisory Board); the Health Board; and Mr Somers at a meeting called by the Environmental Protection Agency (EPA). As a result, a major investigation was launched. However, despite a further twenty-five farms where unusual animal health problems had developed being brought to the attention of the Department of Agriculture, Food and Forestry, several things happened that appear questionable.

The department bought a badly affected farm, which coincidentally was adjacent to the Wyeth baby food factory, where 500 people were employed. The department also leased Mr Somer's farm, employing him as farm manager. The committee felt seriously constrained by the need to avoid too much publicity, which would have affected sales of agricultural produce from the area.

Although sulphur dioxide appears to be the biggest single emission in the area — half of this coming from a natural source, the Shannon estuary itself — the EPA does not appear to have identified what else to look for. In their study of sulphur dioxide, it was the natural and not the *un*natural source on which they concentrated. A forestry inspector's report on tree damage in the area being caused by aerial pollution was ignored by the authorities. Findings by a team of scientists from University College, Galway, that small rodents in the area had liver enzyme abnormalities was also dismissed.

The committee continued to press for a closer look at cattle livers, and accidentally discovered that livers taken for testing had not been frozen soon enough after slaughter for the tests to be made. At one stage, locals believe, it looked as though the Department of Agriculture was waiting for the EPA to tell them what to look for in animal tissues, while the EPA seemed to be waiting for the department to tell them what to monitor in the air.

The committee bought an air monitor and identified caustic soda, chlorine, fluoride and oxalic acid, sometimes in very localised, short-term emissions, but their reports were discounted by the Department of the Environment. Perhaps this was because the EPA had failed to find similar emissions. In May 1997, the committee withdrew its co-operation from the investigation because the Minister for the Environment refused to meet them. His Department had also failed to address any of the serious deficiencies identified by the committee and their advisors in the investigation to date. Similarly, because they felt the EPA had not dealt with the committee's complaints on behalf of local farmers, the committee also withdrew from an oral hearing about an integrated pollution control licence applied for by Aughinish Alumina. But farming families who have had severe animal losses over recent years continue to make first-time contact with the committee.

While the committee feels it has met with obstruction and a lack of integrity on the part of the authorities, they rightly claim that it is because of their efforts that local industries have been forced to spend about £20 million on controls to reduce emissions since the problem surfaced. Since these controls have been introduced, animal health has, coincidentally, improved markedly.

It is evident that some improvements have occurred in the treatment of disease resulting from air-borne pollutants as well as reductions in industrial emissions as a direct result of pressure brought to bear by interested groups. Much more remains to change. Expectations of uncritical acceptance of the benefits of science and technology have to be reviewed. Scientists and technologists have to examine the directions of their research and development with a greater social consciousness. Manufacturers, distributors and salespeople have to ensure that their accounting systems include not only profit and loss, but social and environmental concerns as well.

Companies making and selling organic cosmetics, not tested on animals, represent an example of a change to benign production. But we also have to look at the *need* for cosmetics. Why do women paint their faces, dye their hair or colour their finger nails? What are they hiding from? Why do they perceive a need for change in their appearance? Do we *need* perfumed deodorant or any of the many other products derived from the petro-chemical industry? If vehicles were made that didn't use fossil fuels, there would be no profitable by-production of such things.

Several countries are now making electricity from renewable, non-pollutant sources. Can we not press for faster development in this direction — and examine our use of electricity as well?

Are we not mature enough to try selling our arguments without killing one another? It is time our governments realised that nuclear weapons are obsolete and that they should dismantle those that are left.

PEGS, PAIN, the Askeaton/Ballysteen Animal Health Committee, Adi Roche and the Dundalk Four are just some of the groups created by sufferers and their sympathisers who are prepared to lobby for change. These and other similar pressure groups are the force that will succeed. At the end of the day, it is us, the people, who have control.

Four

SOUND AND MUSIC

*It is said that in the old days all the important songs were
composed in dreams. A song usually came to a man in
his dream; he sang this song in times of danger or
necessity. Songs composed in this manner were used
on the warpath, in the practice of medicine and
in any serious undertaking of life.*

Ojibwe belief

In the womb, the sound that is ever present from the moment
of conception is the beating of the mother's heart. As though
in response to that sound, but before the embryo has a hearing
mechanism and before its own heart starts to beat, the four limb
buds begin to pulsate, like a dancer responding to the beat of a
drum. This rhythmic response to a rhythmic stimulus is just a
beginning. We spend the rest of our lives producing rhythms in
response to stimuli which are also rhythmic. The stimuli and our
responses can become very many, very complex and very subtle.

Of our five senses, smell, taste and touch require particles of
substances to stimulate them. Sight and hearing, however, are
stimulated by wavelengths and frequencies that come to us
through the air. Sound, light, x-rays, radio waves and so on are
all part of a quantifiable series of frequencies on a waveband.
Each is rhythmic and is detectable by electronic gauges, when the
frequency is beyond the human gauges of ear or eye. We have
another gauge in our brain which emits electronic impulses in
response to stimuli. These impulses can be detected by a tool
called an electroencephalograph, or EEG.

There are four basic patterns that can be detected as responses to stimuli and they have been named after letters of the Greek alphabet. *Delta* is the pattern discernible when a person is in deep sleep. Here the range of the brain's electrical activity repeats itself from one half to four times every second. *Theta* is the pattern when a person is awake, but relaxed and not thinking about anything — a state of being without doing — when the brain's electrical activity repeats itself from four to seven times per second. *Alpha* is the rhythmic repetition of the brain's electrical activity that has been stimulated by the mind being creatively occupied, but at ease, when the rhythm of repetitions is between eight and thirteen times every second. *Beta* is the pattern when the mind is in overdrive. The pattern of repetitions ranges from thirteen to twenty-five times each second and occurs when there is energetic activity involving varying challenges from conversation to agitation.

A meditator can reduce the brain's rhythm to Alpha, just by the (non) activity of meditation. One of the simplest ways to achieve this is to close or half-close the eyes, at least to the point where they are not focused on anything (some meditation teachers feel that by closing the eyes it is easier to fall asleep than to meditate), and to watch the breath. Count each cycle of inhalation and exhalation up to ten times, then start again at one. If, at any stage, the mind wanders off and then recognises that it has done so and stopped counting, counting should recommence at one. The rhythm of the breathing pattern in the absence of conscious thought induces a rhythmic response in the electrical impulses of the brain. Without any knowledge of electronics, it is still possible to detect changes in our mental state. The meditator who meditates on a regular basis, will know that the state of mental and physical relaxation experienced during meditation will give benefit throughout the day. However, without any tools to give us any feedback on the brain's frequencies, our reactions to stimuli are largely unconscious, but nonetheless predictable. For example, being in the Beta state for prolonged periods creates undue stress in both mind and body. Sound, especially rhythmic sound that does not synchronise with body rhythms, can do this.

What is sound and how does it differ from noise? I define sound as coming from some natural phenomenon, such as the wind, the ocean, birdsong, or the human voice. Also, whether natural, or not, I define it as the result of deliberate action, the playing of music, or the performance of some job, like sawing wood. Noise, on the other hand, I define as coming from some unnatural source, from a random activity or machinery — even the rhythmic action of a pile-driver to me comes under the heading 'noise' rather than 'sound'.

There is a point too, where aesthetics, such as in musical taste, can cause a difference of opinion: what is sound to one person may constitute noise to another. And noise, rather than sound, is the word applicable to loudness, or high decibel output. Sound comes within the normal range of perception. Noise challenges the hearing by its excess, even when it is music.

There is something inherently harmonious about sound and something inherently cacophonous about noise. I remember attending a wedding reception where, after the meal, while the band was setting up, a group of eight or ten little children were happily playing together on the dance floor. The band suddenly began to play with full amplification. The noise terrified the children, who ran, screaming and disorientated, their brains doubt-less producing Beta rhythms! While trying to calm the children, several mothers remonstrated with the musicians, asking them to reduce the volume. Eventually they prevailed and the children recovered.

There are, in the spiral part of the ear, tiny filaments like fine hairs which are called the organ of Corti; their function is to convert sound waves into the electrical signals carried by nerves into the brain. Also situated in the ear is the mechanism of balance. Studies have shown that two things can occur after a prolonged period of time spent close to the source of a high-volume sound, such as being in the bell loft of a church while the bells are being rung, or staying in a room where very loudly amplified music is being played. As a short-term effect, balance can be impaired and long-term, the filaments in the organ of Corti can be partially or entirely destroyed, resulting in complete or partial, permanent hearing loss in some people.

In addictions such as smoking, or coffee, tea or alcohol drinking, or any other addictions, the brain responds to the stimulus of the 'fix' — the cigarette, the drink, the injection — by going into a high state that feels comfortable. When the stimulus ceases to have effect the brain goes into a low state that can induce symptoms such as depression, ill-humour or agitation, indicating that the stimulus has to be reapplied.

It is generally recognised that addictions are damaging. What is not generally recognised is that humans have become addicted to persistent noise. This is revealed when we only notice a 'background noise' when it stops. This addiction is fostered and fed in many public buildings by the habit of playing music in banks, hotels, doctors' and dentists' waiting rooms and in shops. Supermarket managers manipulate us, after employing psychologists to research the subconscious responses people generally have to different types of music. It appears to be the rhythm, rather than the melody to which we respond. In simple terms, we move along briskly to a march — a helpful feature when the shop is packed — but we slow down to blues and waltzes, at which time we are more likely to pick up the random items, not on the shopping list, that will increase the bill at the check-out. I suppose this could be regarded as a fairly harmless subterfuge on the part of supermarket management, but it remains a manipulation of our responses for someone else's gain and could be used in more sinister ways.

Of course, there are times when we seek out the message of the music, or occasions when it leaps spontaneously into our lives. On a sunny spring day, I was sitting among twenty-two other people in a friend's house in Tunisia. Our ages ranged from about three years old to late fifties and we were all female except for a little boy of about five, who had arrived with his mother and the small drum she'd bought for him at the town festival earlier in the day. A girl in her twenties reached for the drum and, tucking it under her arm as she sat cross-legged on a couch, began to play.

It soon became apparent that her hands were too big to coax the sounds she wanted from the miniature instrument, so another girl ran out to the kitchen and returned with a square, five-litre plastic bottle. The mood was set and while the girl stroked and battered the bottle, making spirals and cascades of rhythms and cross-rhythms, women got up in ones and twos, tied their scarves around their hips and danced those tantalising, bum-wiggling, toe-stroking, hand-turning dances peculiar to North Africa. For the next hour, small groups or single experts got up to dance as others, exhausted and laughing, gave up and sat down again to watch . . . all to an improvised rhythm that induced a seductive sense of pleasure.

Downhill on the further side of the little town, different, male dancing was going on in the plaza outside the mosque, but there was nothing impromptu about this. An elderly black man played a reed pipe among a group of other men beating on big drums while, among the dancers, one or two others fired ancient blunderbusses into the air at intervals. Here the pace was frenetic and loud, raising a fanatic energy for some ancient rite that their forefathers had spliced onto Islam when it arrived and which they still perform at this festival each year.

How different from the gaiety and sinuousness of the women dancing in the house! The rhythms here generated individual agitation almost to the point of stupor. The evocative use of drums to establish harsh beats, out of synchronisation with natural, bodily rhythms is a feature of modern 'popular' music. It is a beat designed to take over the mind, like the music that influenced the men at the African festival. This rhythm, however, is not truly musical in itself and initially might not appeal so much to its audience were it not for the inclusion of other instruments and the voice with some form of melody.

The beat owes a huge amount to ancient, shamanic drumming. Shamans are able to change their own state of consciousness, and sometimes that of other people, by using drums or rattles to create specific rhythms, which modern science tells us alters the timing of the repeated electronic impulses that the brain emits.

Traditionally, for as far back as history can inform us, it has been the role of the shamans in indigenous communities to use their skills beneficially in family and community rituals, in initiation rites for the young, in processes to create recovery in sick people and in divination. Drumming is also a feature of military life, ancient and modern and here the intention is anything but beneficial — for the enemy, that is. The combination of drumming and feet marching in unison is intended to engender a sense of aggressive invincibility in the warriors.

I witnessed a shamanic divination by the Oracle of Lhasa in 1995. The Oracle is a lay woman. She was, like me, at a place of pilgrimage. She'd come to listen to the Dalai Lama teaching in South India. She wore the neat, floor-length *chuba* (a wrap-around, sleeveless dress) over a blouse and the striped aprons typical of the traditionally dressed woman of Lhasa. She looked like a twinkly-eyed grandma. But as she donned her robes, tunic, boots, cape, crown and ring, she began to change. Her breathing rhythm altered to become loud and laboured.

Once she was robed, her assistants seated her in front of a table bearing two metal goblets, one full of water, one of milk. Then she began, with the big thumb-ring she had put on, to beat a large, ornamental metal plate suspended over her solar plexus from a cord around her neck. The air in the temple was full of incense to cleanse us, the supplicants and observers. The flagged floor seemed charged with some electrifying vibration where I stood in bare feet. The sound of the simple percussion was augmented by the Oracle's breathing. Once she began to answer questions from supplicants, she spoke in a high-pitched, rapid voice, punctuated by single, shrill, bird-like cries, until after some minutes, she fell back in her chair unconscious and we were ushered quickly away while her attendants removed her ritual regalia as fast as they could.

Mica Pogacnic is a professional violinist whose playing induces a different state of consciousness from that induced by shamanic or military drumming. He is highly skilled, playing concerts around the world, but is little known outside these audiences, because he refuses to allow recordings of himself playing. No single piece of music ever sounds *exactly* the same each time it is played and, knowing this, Mica demands the attention of a live audience in response to his live playing.

Mica may be unique among concert performers for this prejudice, but his stance draws attention to the public regard for music — or our lack of it. Do we actually listen to the musak in the bank, the hotel, the supermarket, or are we content to be subliminally manipulated while wrapped in aerial vibrations? When someone turns the music off, how soon do we notice and what is the response?

Mica thinks music has a purpose that is purely personal. The music fills the air between the performer and the listener, to create a chosen link between them. Listening to and performing music is a special event, a celebration, fulfilling a special human need. It requires our full attention, whether we are simply listening to it, or following the flow of the sound as we dance to it, or sing to it, or whether we are responding to a shamanic urging. Music, like the visual arts of painting and sculpture, is transcultural, a common language for all of humankind. It is a language whose first dialect was drumming and whose syntax is based on that first repeated, rhythmic sound any of us heard, the beating of our mother's heart as we grew inside her.

Music accompanies all our celebrations, public, formal or personal, at parties, festivals, weddings, funerals. Our youngest daughter and her husband spent several of their early years together living in a mobile home, long since rendered immobile by its age and fragility. After an interminable wait on the council housing list, during which their family had grown to three children, they were awarded a brand new council house. When Miffy was a tiny girl, she sang melodies for months before she began to speak, so I suppose it was natural for her that on the day they moved their scant possessions into their new home, she opened the case of her guitar, sat on the floor with boxes and bags around her and filled the air of the empty house with song, long, loud and lustily, out of sheer joy.

Miffy's singing was a personal response to a personal event, but we also respond to events that do not involve us personally. I am always incredulous at the arguments brought forward about violence on television and the denials that it has any effect on people. Surely, if television advertising had no effect, it would not be a part of the budgeting of multinational manufacturing companies? To deny that what they see on dramas or documentaries has any effect on viewers, is to deny that advertising effects them as well.

I also believe that television news has become a spectator sport. Even the most incorruptible journalist is going to select pictures, or, if on radio, give descriptions, of events that make an impact. As years go by, it takes more spectacular images, visual or audial, to make that impact. And while journalistic news transmission is developing, we, the audience, are becoming addicted to news. Our addiction, though, is to negative news, the only sort most of us hear or see. What is it in our collective psyches that attracts us to watch the face of famine, ogle the results of murder and mayhem, gawp at the devastated lives and homes of people harrowed by some natural disaster? Is it a sense that we are luckier than they? Is it that others can fulfil the role of victim and that by watching or listening to their experiences we can congratulate ourselves that we have not experienced what they have? The only news worth telling seems to be bad news, crime figures, road-death rates, 'terrorist' activity, political scandals and frauds.

A number of the major news bulletins are broadcast at the times of main meals. Maybe it's no accident, either, that transmission strength, particularly on radio, is greater when news is being transmitted than it is for other programmes; I notice this when BBC 3 is 'lost' at those times. Have you also noticed how we phrase our reactions to the news? It was 'sickening', it 'turned my stomach', 'if you swallow that, you'll swallow anything', 'what a load of crap' — just some of the visceral language we use about the news. When it is broadcast at meal times, for example 7 and 8 am and hourly in the evening and we listen to it as we eat, our reactions are not just verbal. The language we use actually *does* reflect how our bodies react. The musculature of the solar plexus makes subtle movements reflecting what we hear and this affects the production of digestive secretions in all the organs in the solar plexus area: the stomach, the gall bladder and the pancreas. We are eating what we hear and see of the news and its negativity is becoming a part of us. As we digest our food, so we are digesting what we are being 'fed' as news. By recognising the addiction you can prevent this from happening to you by turning off the radio and the television while you are eating.

If you were to write to your favourite broadcasting station to ask for good news, you could point out that in Denmark, at the end of the 6.30 news bulletin each evening, there are a few minutes of news about positive or humorous events, as also on the British station, ITN. In Holland, in the province of Brabant, the daily newspaper, *Eindhovens Dagblad*, produced its issue of Tuesday, 15 October 1996 with a brand new supplement. The editor-in-chief and his team of sub-editors had decided to produce a newspaper that would reflect more accurately the world as it really is, a mixture of good and bad. In some instances news appeared twice, once in the conventional, negative way, for example describing the loss of profits for the Dutch electrical firm, Phillips. In the supplement, a different 'spin' was put on the same story by showing how Phillips was proposing to tackle the down-turn in profits. They used the same approach in a report about the Catherina Hospital; in one report it was announced that the hospital was 1.3 million guilders overspent over a period of eight months, while the other report announced that the same hospital had treated 2000 more patients than the budget allowed for, showing that the hospital staff were more concerned with helping human need than balancing the books.

As a follow-on to the *Eindhovens Dagblad* good news supplement, a survey was undertaken by the same newspaper to estimate the public reaction to good news. Two hundred readers claimed it gave them a good feeling as they sat over their breakfast reading the day's news. Three readers were not impressed and one said, 'The paper must not leave its position as a watchdog.' The editorial staff themselves felt it was a success, but they also had difficulties in finding good news and also in putting a good news 'spin' on otherwise negative news. Maybe this is due to journalistic habit, but if good news became a regular feature of reporting, there would be less resistance both on the part of journalists and readers.

Our addiction to bad news, I believe, contributes to its continuance. News broadcasts affect the susceptible just as advertising does, which is why some crimes are repeated after a report has been publicised. If psychologists are employed by supermarkets to study our reactions to the music in the air when we're shopping, how much more would the community benefit if they were to study the effects of negative news bulletins? I challenge any broadcasting authority or station to try transmitting only good news, or news with a positive 'spin' to it, for a whole month. I'm sure results would include a drop in the crime rate within the area of the audience and, similarly, a drop in the diagnosis of depression.

When Concorde began to fly from Europe to America, it did so beyond the speed of sound, but it had to work up to that speed after take-off. From test flights of military aircraft flown at supersonic speeds, it was already known that at the point where the plane begins to go faster than sound travels, a boom is heard that resembles a huge explosion. This percussion that signifies the moment when a moving object passes through the sound barrier caused fears expressed by Church officials that the ancient fabric of cathedrals and churches might be damaged by the force of the boom. Farmers' organisations complained of the effect that low flying, high speed military aircraft were having on cattle, sheep and horses as they grazed. Animals startled by the sudden boom would run, terrified and hysterically disorientated, like the children at the wedding reception. In pregnant animals, this often resulted in young being aborted. Eventually, a compromise was reached in the UK: sub-radar practice flights continued, but only on week days. However, when a complaint was made to the military airforce authorities by a Reverend Howell Evans after an RAF plane had repeatedly 'buzzed' a funeral he was conducting on a hill above Dolgellau in the 1970s, it was made clear by their reply that they effectively avoided keeping another part of the agreement because they denied civilian sightings of planes flying below 200 feet above the ground on the following grounds:

- a complainant had to quote the number painted on the fuselage of the plane;
- a reported sighting made with the naked eye was disallowed because it was not made through binoculars — if it was a sighting reported after being seen through binoculars, it was disallowed because it wasn't with the naked eye;
- the authorities deemed civilian sighting notoriously unreliable;
- it was against the national interest to admit any flights below 200 feet.

But the civilian airliner, Concorde, was slowed down so that it didn't break the sound barrier until it was well out over the Atlantic.

This controversy over military and civilian flights and their effects at ground level was revived many times during the years we lived in Wales. The valleys in that country are mostly deep and narrow and we never got used to the explosive intrusion from the sound of a supersonic flight by a plane that was definitely not more than 200 feet above the ground when it came over the high land on one side of a valley before disappearing, so fast you often did not see it, over the height on the other side — just the deafening boom to say it had passed. I was nearing the delivery date of one of my babies and threw myself to the floor one day when I heard that noise. That sort of reaction is too fast for rational thought and I sympathised with the terrified sheep and cows I'd seen race around the fields for the same reason.

The booms also seemed to have another effect: rainfall appeared to be more frequent. Could the noise of planes breaking the sound barrier precipitate rain? I think so. My paternal grandmother was born in 1884 and she went as a teenager to South Africa to work as a lady's maid. She stayed there throughout the Boer War at the turn of the last century, at sometime leaving her job in a bishop's household to work for the Portuguese Consul in Port Elizabeth. She was always fascinated by people and a very friendly person. She would regale us for hours with stories of her fellow workers, black and white, of her encounters with Zulu women and their babies and the practice of the Afrikaner farmers when drought prevailed: as soon as any cloud appeared, each farmer shouldered his gun and went to the highest hill in the area — a destination preordained between local men. Once assembled, at a given signal each man fired into the air. The percussion caused water droplets in the cloud to hit one another, thus combining until heavy enough to fall as rain. No doubt the boom of the con-certed gunfire was as horrific on the eardrums of the Afrikaners as the boom of Concorde was for dwellers in South Wales. The difference was that the Afrikaners knew it was coming!

Mechanisation has brought a multitude of noises into our lives. Aircraft and road traffic noises are particularly invasive and can carry great distances on the air. In public buildings we are con-stantly assailed by the noises of automatic doors, alarm bells, cash registers, trolleys, telephones, musak and many other noises. When a household is sleeping and the television, radio and the gadgetry in the kitchen has been turned off, the electrically wired house will hum and the thermostatically controlled refrigerator can be heard switching itself on — after which it adds its louder hum to the background hum — and off. The brain, when it becomes accustomed to a persistent sound, has the ability to stop responding to it consciously. However, if a sound to which the brain is habituated stops, the conscious response will recommence. This is perhaps the reason why so many of the visitors to our electricity-free house use words like, 'peaceful' and 'quiet' when they volunteer their response to it.

Once we are able to create tranquillity, we may come to awareness of other pulses. Mother Earth herself has a pulse of 7.83 beats (Hertz) per second, which have been called 'Schumann waves'. There is also a phenomenon in the buds of plants, especially trees, whose buds are usually visible from leaf fall in autumn to the spring. Slowly, over a period of several days, the buds elongate and then return to the earlier shape, then elongate again, then return to the earlier shape in a perceptible rhythm which Lawrence Edwards has observed and documented over many years near his home in Scotland. The pulse, for this is what it is, that the buds are making appears to be related to a frequency that emanates from an alignment of planets, which he has also observed and documented in his book *Vortex of Life*.

There is quiet, but there is no true silence, no total absence of sound. Even in the absence of external sounds, we hear the sounds of our bodily functions, breathing and heart beat. But how often do we sense that state of quiet? Maybe Mica Pogacnic's one-man crusade against recorded music shows a way for us to respond consciously to the sounds around us. No matter where anyone lives, it is possible to bring about relative quiet. By turning off the radio, the television, unplugging the fridge and the telephone, such noise as remains audible will be from outside. Stillness will come to the air in the home. Chosen stillness. It calms the mind. It relaxes the muscles. It brings peace. By returning selectively to the available sounds around the home, we can do so consciously and they can be turned off again when they no longer appeal to our conscious minds.

If the drum or the rattle can induce shamanic trance, because of the way the rhythm influences the pulse of the brain, thereby creating a specific state of consciousness, so too can anything we hear affect our consciousness. Perhaps, when we recognise how we are impeding our own development, both individually and collectively, we will start to be selective about the sounds to which we expose ourselves.

Five

ON THE AIR

*Self-confidence, courage, determination and optimism
are, I think, essential in order to gain the day. If right
from the start you tell yourself it isn't working, if you
give way to discouragement, if you adopt a pessimistic
attitude, even if what you desire is easy to obtain,
you will not have it, it won't work. For the human
community and the individual alike, hope is
vital . . . what matters is to do one's best.*

His Holiness, the Dalai Lama

Materialism is defined in the *Shorter Oxford Dictionary* as 'the doctrine that nothing exists except matter and its movements and modifications'. We are well indoctrinated with this 'superstition', as Deepak Chopra calls it, because, unless as individuals we have a special reason for gauging them, we ignore anything that we cannot touch, see, hear, smell or taste. My mother had a saying, 'Believe nothing that you hear and only half that you see', which encapsulates the common acceptance of the materialist superstition with admirable brevity. We do well to break out of this mind-set, because there are many aspects of our world that cannot be tasted, smelled, touched, seen or heard, but which have a powerful bearing on our existence.

Electro-magnetic frequencies come within this category. They surround us and without them we would not be living. They come to us from the most distant celestial body in the universe and from the earth beneath our feet. From a low point on the spectrum, this includes the naturally occurring frequency that man has imitated and manufactures in electricity generating stations. It extends to a broad range of radio waves embracing what we call 'long', 'medium' and 'short' wave to VHF (Very High Frequency), UHF (Ultra High Frequency) and television frequencies to micro-waves: after this comes infra-red light and the narrow band of frequencies from sunlight. Even the frequencies within this light have a definable sequence, from the longer waves of red, through orange to yellow, green, blue, indigo to the shortest, violet. Beyond the visible light that we receive comes ultra-violet and, over an increasing range of frequencies, x-rays, gamma rays and cosmic rays, all in that order.

We have adapted to the variety of frequencies to which we have been exposed, as a species, for the whole of our existence. Electro-magnetism is energy and electro-magnetic energy is the matrix for all forms of life on earth.

Electro-magnetic energy also emanates from quartz- and silica-bearing rocks and from water within the crust of the earth. Less attention has been paid by conventional science to this form of electro-magnetic field than has been paid to the higher range, described earlier. Orthodox, Western scientists denied for years that any energy existed in the linear system (translated as the 'meridians') that Chinese sensitives had detected on the surface of the human body and which has been used for thousands of years to access medical healing in sick people in China. Acupuncture and acupressure had, supposedly, no validity until an electronic tool was devised that could detect the subtle electro-magnetic field that flows in the meridians and that could also detect the areas of lowered electrical resistance which indicate the sites of acu-points, the places acupuncturists and acupressurists access with needles or fingers. By the same token, scientists are reluctant to admit the existence of the circuits of electro-magnetic energies detectable — by sensitives — around the surface of the globe, similar to their counterparts in the human body.

The meridian system is only one of a web of co-ordinated frequencies in and around all living beings. Another is the series of vortices of energy that emanate from sites on the body close to adjacent endocrine (chemical) and nerve plexus (electrical) control centres of the body. The Chakras wheel their way from the surface of the body out to the edge of the aura, which is the general electro-magnetic field that surrounds the whole body. These frequencies and a myriad others, both discovered and as yet undiscovered, all interact with one another, with those from other living beings, with those from the earth and with all others. Some environmentalists are claiming that the increase in incidences of whales beaching and becoming stranded is due to the disturbance by man-made terrestrial and satellite transmissions of their solar system-dependent navigational organs.

Moderate amounts of any of these natural frequencies, amounts to which we have adapted through the generations, mostly appear to be beneficial. But excess can be damaging. For example, when a white skin becomes tanned on exposure to the ultra-violet frequency in sunlight it is a precursor of the excess that causes burns and excess exposure can result in the growth of a melanoma. The frequency emitted by a colour can also have an effect when absorbed by the body. A lot of red in the decor of a room can cause aggression; amethyst or violet, on the other hand, can be calming, while pink is reassuring and relaxing. It follows, then, that overexposure to other frequencies on the long spectrum of frequencies is also potentially damaging.

Electro-magnetic frequencies are measured in Hertz, the name of the man who first defined these measurements. Hz — being the abbreviation for Hertz, followed by a number — is the way the oscillations per second of a wavelength is stated. The number of such oscillations is what is referred to by the word 'frequency'. There is another measurement related to a frequency and that is the amplitude. If an imaginary line could be drawn that joined all the crests of the waves in a particular frequency and then another line that could join all the troughs in the waves of the same frequency, the distance between the two lines would be the amplitude.

At the lower end of the spectrum of frequencies, not far above the frequency of the energy humanity has harnessed and calls 'mains' electricity, the wavelengths can be measured in kilometres. To differentiate between this and higher frequencies, Hz has 'k' added and becomes kHz. Above this level, the wavelengths start to be measurable in metres, thus MHz; above this in centimetres and millimetres, hence GHz. Each will be followed by the number which distinguishes the exact wavelength oscillation per second.

All the wavelengths below visible light are referred to as 'non-ionising' radiation. In the ionising range, we are accustomed to the burning effect of ultra-violet light, which is visible on the skin and we accept that overexposure to x-rays from medical diagnostic tools and gamma rays from the cathode-ray tubes of television sets can cause cancer-forming burns on the inside of the body. Non-ionising radiation, which is emitted by the wavelengths below visible light and which is employed for telecommunications and broadcasting, was not, until recently, thought to be harmful. However, man-made sources of non-ionising frequencies, which represent exposures over and above what nature provides, are having effects, evidence for which is very slowly being accepted by orthodox scientists. There are quite a few *un*orthodox scientists who have no difficulties in accepting the evidence.

Fifty years ago Ireland had one radio station and few houses had an electricity supply. Until the mid-1980s, most countries had no more than two or three television channels. Each radio channel and each television channel transmits a slightly different wavelength from another. By the 1990s, each national broadcasting company had several different channels, both radio and television as well as innumerable local transmitters. In addition, wavelengths being transmitted from many other countries are also available. On top of all this, there are the telecommunications systems that connect points within each country to one another and also to points outside each country. Each of these uses a slightly different frequency from all the others. *Each* transmission, whether radio, television, telephone or radar (which also comes within this area) represents a gross increase on the natural exposure that all life has adapted to over millennia.

If you sit beside a pond on a calm day, the surface of the water will be like a mirror, smooth and flat. If you throw a stone into the pond, a succession of waves form in a pattern. If, before the first pattern of waves has subsided, you throw another stone into the pond, a second pattern of waves will be formed that will disrupt the first one. To use another illustration: during the Cold War, it was common in some countries for the radio transmissions broadcast from other countries to be 'jammed'. This was done by broadcasting unintelligible sound from another transmitter at the same frequency. Using the same analogy, the many and varied frequencies transmitted by the electro-magnetic currents and fields in living beings are now exposed to a huge range of potentially disruptive, man-made frequencies to which none of us has had the time to become adapted.

To return to the 'materialist superstition'; this has acculturated most people to ignore, or even remain unconscious of, intuition or any of the feelings or individually sensed phenomena that fall outside 'normal' (within the superstition) experience. Thus, scientists, who are more deeply indoctrinated into the materialist superstition than ordinary people, find it virtually impossible to recognise that such phenomena as panic attacks, chronic fatigue syndrome, sudden and inexplicable fear, loss of consciousness in events that have the appearance of epilepsy, hallucinatory-type visions and other emotional disturbances, including headaches, could be caused by man-made electro-magnetic frequencies.

For a growing number of people, a link can be made between the date of commencement of radio or telecommunications transmissions near their homes, or in line-of-sight to their homes and the date on which their symptoms began. Enda d'Alton, a middle-aged man in Dublin, tells how he suffered from chronic fatigue syndrome for four years before he discovered what he believes to be the reason. After many periods spent in hospital, including two months as a voluntary patient in a psychiatric hospital, Enda met a man whose symptoms matched his own. For both of them, the onset of the symptoms had been sudden, in mid-December 1989. Both men were acquainted with electronics and radio engineering. They decided to run an experiment. They enlisted a total stranger who knew how to use a frequency meter which is used to detect radio transmissions. With the meter-reader in the back seat of a car and themselves in the front, they drove across Ireland from Dublin to Galway. Taking it in turns to drive, Enda and his friend noted when they felt unwell and the front passenger recorded the place on a map. Using a copy of the same map, the man in the back seat recorded on it the places where radio transmissions showed on the frequency meter. They took a different route back to Dublin, but the records were maintained on both outward and return journeys. Back in Dublin, the two maps were compared: they matched. For Enda and his friend this evidence was conclusive: their symptoms had begun on the day that microwave transmissions for mobile phones had begun, 18 December 1989. The maps verified that it was these frequencies that disturbed their health and well-being.

Microwaves are used not only to transmit telephone calls via mobile telephones, but also to transmit television signals in some systems (although lower frequencies are also used) and, by virtue of the way they behave, they are used in cookers. Microwaves are in the GHz range. In this range the waves wriggle, or 'oscillate', to use the correct term, over distances from some centimetres to some millimetres between *one billion and one hundred billion times per second*. Bearing in mind that the crest of each wave can be identified as the north pole of the wave's magnetic field and the trough is the south pole, each oscillation represents a complete change of polarity — a major event — which happens billions of times every second.

Separate studies by the biochemist, Freeman Cope, and by Jacques Benveniste, an analytical scientist, have shown that water is structured. The oxygen atom in a water molecule is the most sensitively reactive natural substance. The structure of the oxygen atom is torn and deformed by the rapid changes of polarity in the oscillations characteristic of a microwave frequency. The by-product from this frenetic activity is heat. The longer the activity lasts, the greater the heat generated, which is how a microwave oven works. Water is a major constituent of all life forms — plants, insects, reptiles, fish, birds, animals and people; up to at least three-quarters of each body is water.

In telecommunication transmissions used by the police, the military, or the utilities such as water, gas, electricity and forestry, microwave is often used, because it remains a dense shaft of power and doesn't disperse, provided there is no obstruction between the transmitter and the receiver. Microwave transmissions for television or mobile phone users, on the other hand, are transmitted in a deliberately dispersive way to provide what is called 'blanket cover'. Some countries, Ireland among them, have chosen to licence companies to provide this blanket cover over the whole of the state (Northern Ireland, a province of the UK, uses UVF to transmit television signals).

Satellites are already in use to bring television transmission to parts of the world far from the point of origin, simply because microwave travels in a straight line and the curvature of the earth reduces the feasible range of any transmission. A beam from the transmitter can be received by the satellite and re-transmitted to parts of the earth's surface otherwise inaccessible. Terrestrial systems require also to be re-transmitted in order to cover large areas and, for this purpose receiver/transmitters — like relay stations — are mounted on high places, often purpose-built metal towers, or masts, within range of one another. Each channel utilises a different frequency whether it is transmitted by a satellite or by a terrestrial system.

Mobile telephone companies erect networks of masts in hilly areas, each mast transmitting over a distance approximately ten miles in diameter. Where there is more than one mobile telephone company in a given area, each will have its own network of transmitters. A finite number of subscribers can be served by one transmitter, so, as the number of subscribers increases, so will the number of masts; now at ten-mile intervals, they will later be at five-mile intervals. There are plans to take microwave transmissions for mobile telephones onto satellites as well. Sixty satellites are calculated to be needed (to begin with) for users to be able to contact one another to and from anywhere. This system is predicted to be in use early in the twenty-first century.

It is common for sites on masts already transmitting to be leased out to facilitate other transmissions. For instance, Telecom Eireann, the semi-state national telephone company in Ireland, which was the first company to erect masts for mobile transmissions, subsequently leased transmitter sites to companies operating Multipoint Microwave Distribution Systems (MMDS), also known as 'cable TV'. The transmissions continue, twenty-four hours each day, whether the television set or the mobile telephone is switched on to receive them or not. What an incredible amount of hardware there will be circulating in the upper atmosphere, not to mention that making the surface of the earth look like a metallic porcupine! What an extraordinary number of invisible, man-made electro-magnetic frequencies from kHz, to MHz, to GHz are filling the earth's atmosphere. And what damage to the natural frequencies that have been here since the earth began?

There is a small minority of people who cannot tolerate even the circuitry of mains electricity in their homes. Some of these sufferers, many of whom have to move into electricity-free accommodation, have formed CIRCUIT, a support group. Enda d'Alton and Colette O'Connell plan to bring a test case on health grounds backed by the Irish Campaign Against Microwave Pollution (ICAMP), hoping to create a precedent for people suffering as they do.

Health issues concerning microwave transmissions have only become an area of public interest as a result of protest about them on quite different grounds. In the late 1970s, people living in the hilly parts of the West of Ireland began to feel cheated because the landscape interfered with their television reception. As a result of public meetings held all over the region, large numbers of non-profit, community groups organised themselves and erected equipment known as deflector systems, which enabled all households to receive television signals. Each household paid a modest annual fee towards the maintenance of the equipment. There was no licensing authority for such systems, but both county councils and central government turned a blind eye to the situation until the early 1990s.

Altnagapple is an obscure hamlet of half a dozen houses on a hillside in South West Donegal. Co. Donegal is on the Atlantic fringe of Europe, at the top left-hand corner of Ireland. Because of its altitude and its visibility from so many points around, the hill above Altnagapple was chosen by Telecom Eireann as a site for a mast in their mobile telephone network. The mast was built in 1992 without planning permission and therefore with no forum for public discussion. This was not against the law, because at that time the government did not demand planning permission for public utilities such as this.

Tourism organisations claimed that the mast marred the skyline and local people grumbled about it, but no-one took any action, until 1995. By then, a number of companies had been formed to provide blanket cover by microwave transmission of television signals over the whole country, including the areas hitherto served by the community-owned deflector systems (which had transmitted on VHF). The companies were formed to make a profit. Cable Management Ireland (CMI) was the company that had negotiated to lease a site for its transmitter on Telecom's mast at Altnagapple.

The system planned by CMI and the other cable TV companies requires each subscriber to rent a 'decoder' box supplied by the company and to pay an annual service charge for the signal. Non-payers would have the signal 'scrambled' — via the decoder box — until they paid up. When the charges were calculated, they proved to be approximately twenty times higher than the average of £10 to £15 paid by most households under the community schemes. Central government had designed a licensing system by which it would receive about twenty per cent of the revenue earned by the new companies.

Overnight, the community deflector systems organised, erected, paid for and maintained by local people up and down the country to serve each locality for nearly two decades were rendered illegal, without any consultation, let alone public debate.

The community that would be covered by the signal from Altnagapple already had very good cover from the service they had been providing for themselves for almost twenty years. At a public meeting to discuss Telecom Eireann's leasing a site on the mast to CMI, it was decided to mount a picket at the entrance to the mountain road leading to the mast, to prevent CMI from erecting their equipment on it. Meanwhile, the community deflector system continued to function. For eleven months, local people in twos and threes or more maintained the picket. CMI took action through the courts and obtained an injunction against named persons to abstain from picketing. The picket, always within the law and behaving with admirable good nature and within the true tradition of peaceful civil disobedience, finally abandoned the action.

The same people were far from abandoning the issue as a whole, however: as a general election loomed, by way of creating a platform for further debate, the Ardara and Glenties Anti-MMDS Group adopted a candidate to represent their interests by standing as an independent. Protest groups in other parts of the country followed suit by selecting their own candidates. There was considerable press publicity after a meeting in Athlone of delegates representing groups from all over Ireland, after which the Minister for Communications, Alan Dukes, promised to review the situation. Unwisely, some protesters thought, all the candidates were withdrawn, except the candidate for South West Donegal, Thomas Gildea, who had been adopted by Ardara and Glenties.

Once the date of the general election had been announced and the date for the registration of nominated candidates had passed, Alan Dukes announced that a system had been worked out which would allow the community deflector systems to continue functioning. They would from then on, however, be subject to the same licensing scheme as the cable TV companies. In other words, the households that had hitherto helped to maintain their own VHF television reception were to be charged as much as the commercial microwave systems. Many anti-MMDS protesters regarded this as government duplicity. Feelings ran so high that by the time the votes had been counted at the end of the general election, South West Donegal had a new, independent representative in the national parliament, Thomas Gildea.

Six months later, it was estimated that none of the households were subscribing to CMI, even though the deflector system was closed down by the community, who refused to accept the terms of the government licence. The increased awareness among the population about the health hazards from high-frequency transmissions has resulted in a succession of meetings, local and national. Colette O'Connell has joined Enda d'Alton in preparing a case for the High Court to challenge the government on its neglect of the health and democratic rights of the nation.

Commonly, we talk of someone being 'on the air' when we hear them on radio, but the frequency that brings their voice to the receiver is 'on the air' whether the receiver is switched on or not. Commercial consortia, like CMI, don't air their views about their business interests or profit expectations. Difficulties arise when ordinary people with neither business nor political interests feel that decisions are being made that affect their lives, although they are not being informed or consulted. However, it is a paradox that the very telecommunications systems that are posing health hazards are also the means by which many of those affected are able to contact others and gain information that can open up the perceived secrecy.

Many people believe that the technological wizardry which fills our homes and public buildings is tangible evidence of 'progress'. 'Progress', however, is an illusion. Humankind has survived for more millennia than there is written history to describe. We have come through profound climatic and political changes with ingenuity, courage, strength and intelligence. Today's people wonder how earlier humans achieved the relics that remain of their 'progress': the Pyramids at Giza, the ziggurats of Central and Southern America, the vast astronomical calculators in India, Stonehenge, Carnac, Newgrange.

Among the indigenous tribes whose qualities have allowed them to survive into the twentieth century without the technologies that Europeans have invented, there remain skills which the materialist superstition has denied. A small but increasing number of people from technological communities are rediscovering and practising these skills. Maybe this is a sign of a renaissance for co-operation with natural energies, which might take the place of the potentially damaging technologies and the accompanying unwelcome domination and manipulation of the lives of ordinary people?

Six

A SPACE TO BE

. . . your consciousness is the consciousness of all humanity because you suffer, you are anxious, you are lonely, insecure, confused, exactly like others, though they live ten thousand miles away. The realisation of it, the feeling of it — the feeling in your guts — is totally different from verbal acceptance. When you realise that you are the rest of mankind, it brings a tremendous energy, you have broken through the narrow grove of individuality, the narrow circle of me and you, we and they. We are examining together this very complex consciousness of man, not the European man, not the Asiatic man, or the Middle East man, but this extraordinary movement in time that has been going on in consciousness for millions of years.

J. Krishnamurti

My friend Márie had a brother who went to Japan to teach English. There he met a Japanese girl who had learned English as an *au pair* in Dublin. They married and had two beautiful children, Japanese children with Irish names: Sorcha and Donacha. John became ill and cancer was diagnosed. His family and friends in Ireland organised dances and whist drives so that he could come home for the treatment that in Japan was too expensive for him and his wife, Reiko, to afford. The money raised included the fare for Reiko and the children. Sadly, having returned to Ireland, John died. Reiko and the children stayed on with Márie for a couple of weeks after the funeral. The children were accustomed to the cramped conditions of an apartment block in a busy Japanese city, not the space and quiet of a farm in the West of Ireland. One day, Márie looked out her kitchen window and saw eight-year-old Sorcha, her eyes shut and her arms outstretched as far as she could reach, slowly turning round and round on the lawn in front of the house. She was *feeling* the space around her.

Many children live in far more cramped conditions in cities around the world than Sorcha in Japan. Children grow up in barrios in Mexico, in shanty towns in Africa and India, in high-rise flats in Paris, Cologne, London, Dublin and all the other huge cities of the world. How wonderful for a child, so used to the proximity of other people twenty-four hours a day, every day, to experience the space to stretch herself both physically and emotionally! So few children would have that chance. However, some may — in Ireland, at least, through the brainchild of Jim Connolly, who has created the Rural Resettlement Ireland (RRI) scheme that offers city-dwelling families the opportunity to live permanently in a rural area.

Jim, who lives in Co. Clare, recognised a dual need. On the one hand, the drift of rural dwellers to the town causes depopulation of the rural areas and the consequent loss of primary schools, village shops and local authority services as populations shrink; on the other hand, many people feel themselves to be trapped in an urban environment and that they and their children would have a better quality of life in a rural area. In 1990, Jim created RRI, a non-profit-making company, which is limited by guarantee and has no share capital. Its two main aims are: first, 'to encourage and assist families to relocate in depopulated rural areas in Ireland', and second, 'to seek financial aid from Government and other agencies to assist the relocation programme'.

By June 1997, RRI had helped an estimated 284 families to move out of cities into nineteen of Ireland's twenty-six counties, often into houses that had ceased to be occupied and were liable to become derelict. Local committees, in areas where the community has entered into the spirit of Jim Connolly's intentions, have tidied overgrown gardens, as well as cleaning and repairing the empty houses about to be occupied by people moving from a city. They also establish and maintain friendly assistance to families who relocate.

In addition, by mid-1997 it was estimated that more than 140 houses have been made available to city housing lists, mostly in Dublin, through the departure of families who have moved to the country as a result of the help provided by RRI. This initiative now has government approval and financial assistance. It is actively helping over 3,500 more families wishing to move into the country and who have answered the questionnaire that puts them on the RRI waiting list.

For a few people at least the rural drift to cities has been reversed. Rural drift is a phenomenon of industrialisation and mech-anisation, before which the size of the family farm used to be gauged by the distance from the byre that a person could push a barrow full of manure; this gave the radius of the farm at a time when there was hardly any farm that wasn't run by a family. All the work on the farm was hand work and there would be plenty to occupy everyone from children to grandparents. It wasn't all drudgery and it was also seasonal, so that at some times of the year there was a lot of work and at others far less.

Industrialisation is oblivious to the seasons and the tractor, because of its mobility and carrying power, has stretched the poten-tial size of the farm. The tractor has also revolutionised work by providing a constantly available power source for lifting, sawing, hedge-cutting, mowing, ploughing, harvesting and transporting produce. One person with a tractor has demolished the work of ten people — and negated the skills they had. It is no longer necessary to be able to milk by hand, to mow with a scythe, to cut and lay a quick (live) hedge, to make tool handles from ash wood cut from that same hedge, to judge the weather, or to do those many jobs that required judgment, accumulated wisdom and *skill*.

Mechanisation has dispossessed the country person, not only of work, but also of the abilities that generations had refined and handed down to daughters and sons for as far back as anyone can remember. Their skills no longer relevant, the dispossessed left for the centres of industrialisation, hoping to find security of income in a factory job. They settled where they could — where they continue to settle, for this movement persists around the globe — in shanty towns or high-rise flats where they become ghettoised as the (often) unemployable, because few of them find the well-paid work they seek.

Before mechanisation, every job was related to natural rhythms and processes. Thus, the late winter was the season for laying a hedge or harvesting a piece of woodland involving coppicing skills. These skills included the laying aside of ashwood for tool handles; hazel and willow wands for making baskets, hurdles or furniture; fine twigs for making faggots to fire a bake oven; chestnut for poles and charcoal burning and the use of judgment that allowed the wealth of the woodland to be used without removing the possibility of it renewing itself. There was no wastage. Sustainable woodcraft is only one of the practices of country living that always were sustainable, that is, before country work became industrialised with a harvest of monetary gain and wasteful practices that make such work *un*sustainable unless profound revisions of methods and means are found.

In Ireland, over 150 primary schools are currently involving children up to the age of twelve in a Wildlife Garden Scheme in which old ways are being revived. A very informative book called *Go Wild at School*, helps teachers and children to design, plant and maintain a garden with native trees and shrubs, herbs, flowers, vegetables, ponds and even rotting logs as a habitat for insects and fungi. In these gardens the children are learning how to relate to the seasons, to plants, insects, animals and birds, to the earth and to one another. They are using their hands as well as their heads, and thereby discovering skills they've never met before. They are able to apply the academic lessons of the classroom in this outdoor learning space — arithmetic in measuring, weighing, calculating germination and harvest times and writing to record their increasing familiarity with the piece of growing planet in their care. They are learning that nature has no waste products, because every discarded body becomes food or home for other creatures. Patrick Madden, the imaginative teacher who is the innovator of this movement sees this as a means for children to learn commitment to and responsibility for the world 'in which they have been placed as caretakers for a brief amount of time'.

Just as the children learning on the Wildlife Garden Scheme are applying the sums and writing learned in the classroom to the jobs they do in the garden, there is hope that the lessons of natural regeneration and waste disposal will be applied in the years ahead in their homes and places of work. Social and political changes are taking place and the Garden Scheme is one of them. The complex mixture of social and political changes that occurred as industrialisation took place drove many country dwellers into cities and altered everyone's life to some degree. Until then, a very small proportion of the population lived in cities, which were, by twentieth-century standards, very small. The wastes produced there were similar to country wastes: broken pottery and glass, scraps, all from natural sources to which they returned via the cities' rubbish pits that modern archaeologists have explored. Animal dung — the traffic effluent of the time — along with human dung and stable sweepings, could be carried to the fields around the city, as they still are in 'underdeveloped' countries. Post-industrialisation, there is still manure to dispose of — mostly human — which is seldom used on the land, but rather discharged from sewers, often untreated, into the sea.

By the end of the twentieth century, nearly one third of the population of any industrialised country will be city dwellers. It is well for Sorcha and others like her to feel the space around them, but much of what is in that space cannot be felt or sensed until many years have passed: this is the hidden waste. The most visible waste is the packaging from the things we buy, most of which are, like the packaging, made from unnatural materials invented by science and technology. There are thousands of chemical compounds assembled by science that owe nothing to any natural substance, that do not return naturally to the earth.

Many of these substances are proving to be far from benign in their production, their use, or their disposal. The origins of some of the commonest are as by-products of major industries: chemical dyes to colour cloth were first derived from coal in the nineteenth century; plastics have been derived from petroleum.

Consumer goods were never intended to harm anyone, nor was their packaging, but the emerging effect is potentially very harmful indeed. By skin contact and by inhalation, tiny, molecular particles of these chemicals are entering the bodies of all living creatures, mostly because of our messy disposal techniques and our ignorance. Phthalates, an ingredient in plastics, were in the news in late 1997. Alkylphenol polyethoxylates are ingredients in plastics, detergents, washing powders and washing-up liquids. Dioxins and their close relations, the furans, in whose company they can often be found, come from pesticides — fly-sprays, weed-killers and wood-preservatives — and from the manufacture *and* destruction of substances that incorporate chlorine in some form, especially when they are burned.

Polychlorinated biphenyls (PCBs), of which there are 209 kinds, are found in these products, as well as being used as coolants and in non-flammable treatments of timber, in electrical trans-formers, lubricants and liquid seals. There are 135 sorts of furans, along with the seventy-five dioxins, including the one identified by the tag 2, 4, 7, 8 — TCDD, which is known as the most toxic chemical on earth. It has been implicated in birth and behavioural defects in the children of American soldiers who had been exposed to Agent Orange during the Vietnam War, when they sprayed it as a de-foliant over millions of acres of Vietnamese forests. There appear to be no studies to consult about the effects on the children of the Vietnamese people who were also exposed by virtue of living beneath the trees.

In their book, *Our Stolen Future*, Theo Colborn, Dianne Dumanoski and John Peterson Myers explain, as in a detective story, how the discoveries were made that led to an understanding of how these chemicals are damaging life on earth. I will stick to the effects on the human body here, but they are similar throughout all animate creatures. The seven major endocrine glands in the body produce hormones, the potent secretions required in tiny amounts to control body size, colour, gender, activity, metabolism and reproduction, which they do by activating the potential in the DNA within relevant body cells. The activation occurs when a specific hormone molecule attaches to a hormone receptor, ready to accept only that specific hormone, within the cell. This is called the 'lock and key' mechanism; when the hormone, equated with the key, engages with the hormone receptor, equated with the lock, the key can be 'turned', so that the two can enter the nucleus of the cell to instruct the DNA to release the required response.

It is now recognised that when many man-made chemicals are ingested — including those listed above — they behave in one of two ways: as a hormone-mimic or as a hormone-blocker. Hormones are only released from their respective glands after complex trigger mechanisms have been activated by the 'master-gland', the hypothalamus in the brain. Hormone-mimics are not subject to the trigger mechanisms, so, like any maverick, they go into action and cause disruptions within the system. Hormone-blockers get as far as the lock and key fitting together, but the key can't turn, so the unit can't move into the nucleus, which results in no response. The problem here is that the site occupied by the hormone-blocker is rendered unavailable to the real hormone.

The observable results of this chemical interference are not immediate. In fact, they may not show up for another generation. It is in the offspring of parents who have been exposed that reproductive abnormalities appear and then only once those offspring have attained maturity and breeding age. In men, the sperm count is drastically reduced and the penis often foreshortened, with one or both testicles failing to drop after birth. In women, the uterus and fallopian tubes may be misshapen or absent and ovulation may be affected. These people will never be able to reproduce. The young of exposed parents may have other characteristics, from hyperactivity to lowered intelligence and faulty reasoning abilities, all of which suggest that the thyroid gland and some part of the brain are affected, in ways that are not yet fully understood. Immunity suppression has also been detected as an effect, though why is also unknown.

A human generation is thought of as twenty-five years, so it may be another century before clear evidence of the eventual effects of these chemicals can be assessed. The alarming realisation arises that most of the things that fill the spaces in our homes, in offices, hospitals, schools and other public buildings, as well as the articles that impregnate the air around the apparently empty air around us are now, or will be, a health hazard.

Not In My Back Yard (NIMBY) is no longer a defensible stance — this is in *everyone's* back yard. All items that are discarded, because they are broken, worn out, or out of fashion, if they contain plastic, or any form of bleached paper — a process using chlorine — are likely to arrive at the corporation dump, or landfill site, millions of cubic acres of which are filled annually, where they may be burned, compressed and buried. Blister packs, paper handkerchiefs, shrink-wrap, kitchen towels, drinks cans, milk cartons, tampons, sanitary towels, disposable nappies, computer print-outs, fast-food packaging and plastic shopping bags are just *some* of the daily detritus from the average home or workplace.

This list makes it apparent that each of us can do a number of things about changing this situation. It requires only a bit of forethought to use a cloth shopping bag, to use cloth handker-chiefs and rags as wipes in the kitchen; these are some of the non-vocal ways toward change, but vocal ways are also needed. Demand your liquid foods, milk, juices, soft drinks, in returnable bottles. Make your wishes known to the person in the corner shop, the milkman, the manager of the supermarket. Talk about it with your neighbours, in the pub, at Rotary, Merched y Wawr, the ICA, the WI, the Church — ask all you know to join in and explain why. Use natural soap to wash your clothes and stop using washing-up liquid. When I was a child, I remember my mother using a small wire cage attached to a handle, into which she put the toilet soap scraps. When the washing-up bowl was full of hot water, she used to swish the cage about in it to make it soapy, before immersing the dishes. In our house, we don't even do that: we wipe our used dishes and rinse them with cold water, before immersing them in near-boiling water — there's a knack to removing them without burning the fingers!

Demand unbleached sanitary towels or tampons, or better still, use re-useable sanitary towels. And use terry-towelling nappies. It looks like hard work, doesn't it? But the hardest work is changing the way we think and the habits we have. Once the change is made, the work becomes a matter of course. I know, because I've done it.

A starting point for discontinuing the use of plastic in the home is to seek out stainless steel, or enamel, for bowls and buckets, baskets made from wicker or other plant material, ceramic plant pots and coir, rather than plastic mats, brooms, or brushes. The dangerous chemicals in synthetic sprays or impregnated slabs to kill insects can be replaced by deterrents such as bunches of sweetpeas or spearmint — both much disliked by houseflies at the time of year when all three are at their most prolific. All of these materials decompose naturally and return to the earth once their usefulness has passed. It's a matter of choice.

I have heard people disclaim responsibility, saying the adverse effects of some action will not occur in their lifetime and they don't care after that. Such irresponsibility is not humane and may easily deny others a choice that they are entitled to. The ecologically based philosophy of the First Nations of Turtle Island was to judge an action or an acquisition by its perceived effects on seven future generations. If the outcome could be seen to be adverse, the action was not undertaken. By adopting this way of assessing our actions and possessions, we could turn the tide very quickly. If we make the choice to turn away from chemical consumerism, we have to talk about it, write letters about it, make our needs and wishes known; the more of us who do these things, the more attention we will get.

All these issues and many others are tackled by the Women's Environmental Network (WEN) in its campaigns. This registered charity was created to inform, educate and empower women who care about the environment. It is women who are the shoppers for most households, who push buggies, change nappies, do the washing. Through WEN's campaigning, nappy-washing services have become available in many urban areas; they also promote the tailored terry nappy, which combines the convenience of the shaped disposable with the advantages of the towelling nappy. WEN's literature also points out that the wood pulp from which domestically used, disposable paper-based goods are made, comes in the main from Scandinavia and Canada. Flying over forest areas of Canada, I remember looking down on the spaces left by clear-cut, where the timber has been removed, leaving an effect similar to the bald patches on the head of someone with alopecia. It's unnatural and likely to get worse if we do nothing to stop it.

To reduce use is to reduce waste, but to minimise even that is essential; to this end, WEN have lobbied for the Waste Minimisation Bill, 'To enable certain local authorities to make arrangements to minimise the generation of waste in their area: and for related purposes', which was presented to the UK Parliament in December 1997.

WEN's aim is to be pro-active in creating environmental awareness and caring behaviour. This is a form of overt education, but by subtler ways other organisations are creating appropriate awareness, especially among children. The movement to establish city farms began in the 1970s, when derelict spaces in cities throughout Europe were taken over and cleared by volunteers to make grazing areas and housing for animals and poultry. Now in their second generation, school groups and family groups have brought children to them who would otherwise have had little or no opportunity to learn about the sources of their food, nor to experience animal and bird husbandry.

Forest School Camps take children out of the city altogether, usually to secluded country spaces where their resourcefulness, observation, hand-skills and creativity can develop unimpeded. The grandchildren of the founders can now take part in collecting firewood, cooking, orienteering, plant identification, weaving and playwriting, among many other occupations. They learn compan-

ionability, self-confidence and an appreciation of the many unob-
trusive wonders that the earth has to offer.

A newer movement involving whole families is toward eco-
villages, in which spaces are created for living with ecological
awareness. These ventures will pave the way for future home
designs, by being constructed from readily available local materials,
rather than those requiring chemicals in their manufacture, such
as chipboard or plywood, both of which continue for years to
release poisonous formaldehyde from the bonding. A whole range
of ideas is being used to design these villages and the houses in
them. Starting from knowing what is *not* wanted, the designers
and builders include sustainable, beneficial, stimulating and enrich-
ing features, such as organic gardens or allotments, on-site bakeries
using organic, native flours, reed-bed sewage disposal leading into
ornamental waterways (with purified water), communal meeting
places and 'green' businesses. They appeal to people with a
variety of skills and aspirations, first among which is the desire
to create a space in which they and their families can live harmonious, productive lives.

Harmony is not a natural outcome when individuals, businesses
and sections of the community concentrate on competitiveness and
on killing the opposition. The first reaction of most people to an
unknown or disliked creature entering their space is to kill it.
Ultimately, it is our materialist superstition, our greed, our naiveté
and our cupidity that have brought us to the present situation.

We, the ordinary people, have strengths. It was the strength of
ordinary people that reduced the Berlin Wall to rubble; it was the
strength of ordinary people that released Nelson Mandela from
prison and made him President of South Africa. Our grand-
daughter, Naomi, was six years old when Nelson Mandela was let
out of prison. I'm not sure how she first learned about him, but
I know she had been praying for his release every night for about
six months before it occurred. When she learned that he was free,
her blue eyes grew huge and between laughing and crying, she
was convinced that she and God held full responsibility for what
had happened. This heartfelt belief that what we want very much

can happen, if we want it enough, keeps alive all the hopes and aspirations of exiled individuals, suppressed nations and those of us who wish that our world could be a better place. We can make our own decisions about what we own and use and where we obtain it. We can give up our dependence on 'them' — scientists, politicians, advertisers, priests, lawyers, doctors or teachers. We do not need slavishly to obey. We can consult with and make our opinions known to them: we can because we know we can — the absence of the Wall in Berlin and the presence of the President in South Africa confirm it.

Part Two

WATER

Seven

WATER IN MANY WAYS

*The violet growing along a mountain path blooms for
no-one in particular, but people cannot overlook or forget
it . . . I am fortunate to have grown rice and barley.
Only to him who stands where the barley stands and
listens well, will it speak and tell, for his sake what man
is . . . A university professor told me, 'It's best to keep
philosophy and religion out of the world of science.'
If the barley had heard it probably would have answered,
'Don't bring science into the world of barley.'*

Masanobu Fukuoka

A family of Londoners arrived about twenty-five years ago in
the area where we lived in mid-Wales. As they settled in on
the small caravan park they'd bought, we got to know one another.
John was fascinated by wildlife and one of the stories he told has
remained in my memory. He and his wife had lived near Clapham
Common in London. One spring day, he saw frog spawn for sale
in a pet shop. He bought the frog spawn, took it to the Common
and 'seeded' the ponds with it. He could remember frogs living
there when he was a lad and he missed them. For the few years
they continued to live in Clapham, John, his wife and their little
girl used to go to watch and enjoy the frogs.

This story has stayed with me because I love frogs too, from
the guttural warblings of their mating calls in February and March,
to the slimy wobble of their spawn, to the wriggle of tadpoles'
tails, to the look of impassive wisdom on the face of a mature
frog. We see lots of frogs in our garden and in the fields around

our house. Just recently, Jeremiah and I were walking home from our postbox one morning when a movement caught my eye. For a moment, I could not discover its source, until I recognised, camouflaged by the grit and pebbles that form the surface of our unmetalled lane, a tiny frog. He was perfectly formed, but less than half an inch long. He was making determined and enormous leaps of at least three inches at a time to get across the lane. Like all babies, as they learn to move about their territory, he stumbled and fell on most of his landings, but got up each time to try again. We were careful not to let our shadows fall on him; I am not sure that he was even aware of us, but we watched him for many minutes with great delight.

Frogs are watched by scientists too, because their survival rate provides an indication of degrees of pollution and changes in land use by the drainage of wetlands. Frogs, amphibians at home as much in water as on land, have an obvious need for clean and ample water. It may not be so apparent that we and all other life forms are also dependent on water. Every cell of our bodies has a greater or lesser percentage of water in it, to the extent that our bodies are more than eighty per cent water and without water to drink to maintain this level, we would die in a few days.

Of all our natural resources, water is regarded with reverence on the one hand and contempt on the other. In rural Ireland, for example, every parish has at least one holy well, or spring source of water that is dedicated to a saint and conferred with some special attribute, usually of healing. In every parish, there are also streams and rivers abused by people who habitually throw their rubbish into them. By the same token, water is sanctified for baptising Christians, but everywhere it is possible to find public amenities, such as toilets, or private businesses where, for want of proper maintenance, water is leaking away. I have seen prodigal wastage of water in both a cheese factory and a fish processing factory, where hoses, when not in use, are left lying on the ground, still flowing.

Poor maintenance of equipment alone accounts for twenty per cent daily water loss in Bangalore, South India, where domestic water is frequently available for only one hour a day. Industry and the irrigation necessary for the new-style farming of cash crops for export which now occurs over much of the water-catchment area that should serve the city accounts for consumption for the remaining twenty-three hours of the day. At one time, Bangalore was called the City of Parks, because of its abundance of trees, but in 1995, I saw poor people using poles to dislodge dead branches from those trees to sell as firewood.

Before Christianity arrived, with its doctrine of human domination over all 'God's creation', springs and wells were sacred. So were streams and rivers, just as all rivers in India still are; the River Ganges is called Mother Ganga and revered by all the non-Abrahamic religions in India. When Christianity arrived in the islands of Western Europe, the new faith took over many of the existing religious beliefs and practices. The Yule, or mid-winter feast — the Solstice celebrations — became Christmas, while the spring festival to honour Oestus, or the surge of new life, became associated with the death of Jesus and the new life he had in the Resurrection, so similar to the return to life of plants and the spring birthing of animals.

The Christians took over the old practices so well, however, that they have allowed no hint of the way these events are graftings from earlier traditions. For example, when I was a little girl, I inferred from the New Testament stories that Jesus was the only person ever to walk on water. When I was in my early fifties, I attended a lecture given by an eminent Japanese professor. With doctorates in psychology and electronics, he is also a Shinto priest. He was brought up by his mother and a priestess, both very devout women who practised advanced meditation techniques. When Dr Hiroshi Motoyama was a little boy aged six and first went to school, he was surprised to discover that not everyone's mummy walked on water, like his did!

Like our own, the bodies of trees are eighty per cent water. Any mature oak, ash, or sycamore will use roughly 500 litres of water every day while it is in full leaf. The water will carry sustenance to the tree's flowers, fruit, leaves, twigs, branches and trunk and it will be transpired from the leaf surfaces to maintain homeostasis in the body of the tree. This ascent of water up the tree from its roots is anti-gravitation — it is levitational. When Newton asked how the apple fell from the branch to the ground, he could well have asked how did the apple get on to the branch in the first place? If he had asked the second question, instead of the first, if he had created the foundation for a science to study the raising of form and spirit that is imbued with life force, instead of a science based on gravity, weight and quantity, we might be living in a very different world.

Newton's question about the apple, leading to a relationship of gravity with weight, was a precursor to our present culture's obsession with weight and size and therefore with quantity instead of quality. The phrase, 'standard of living' relates to nothing more than size of income, quantity and monetary value of possessions, taking no account of the quality of life, a subject I will return to later.

If we continue to use the example of trees and plants, it is easy to detect if they grow on polluted land. They will be stunted, malformed and they may die. Different plants, even of the same species, may be affected to a greater or lesser degree on the same piece of land. It is the water in the soil that carries pollution into the plants. Water, with its amazing bonding capacity and the fluidity which depends on spiral and vortistic movements, is the carrier of nutrients into and out of the soil — and of the poisons that enter the soil as well.

Before looking any further at the way water has been polluted, let us look at water itself. Of all the substances in our world, it is, in one or another of its manifestations — steam, liquid, ice — the one that shows best how energy moves. Accompanying the diagram of how energy, through spiral flow, becomes form, Callum Coats writes: 'Energy creates the form in which it wishes to move. The form is therefore the mirror of the energy flow.' Later he writes,

> As the energy moves along its desired path, it draws matter into its wake and forms the vessel through which it wants to move. A river does exactly the same thing. The capillaries in our bodies likewise. The blood is the external manifestation of an energy

Form is Secondary – The Effect

Energy creates the form in which it wishes to move.
The form is therefore the mirror of the energy flow.

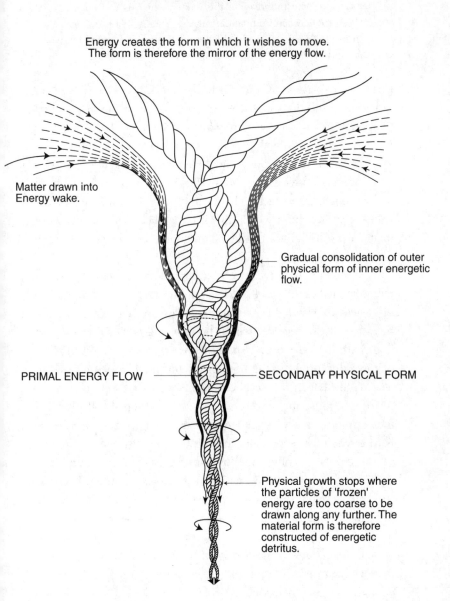

Matter drawn into
Energy wake.

Gradual consolidation of outer
physical form of inner energetic
flow.

PRIMAL ENERGY FLOW —————— ← —— SECONDARY PHYSICAL FORM

Physical growth stops where
the particles of 'frozen'
energy are too coarse to be
drawn along any further. The
material form is therefore
constructed of energetic
detritus.

Energy and Form

path. What we see is the blood, but we do not see the energy that moves it. The blood is all the matter which is too coarse to be taken to the energy's final destination. Energy therefore creates the form of the path through which it wants to move and along which it can move with the least resistance.

Coats also explains how Viktor Schauberger detected the differences in viscosity and density that water adopts at even subtly different temperatures. It is at +4° centigrade (or celsius), that water is at its most dense and lively. In its natural state and at that temperature, water flows in longitudinal spirals of alternating sun-wise and counter-sun-wise directions. These directions in the flow of the current are the factor that continually cool and recool the water as it flows and which give it the ability to lift fragments of matter from the bottom of its channel and to keep it within the defining sides.

This flow pattern gives rise to the winding pathway that water naturally makes for itself. No natural waterway is straight. No blood vessel is straight. As water levitates up the stem of a plant or a tree, it does so in a spiral flow. As the water flows out of your bath, it does so in a spiral flow and the spiral is sun-wise, or toward the right in the northern hemisphere and sun-wise, or toward the left in the southern hemisphere. This is not contradictory, because the sun, seen from the northern hemisphere of the earth, appears to be moving toward the right and the reverse is true when it is seen from the southern hemisphere.

These polarities of energy flow must be telling us profound facts about the energy vortices with which we are surrounded. The structure of snails' shells, escargot or winkles, is spiral; the structure of animals' horns is spiral; the galaxies are spiral in shape and rotate in that pattern; strands of DNA are arranged in a double helix, which means they are in a pattern of two intertwining spirals of matter. Because a rotating projectile carries further and truer to course than one that does not rotate, the feathers that make up the flights of arrows are attached to the shaft in a spiral pattern. This is a feature noted by gun makers, who construct rifles with spiral grooves inside the barrels (the 'rifling'), so that the bullet will emerge from the barrel rotating. Archimedes invented a device to raise water. It was called a 'screw' and took the water on a spiral path, vertically. The latter appears to be one of the few benign uses to which this natural motion has been applied by humankind. Water shows us this pattern in all its activities and yet it is ignored. It is as though science sees water as too commonplace to be important, instead of recognising that, by its very ubiquitous nature, its characteristics are of supreme importance to our understanding of our universe and also of our environment.

Years of observing water in its natural environment, the forest, taught Viktor Schauberger that egg-shaped objects move through water with far greater facility than objects of any other shape. In fact, the section through a fish's body is, for many species, an elongated egg shape. Schauberger also realised that vessels made in the shape of an egg can be used to improve the state of water. He invented such a vessel. Its internal shape caused water, initially, to move downwards between two matching, egg-shaped 'skins' (the exterior skin and another that fitted inside), and by percolation into another section inside the second skin, which was placed in the bottom half of the vessel at the pointed end. This latter section was again of two almost matching skins, but only half-of-an-egg shape, and with a rippled surface which would create a cycloid oscillation in the water that made it move upwards. During this process, small amounts of naturally occurring minerals that Schauberger called 'noble salts' and carbon dioxide were added to the water that ultimately ascended a long pipe to the top, no matter how high that was, to emerge with all the qualities of natural spring water.

As untreated water constantly flows in and treated water emerges at equal speed, it would take only a small machine to create a large quantity of life-enhancing natural spring water for the benefit of animals, plants and people. Coats describes in detail the function and structure of this 'spring water machine', calling it, as Schauberger did, the Repulsine. More recently, several people, independently studying Schauberger's theories in England, Ireland and India, have developed water energising appliances that can, by vibrational transfer, harmonise the energies of water exposed to them. The effect of these appliances can be compared to the effect of a bugging device on a telephone line, although, instead of drawing the vibrations towards itself, as would the bug, the water energiser transfers a harmonious energy to the mains water so that the negative dominance of dangerous chemicals becomes innocuous.

Trees and plants can only express choice about the water they consume by dying, or by seeding themselves in unpolluted places. Many people would question whether life forms such as trees or plants can express choice, but these living things are not dependent on an invented technology — they follow nature. People, on the other hand, are dependent on a technology developed from orthodox scientific thought. Although this is not the only science that exists, it is the only kind the scientific establishment has under review — so the scientists release their findings and their acolytes in politics and industry implement them. The result, in terms of the public water supply, is 'clean' water.

The earliest additive put into public water supplies was the chemical, chlorine. This water can be termed 'clean' because the chlorine kills two organisms dangerous to human life, the bacteria that cause cholera and typhoid. These can become rampant where people live in close quarters to one another, as they do in towns and cities. In this context and in all others, the route of orthodox scientific endeavour is always toward destruction, in this instance to destroy living organisms. If scientists were interested instead in seeking out life-enhancing phenomena and machines, the water wouldn't contain the organisms that cause cholera and typhoid in the first place.

Schauberger was denigrated by academic hydrologists, whose work was exclusively confined to the laboratory, while his explored water in all its forms, in its natural habitat. If his observations about the optimal temperature of living water, for example, had become accepted within orthodox science, the provision of wholesome water to the public might have taken a very different form. For reasons that I believe have to do with the centralised form of government, public utilities arrive in the home from a central source, or a number of sources controlled from a central place. This has led to a form of gargantuanism that ignores improvements that could result from a reduction in scale, as well as improvements that become possible because of developments in other aspects of life. While cholera and typhoid are likely to occur where there is a high density population with no sanitation system, or with an inadequate system carelessly used, these diseases tend to disappear when improved sanitation systems are introduced. Whilst huge schemes to bring running water to city homes were being developed, flush toilets were being installed in every home. Improved hygiene and better nourishment from cleaner food also contributed to the elimination of many formerly mortal illnesses.

City households, miles from the sight of a spring or river, are entitled to water of the quality to be found in a mountain spring, deep in a forest, far from the influence of pollutant chemicals or random bacteria, the sort of water that many country dwellers take for granted. At present, such supplies for cities seem impossible, using established systems, but as Callum Coats' elucidation of Viktor Schauberger's experiments and inventions of earlier this century have illustrated, it *is* possible. We need to detach ourselves from the ideas that create the huge and complex distribution systems that we use for the present forms of electricity and water supply and sewage disposal. If instead we made small units, ranging in size from those suitable for a single household to those suitable for, say a tenement building housing 100 families, Schauberger's technology could be used to supply regenerated spring water containing no hazardous additives or bacteria to every household, no matter how deep in the city jungle it might be.

Clean water is good news, but it relates solely to the state of the water *before* it enters the human body. The water that can be drawn from any domestic mains water system is unlikely to contain the bacteria that cause cholera and typhoid, because it contains chlorine. It has been discovered only in recent years that the human digestive tract contains a huge variety of bacteria and fungi, without which it cannot properly function. Chlorine creates havoc within this population, with the result that the beneficial activity of these organisms is severely impaired. Through the continual imbibing of chlorinated water, day after day, with the resultant damage to the microbial activity in our guts, we become unable to absorb adequately the food we eat. This is one of the contributory facts to immunity depletion and ill health in Western countries — quite the reverse from the original intention!

If the addition of chlorine to the public water supply is an early example of mass-medication, a more recent one is fluoride. It is claimed that fluoride creates stronger teeth and fewer instances of dental caries, especially in babies and young children. This may be true of calcium fluoride, which is a salt found naturally in some rocks and therefore in the water that leaches out of them, providing a protection among youthful populations who drink it. Because the word 'fluoride' is all that is used to refer to this additive, it is not common knowledge that the fluoride used to medicate drinking water is *sodium* fluoride; this does not occur naturally, but is a poisonous by-product of aluminium smelting, one of the uses of which is as an ingredient in chemical insecticides. Sodium fluoride is also added to some brands of toothpaste; this is advertised as an enhancement of this product, although in the US, toothpaste tubes and their packets now carry a government health warning that if any of the toothpaste is swallowed the affected person should go to a hospital casualty unit at once! Children growing up in areas where sodium fluoride has been added to the water supply have been observed to develop brown spots on their teeth and to have an abnormally high occurrence of brittle bones, both signs of fluoride poisoning.

The National Pure Water Association was founded by Lord Douglas of Barloch in the 1960s. With reference to sodium fluoride in the public water supply, Dr Peter Mansfield, the current president of the association, is quoted as saying,

> No physician in his right senses would prescribe for a person he has never met, whose medical history he does not know, a substance which is intended to create bodily change, with the advice: take as much as you like, because some people say that it reduces tooth decay in children.

A considerable volume of research data has been available for several years, including a report by Dr Hans C. Moolenburgh, who wrote about the experiences of ordinary general practitioners before the proven side-effects of fluoridation of water supplies caused the government of Holland to outlaw its use:

> . . . we were up against two difficulties: in the first place the complaints were so general that we didn't recognise them. They were registered under different heads as: dyspepsia, asthma, allergic skin rashes, urinary irritation, spastic colon, arthritis, etc. The second trouble was that where the authorities had solemnly declared that no side effects could be there, the rather orthodox medical establishment was not inclined to believe what they saw before their very eyes.

For similar reasons, the government of Denmark banned fluoridation as long ago as 1977, in response to a recommendation from its National Agency for Environmental Protection. Sweden ruled against it in 1980 on the grounds that there was insufficient knowledge about the combined and long-term environmental effects of using fluoride in water supplies. An advertisement made by the company that produces Endekay Fluoride Supplement, claiming that ninety percent of us don't get enough fluoride in our diet, was refuted by Dr Eggins of the University of Ulster. He concluded his report on his investigation into the truth of the claim by saying, 'I consider this advertisement to be factually incorrect and dangerous, in that it encourages people to ingest excessive amounts of a toxic substance, fluoride.' In view of all this, why is this substance still added to drinking water in *any* country?

In the search for safe water, it might be thought that bottled spring water is the answer. At least it doesn't contain chlorine or fluoride. Water in plastic bottles, however, should be avoided, because the ingredients in the plastic, such as PCBs, can leach into the water very easily. The increase in sales of spring water has led to an increased interest in the product by health inspectors. Even 'natural spring water', as advertised on the bottle, may contain some added chemical substance to destroy, for example, E-coli, the bacteria arising from animal or human manure which can cause life-threatening infection.

Distilled water, also available in the shops, is made by boiling water, gathering the steam and condensing it back into liquid, at which point it is simple, pure H_2O, when it is bottled. Health inspectors have been known to insist that disinfectant chemicals are added even to this! Carbonated mineral water has had carbon dioxide added to it under pressure. Some people like it, some loathe it, but taste is personal, though the choice of chemicals that are added to this as well are not.

Some people prefer a domestic method of water purification, perhaps feeling that they then have more control over the water they use. The simplest method to remove living organisms from water is to boil it for at least ten minutes, to kill all possible bacteria. To avoid increasing any chemical contamination that may exist — boiling will not remove these — the vessel in which the water is boiled should be made from an inert material, such as ceramic, fire-proof glass, or unchipped enamel (powdered glass, fused by heat onto a metal base).

The Schauberger Repulsine seems to me to be the most desirable piece of domestic equipment, but there is a range of more readily available items, with varying degrees of efficiency. Filtration is possible using a hand-held jug, as well as with more permanent installations. There have been some instances of allergic reaction to the contents of the filter material, so it is wise to check the list of contents, before buying. Reverse osmosis is generally regarded as the most efficient method; this is a requirement for people on kidney dialysis, who have to avoid any form of contamination in the water they ingest. Such units are quite compact, but may be several hundred pounds to buy and install. Distillation needs equipment that has to be supervised when in use, and may make the kitchen look like a laboratory. Consumer magazines and 'watchdogs' can be helpful in making a choice, but the user needs to remember that, whatever their choice, the unit will need regular cleaning and maintenance to work efficiently.

Mains water supplies, whether privatised, as in the UK, or public utilities, are frequently not maintained as they should be. Visible, live infestations have occurred in domestic supplies, as well as bacterial and chemical contamination. As in all the utilities, annual profits take precedence over daily care to produce clean, potable water. In the 1970s, the water authorities in England and Wales — as yet not privatised — decided that *all* households, whether receiving mains water or attached to mains sewage disposal or not, should pay a water rate. It was not a large sum, so far as individual houses were concerned, being a little over £3. However, a number of people not connected to either service regarded this as an official iniquity and refused to pay — we were among them. Eventually a non-payer was taken to court in Plymouth as a test case. The water authority lost and as a result, all the authorities were obliged to refund the amount charged to those households who had paid — and, as it turned out, those who had not.

Since the privatisation of water companies in UK, people with their own spring or well source have been charged a water rate, on the grounds that the water they abstract is being taken from the natural reservoir that the water company now owns. We laugh about the window tax levied in an earlier century, but this is equally ludicrous. No-one is obliged to accept any mains services and those who do not should not be obliged to pay for what they do not receive.

Perhaps householders who are connected to the mains but also find it necessary to install purifying equipment, should send a bill to the water supply company for the installation and main-tenance of such equipment. Or those who have a private source for which the water company is making a charge could send a bill to the company for the maintenance of the pump and pipes they use to bring the water to the house? This is no more ridiculous than what the water companies are doing. Or, in the event of a supply that the householder finds is not up to standard, perhaps payment should be refused altogether? After all, the poll tax in UK was withdrawn because it proved to be unworkable due to the high number of people who refused to pay it.

Eight

WATER, WATER, EVERYWHERE

*There is a time when a thing is a heavy thing to carry
and then it must be put down. But such is its nature that
it cannot be set off on a rock or shoulder off onto the fork
of a tree like a heavy pack. There is only one thing shaped
to receive it and that is another human mind.*

Theodore Sturgeon

It was in 1967, when Jeremiah and I moved with our children to live in rural Wales, that for the first time we experienced using fresh spring water on a daily basis. On drinking cups of tea in a café on a visit to town, we recognised the chemical taste of the medicated public water supply. We were no longer desensitised through using it habitually and it tasted disgusting.

Water is not simply H_2O, two hydrogen atoms attached to an atom of oxygen to form a molecule of water — it is far subtler as a compound. In its passage through the atmosphere, as cloud, mist, rain or snow, as well as through the soil and rocks, water changes its character as it absorbs a variety of other substances and as its temperature alters. It 'grows' in maturity, if it is allowed. By boiling water, trapping the resultant steam and condensing it back into water, we can 'distil' it. This process returns the water to its basic H_2O — no additives, no solutes, no character.

At this stage, water is in its infancy and like all infants, it wishes to absorb as much as it can of everything with which it comes into contact. Restricted in its contact and kept 'pure', it would be totally safe for wet cell batteries, but not for human consumption. In its passage through the human digestive system, distilled water can remove more than it leaves; in its greed and eagerness to mature, it seeks out and absorbs electrolytes, subtle amounts of trace elements and minerals that we require in order to function properly. To drink pure, distilled water on a regular basis, is to run the risk of health loss, through subsequent mineral deficiency. However, the use of distilled water to make beer, tea, coffee, or medication is far less hazardous, because the water will absorb all it can from the substances with which it is used as a process medium.

Marginally better than distilled water, rain water is hazardous to drink on a long-term basis. It contains a few minerals that it has absorbed during its life in the air, but in some industrial areas these may be pollutants that are themselves deleterious to health. This water needs to be 'ripened' before it can be usefully absorbed by the body. Surface water and water that has stood on the earth's surface in dammed lakes and reservoirs will have absorbed more minerals than rain water because of its contact with the soil. However, it will be more oxygenated from atmospheric exposure, combined with exposure to the sun's heat. That same heat also draws much of its energy and character from the water.

Water that comes from the ground can be classified as juvenile, adolescent, or mature. It might prove difficult to distinguish between the first two, except perhaps empirically, using taste as the judge of flavour, or by laboratory analysis. Both may emerge from the ground in a variety of ways, as geysers, seepage wells, or from artesian bore holes. The qualities the water contains will depend wholly on the types of rocks and soils through which it has passed and its temperature at the time. Truly mature water, at its beneficial best can sometimes be detected visually, because it has a slightly bluish tinge and a shimmering, vibrant quality. In addition, it will have the highest quota of dissolved carbons, which constitutes the best water. Sadly, sources of this water are diminishing because of the way chemicals and other pollutants are also seeping through soil and rocks.

Medical opinion has concluded in recent years that those of us who live in industrialised societies are seriously and habitually dehydrated. The liquids we ingest, from soup, tea, coffee, beer, wine, spirits to juices, are accepted by our digestive systems as food. Granted, they *contain* water, but in fact, some of these liquids, especially the alcoholic ones, actually accelerate the dehydration process — which is why a hangover often includes a very real thirst. Water, as water, on the other hand, passes readily through the alimentary canal and needs less 'sorting' and digesting; it lubricates and hydrates the canal and is easily assimilated by osmosis into the blood and urinary systems. Osmosis is the process used by the body to transport liquids from one system to another; a fluid with a lesser quantity of solutes can be drawn through a semi-permeable membrane toward a fluid with a greater quantity of solutes (this is the factor that guarantees a one-way flow).

When water arrives in the urinary system, it absorbs the waste material the kidneys have collected from the blood. This process is clearly illustrated when people who have a problem with 'water retention' (oedema), in the form of swollen ankles, hands, or other bodily parts, drink a lot more water than anything else, the oedema is reduced. Water, drunk as water, thus works as a powerful detoxification agent by taking poisons out of the system. Having access to uncontaminated and unprocessed mature spring water is, for me, the sort of privilege a wine connoisseur would feel regarding vintage champagne.

Mass medication of the public water supply is one area where chemicals in water can impinge on both human and non-human life forms; another is from the addition of chemicals during the purification process used before the water is distributed to consumers. A protracted issue in Northern Ireland has been the use of chemicals to precipitate solids that exist in the water at the point of abstraction. Most of Northern Ireland is supplied with water that is soft and drains out of bogland. Its original appearance can be quite discoloured, depending on the amount of plant and mineral material suspended in it. Aluminium sulphate and iron hydroxide are the chemicals most frequently used to precipitate the particles out of the water. A sludge forms at the bottom of the treatment beds; this is composed of a mixture of these chemicals and the substances formerly suspended in the water.

Danny Brown, chairman of the *Neagh and Maine System Game Angling Association*, became anxious when he observed large numbers of young salmonid fish with deformed gill covers, which affected their ability to breathe. He is convinced that this disorder is attributable to the unnatural presence of aluminium and iron compounds in the rivers. Brown has established that some of these compounds originate from water treatment works, while some may come from careless disposal of industrial chemical residues.

In June 1993, James R. Lamont, Director of Environmental Protection at the Department of the Environment in Northern Ireland, in replying to Danny Brown's request for information about the contents of the sludge, wrote,

> . . . filter washing sludge . . . contains aluminium and iron hydroxides which are both insoluble in water. In other words, the aluminium and iron are bound up in the sludge particulate and are not available for uptake by fish, macroinvertebrates, plants, or indeed humans.

In what appears to be a contradiction of this, Minister of the Environment, Malcolm Moss, wrote in another letter in November 1995,

> I can confirm that both aluminium sulphate and locally produced iron aluminium sulphate are used as coagulants at water treatment plants in the Maine river systems . . . in accordance with accepted practice within the UK water industry. Water quality testing ensures that aluminium levels are maintained within the standards set for drinking water by national regulatory limits which accord with those of the EU. They are set with appropriate margins to safeguard public health.
>
> It is not the practice of the department to discharge filter sludges produced as part of the water treatment process to rivers. Sludge from the lagoons at these water treatment plans is disposed of to the public sewer and spread on land within the catchment area.

From here, presumably, it can seep, through natural drainage, into both the rivers and the drinking water reservoirs. There is also the problem of human error in the use of these dangerous chemicals, as was the experience of the population of the village of Camelford in South West England, when, in the 1980s an excessive amount of an aluminium-based compound was accidentally added to the water supply.

Doug Cross is a chartered biologist and a forensic ecologist, whose Camelford home was the first house below the outfall from the waterworks and therefore the first to be affected. In the events that followed, his expertise was a great advantage to that community. The November/December 1990 issue of *The Ecologist* published a paper he had written: The Politics of Poisoning; the Camelford Aluminium Sulphate Scandal (An examination of the effects of aluminium poisoning after the Lowermoor Incident). The paper begins,

> In July 1988, the public water supply to the town of Camelford was contaminated when aluminium sulphate solution, used in the purification of drinking water, was accidentally discharged into the treated tank water at the Lowermoor Water Treatment Works, supplying over 7,000 properties and at least 20,000 local consumers and tourists in North Cornwall.

When this paper was written, legal action in the High Court was pending on this issue against the Water Authority Residuary Body (WARB) — appointed by local government, but answerable also to national government. Therefore any discussion of that body's role in the Camelford incident came under the *sub judice* rules. After explaining this, Doug Cross continues,

> But despite repeated assurances that aluminium in drinking water poses no health hazards, many people did suffer from persistent medical problems, some of which are still so severe that the victims are no longer able to lead a normal life, or operate their businesses. This paper examines the medical and political factors in the Lowermoor Incident.

What led to the incident was partly immediate and partly long-term neglect. The aluminium sulphate was supplied by lorry which under normal circumstances would unload under supervision.

On the occasion in question, the lorry driver found no-one to supervise the unloading, but went ahead, unwittingly pouring the load into the wrong tank. This tank was the one in which chlorine was normally mixed through the water, immediately prior to entering the holding tank from which it would be distributed to consumers. This might not have proved so serious, had it not been for the long-term neglect to clean the sump at the bottom of the tank that received the 27.8 per cent aqueous solution of aluminium sulphate. Because this solution is heavier than water, it could quickly have flowed to the bottom of the sump, had the sump not already been full of solids that had collected over many years.

While initially no deliberate cover-up may have been intended, the lack of knowledge regarding the effects of ingesting high percentage solutions of aluminium salts displayed by water authority representatives is staggering. The assurances given by the authority subsequent to the event related solely to the flavour of the water and recommended the addition of orange juice to mask any unpleasantness. In notes he compiled for the prosecution in the case against the WARB already referred to, Doug Cross points out that when aluminium sulphate solution enters the gut it combines with substances present there to form new compounds. Some of these will make the aluminium more accessible to the blood and one, citric acid, which is present in large amounts in orange juice, ensures rapid take-up of the aluminium by the blood. Sulphuric acid is formed when aluminium sulphate is mixed with water.

No warning was given of the additional hazard resulting from the dramatically increased acidity of the water supplied to consumers. It caused extensive descaling in domestic copper tanks and piping, which released another poison, copper. The more recently the plumbing had been installed, the more seriously the copper corroded. One would have expected that a professional representative who gave inadequate as well as dangerously inappropriate advice to customers would have been prosecuted for negligence, but this never happened.

Doug Cross and a local doctor helped to form the Camelford Scientific Advisory Panel to provide support and information to residents, many of whom began to suffer from mouth ulcers, digestive problems, bone pains and skin rashes, all of which were attributed to the increased chemical acidity of the water. The panel assembled and recorded all the data they could, in order to provide the health authority with expert information for use in the professional epidemiological study that was expected to be conducted, but never was.

As the months passed, other patterns of ill health began to emerge that showed, on investigation, to be caused by aluminium. Impaired memory and concentration were the commonest symptoms which helped to establish the link between aluminium poisoning and the manifestation of Alzheimer's disease among Camelford residents that occurred after the incident.

Early veterinary reports from a number of farms with animals that drank from the public water supply showed similar reactions among the livestock as had occurred among people. As time passed, fertility and foetal development were seen to be diminished noticeably in local herds and flocks. Some farms watered their animals from private sources of water, unaffected by the incident, which made possible a series of comparisons that substantiated the reports of health problems among animals on the farms using the public water supply.

As if this was not enough, local people were thwarted at every turn in their efforts to get clear advice and compensation for the damage done. The authorities, in particular the government, seemed interested only in damage limitation, because of the intention to sell off the water authorities into private business control at the end of 1989. The last thing the government wanted was any kind of adverse exposure. The information suppressed by officials was, however, readily available in the scientific literature and was summarised by Doug Cross in notes he made available. In a handwritten addendum, he classifies the suppression as,

> criminal conspiracy at the highest levels in attempting to support
> the share values of an industry about to be privatised — I see no

difference between the government's action and the 'insider trading' they profess to abhor.

The work of Danny Brown and Doug Cross clearly shows the serious risk to fish, animals and people present in exposure to aluminium in water. Doug Cross's paper has been used in many challenges and has succeeded in preventing some dangerous developments in the use of aluminium in other countries.

Most of the man-made chemicals added to water have proved to be damaging to health, while many of the naturally occurring chemicals have the reverse effect. For centuries, chalybeate and sulphur springs have been the foci for spas — in rural Ireland, chalybeate springs are referred to as 'spa waters'. Spar, or the iron content of this water, was highly regarded as an antidote to anaemia in the days before the patenting of iron supplements for medication. The Roman Baths in the city of Bath in England owe their origin to the therapeutic value of the waters, not only for their chemical content, but also because they include hot springs used as therapeutic baths for people suffering from arthritis, rheumatism and muscular disorders.

Naturally chelated springs are not the only sort of therapeutic bath. From Austria and Switzerland have come the moor-bath. The native custom of using a portion of the black sludge collected from the base of bogland deposits to add to a bath of warm water is now available in many health centres far from the lands of its origin. Bog (or peat, or turbery), forms on a non-porous base of clay or rock where plants have grown and died, regenerated only to die and regenerate again. Slowly, the depth of dead plant material accumulates, holding in it water from the rain and from any surface seepage from springs and streams. This material, sometimes many metres deep owing to its great age, has over the centuries accumulated a store of steadily increasing organic deposits, enzymes, pollens and mineral solutes from the generations of plants. These rich deposits have been traditionally recognised for their therapeutic value.

Jeremiah had a damaged big toe that gave him pain for many years. One day when cutting our winter fuel from the bog (dried bricks of peat being the traditional, excellent fuel in the boglands of Ireland), he was irritated by a leak in his wellingtons, so he took them off. After working for the rest of the day with the soft, black sludge of the bog-base squidging between his toes and staining his feet dark brown, he discovered that the pain in his toe had gone. Our neighbours were not at all surprised by this, such a practice being a recognised local cure for similar aches and pains. When about five years later the pain returned, Jerry went up on the bog and spent only about fifteen minutes walking in the sludge with bare feet. The miracle happened again, and this time the pain has not returned. Just as naturally chelated spring waters have therapeutic value when drunk in small quantities, so too has diluted bog sludge, containing, as it does, the richness from centuries' old pollens and seeds.

The ocean too has many benefits. In some resorts in the nineteenth century, bath houses were erected near the shore, where salt water baths enriched by the addition of kelp and other sea vegetables were offered. Ocean plants retain the heat of the water in which they are placed, so even a long soak might not need a hot top-up as it soothed sore muscles, irritating skin conditions or general debility. Three or four buckets full of sea vegetables, picked at low tide, rinsed in cold water to remove any sand and other detritus, can be used in your own bath. It was in the nineteenth century too, that ocean bathing began to be recognised as both enjoyable and beneficial for minor abrasions, bruises, sore muscles and some skin disorders. Sea bathing would still be beneficial provided no salmon cages or sewage outfalls were nearby!

When Esther, our elder daughter, was about three years old, some friends took her to the seaside. On her return, we asked her what it was like. She thought for a moment, then said, 'It was *very* big and it was *full* of water.' Any quantity of moving water generates negative ions, which are the electro-magnetic polarities of the atoms of gasses in the atmosphere. A preponderance of positive ions saps our energy, making us lethargic and heavy. Negative ions, however, invigorate us and make us feel good. Is it any wonder then that we gravitate to such places, not only for their frequent natural beauty, but also for the energetic benefit we accrue while there?

There is a paradox here. Synthesised, man-made additives and naturally found additives to water appear to have opposite effects. Naturally found, flowing water benefits our energy levels, piped water from a treatment works can do the opposite. Somewhere between the extremes of this paradox lies an area ripe for exploration. The work of researchers such as Schauberger could be brought out of the shadows and into the spotlight to the benefit of all. The radical changes needed in the treatment of water and its distribution must be reviewed without conservatism or protectionism entering the debate. There is no doubt that the dense populations in cities need clean and wholesome water and there is also no doubt that the capabilities exist for it to be provided.

No-one has yet found a way to tax the air we breathe, nor to privatise its supply, but water has been made subject to both, despite being quite as essential to life as the untaxed air. Government-run 'nationalised' water supply authorities and independent 'privatised' suppliers both need to realise the commitment they are undertaking and behave with compassion and honesty, taking a fair profit for fair dealing. We are all water consumers, no matter where we obtain our supply and we can make our needs and wishes known to these authorities.

Nine

WASTE NOT, WANT NOT

It is not, of course, the subject that is or isn't dull, but the quality of attention we do or do not pay to it, and the strength of our will to transform. Dull subjects are those we have failed.

by Wendell Berry

What are People For?

(Quotation from William Matthews)

If we take more care of how we use water in the domestic area — for drinking, lavatory flushing, bathing, dish-washing, laundry and garden hoses — those who work in agriculture and industry will be bound to apply a different and more careful attitude to water use. Our experiences as a household that has lived by choice in a far more basic way, bears out this contention. In centuries past, most people lived as we have chosen to live in the twentieth century. We didn't make that choice about simple living when we were first married — it came to us gradually after we had sampled the amenities the twentieth century had to offer.

During our early years together and while we were modernising a Victorian terrace house we had bought, we took baths in an old hip bath we had bought in a junk shop. We kept it in the back garden and brought it into the kitchen, where we used it in front of the kitchen fire. I remember a particular bath night. I was eight months pregnant with my second child and too large to fold my legs into the hip bath, so I sat, my bottom in the bath and my feet on the hearthrug, gazing into the flames. Jerry and a plumber friend had nearly finished the plumbing and I knew that before my baby was born I would have the choice of a bath or a shower in the warm, wood-lined bathroom at the top of the house. I would no longer have to heat the water in the clothes boiler and tip it into the bath, nor tip it out again after I'd used it. Perversely, I wanted to retain all that hard work, because I loved the fire and there wouldn't be one in the bathroom!

About eighteen months later, we packed all our possessions, loaded our two children and two cats into our VW Microbus and drove away from our modernised, desirable residence in a provincial English city, heading westwards to start a new life in the mountains of Wales. It is since that day, 30 September 1967 that we have had no indoor plumbing in our home. To be fair, it was force of circumstances to begin with. The house we had bought had not only been unoccupied for forty years, it had never had any modern amenities. While we began the necessary restoration work, we rented a farmhouse for a few months; during this time, we erected a secondhand prefab outside our old farmhouse, in which we lived until the restoration was completed. When it was completed, I could once again bathe in the hip bath, but this time in front of the ingle fire.

Given the way we live I have become very aware of the issues around the use of water as a cleaning medium. To begin with, far more is used than is really necessary. Dishwashing is a good example; now that mechanical dishwashers are commonplace, it is not unusual for the soiled dishes from a day's meals to be washed only once a day. We also only wash our dishes once a day, but we do so by hand. Dishwashing machines use several gallons of water per cycle and are not very efficient, because if the food residues are not removed by hand before the dishes are put into the machine, then they are not properly removed by the machine. We clean our dishes of food residues after every meal, either by using small amounts of cold water to rinse the none-greasy ones, or by using discarded paper to wipe the greasy ones. Thereafter, it takes only a very small amount of near-boiling water to finish the job.

After this hand processing, there is no residue of soap or chemical detergent as there is on dishes washed in a dishwashing machine, because we never use washing-up liquid. In our opinion, our technique renders it unnecessary as well as ecologically undesirable. Washing-up liquid in waste water prevents the natural, organic decomposition of the material in the water. If a house in a rural area has an independent disposal system, it is likely to be a septic tank; the basic principle behind a septic tank is organic decomposition. If this is inhibited by washing-up liquid, or any other household cleaner with a chemical base, the system fails to work; it stinks, and the final outflow does not contain clear, clean water as the design intends. Houses in urban areas are served by a sewage drainage system, so that the waste water produced in the home is transported and disposed of in places often quite distant. But the same principle obtains. The presence of soaps, bleaches, solvents and disinfectants prevents the proper decomposition of the solid matter carried in the waste. Very little of this waste is processed to render it either usable or safe for further disposal. Whether it is the effluent from a properly functioning septic tank, the outfall from a mains sewer, or the product from a sewage farm — as sewage processing plants are euphemistically called — this material flows into streams, rivers and ultimately into the ocean.

In our Victorian terrace house, which had a two-roomed basement below street level, we had an experience that made me question for the first time why rainwater — called 'storm water' when it flows into sewers — is allowed to run into the sewer. One day, there was a storm so heavy that the Victorian sewer, burdened with additional drainage from twentieth century houses and increased water usage, simply couldn't cope. The result was a back wash of raw sewage that flowed into our basement to a depth of nearly a foot. It was disgusting and it took days to clean it out. The sole help we received from the city council was the advice to fit a non-return valve to our connection with the main sewer. If it was standard practice for rainwater to be drained off separately, or retained in a storage system for domestic or industrial use, there would be far less need for large sewers.

Furthermore, far less mains water would then need to be piped to houses or factories. Calculating our domestic water usage as a two-person household, we drink or cook with about 2,600 litres (520 gallons), per year and we use 11,700 litres (2,340 gallons) of washing water per year. The combined total of drinking and washing water is about forty litres, or eight gallons every day between us. I'm sure this is far below the national average. According to official figures, the consumption in the United States for every individual is 6,440 litres, (1,288 gallons) each day! One hundred and sixty-one times more than *two* of us use! However, while my assessment of what we use is literal, in that it relates to what we actually use each day, the assessment by the US Department of the Interior, from whom I received these figures, must include *all* fresh-water usage, whether in the home, the factory, the farm, etc. the figure derived must then be divided by the population number. In Ireland in 1998 the figures were 135 litres (27 gallons) per day per head domestically, or 250 litres (50 gallons) per day, per person, at home and in offices.

Flush toilets use an inordinate amount of water to wash away the deposits left in them. With a different system and attitude, one that recognises the value of that waste material as well as the value of the water, some other form of processing could be used to turn human dung into manure for agricultural or horticultural use. Such a system exists in China, where this resource helps to grow food needed for the huge Chinese population. For thousands of years, human dung has been collected and processed by natural fermentation to be used as fertiliser. Some processed sewage is used as fertiliser in the UK, but, because of its chemical overload, it is as suspect as fertiliser derived from chemicals in a factory. Sewage from British houses is washed into pipes along with washing-up liquid, chemical products used to clean and deodorise toilets and any other chemicals a householder may have 'flushed down the loo'. It is a toxic mess, possibly subject to further exposure to chemicals during its processing into fertiliser.

In 1956, it was estimated that ninety per cent of the human dung produced in China was used in this way — 300,000 tonnes of it annually! At that time, this represented one third of all fertiliser used. Throughout China, in cities, villages and isolated houses, it is customary to use either a lacquered bucket or a shallow pit to defecate into. The pit is carefully built and lined with concrete or tiles. It is designed in such a way that the urine does not lie with the solids, but flows into a separate container. This is usually diluted with water and used with no further treatment to water vegetable plots. The solid dung is collected daily by salaried sanitary workers, who use specially designed bicycles to carry this valued commodity to the processing site. There it is stacked in shallow heaps, after having been mixed with animal dung and earth and street sweepings, in roughly equal amounts.

Most processing is by a high-temperature method that destroys any pathogens present; this is achieved by inserting rods during the construction of the heaps. The rods are removed once the heaps have settled and the covering layer has dried, leaving aeration tunnels. Processing times vary from summer, when it is roughly three weeks, to winter when it can be as long as two months. After this, it is ready for use on the land. The attitude toward human dung that prevails in Europe would require radical alteration for such a system to be adopted here, but there is no doubt that it could work, if we wanted it to. We deny the value of dung by denying it in our daily lives.

A growing number of toilet designs have come into use in recent years that either compost the dung, or allow for it to be composted elsewhere. They are usually made to accommodate the product from a year's usage, rather than for daily emptying. Some of them even incorporate two chambers, each with one year's capacity. When the first chamber is full, it is sealed and the contents left to mature until the second chamber is full, by which time the contents of the first chamber should be decomposed and ready for use. Most of these lavatories use more space than the average flusher and may be easier to install in rural rather than city homes. A great deal of effort, however, is going toward the design of lavatories that dispose of urine and dung other than by losing it to an inadequate sewerage system, so it may not be long before more compact systems are available to the city dweller.

In *Designing Ecological Settlements*, a book in which the contributions of several professional designers have been edited by Declan and Margrit Kennedy, attention is paid to the details of sewage disposal in planning any kind of new settlement. The principles can be applied to small units, such as a commune in a country setting, a new satellite for a town, or a new village. All the systems described separate solid matter from water, to allow for composting of the former and sedimentation of the latter. Such a project offers a self-serving water system, in which sourcing and disposal form a continuous cycle, reflecting what happens in nature, ensuring no wastage and establishing harmonious self-sufficiency.

The designs in this book are governed by the premise that 'every waste is a resource in the wrong place', though I would add the rider that the waste has to be of organic rather than chemical origin. However, these designers also envisage a blanket ban on toxic substances entering the groundwater serving the settlement. This implies a new dimension to housing design: the self-conscious responsibility of every inhabitant to ensure they do not contribute any pollutants.

Personal cleanliness is another issue closely related to how we dispose of our personal wastes. I maintain that it is connected to an individual's state of mind. I equate our attitude to personal cleanliness to what I have observed among animals. A healthy, well-balanced animal keeps itself clean. One that is either unhealthy, or abused by humans and therefore unhappy, does not. People are the same.

Most people also equate personal cleanliness with the presence of domestic amenities in the home: if your house has no bathroom, by definition you, the occupant, are unclean. It's a state of mind again. Indians, Africans and many Asians live in homes without plumbing and water is often carried considerable distances, but a small amount in the bottom of a bowl will wash a body and very few people could be considered personally dirty.

I remember one of our daughters when she was about twelve years old arriving home from school to complain that our neighbour's son stank. 'Of what?' I asked. 'Dead knickers and dead socks,' she snapped.

This boy's home had been modernised. He had a bathroom to use and his mother had a washing machine for his soiled clothing. For whatever reason, he didn't seem to use either, but Esther strip-washed in half a gallon of water every day, as well as wearing clean underwear.

By the same token, there is no guarantee that the person with the gold-plated lavatory fittings will wash her or his hands after using the bathroom. Fatal intestinal diseases are spread by unwashed hands. When we have visitors to our amenity-free house and we introduce them to our sanitary arrangements, some of them are quite startled when I insist that they wash their hands after they've urinated, or defecated, or changed the baby's nappy. In the early months of 1997, a serious outbreak of E-coli infection in Scotland caused a number of deaths. A butcher's shop was identified as the source, but I heard no reports or comments that personal cleanliness — or the lack of it — might have been a major contributory factor.

An example of a sewage processing system called the Living Machine has been installed at Findhorn in Scotland. Dr John Todd, a Canadian biologist, used the principles of ecological engineering based on the natural growth processes inherent in the sequence of ingestion, digestion and excretion. By employing all forms of aquatic life, fish, snails, plants and bacteria to perform these functions, Todd designed a method of waste disposal that is not only productive but attractive. Findhorn supplies a leaflet about the Living Machine which describes how it works.

> The first component of the treatment process is three anaerobic bio-reactors buried outside the greenhouse [another part of the system]. Their function is similar to ordinary septic tanks, that is to reduce the organic material and inorganic solids in the waste water.

Grey water from baths, showers, dishwashing and laundry — as well as the dung from the 165 people permanently resident at The Park, Findhorn — is processed by the Living Machine. The volume of this is about sixty-five cubic metres every day. The greenhouse in which the aerobic processes that follow the initial, anaerobic one take place, is full of vigorous plant life; each is chosen for its extensive root system, by which the real processing of the sewage is done.

After a description of the several aerobic tanks in the green-house and how they change the chemical content of the water from hazardous to benign, the leaflet continues,

> The biology is managed as a balanced eco-system. The outer rings of the Ecological Fluidising Beds have floating plants, like azolla and duckweed, to prevent sunlight entering the water which would create algae growth. Snails graze the surfaces and other animals, such as water beetles and fish, complete the ecology. They not only enhance the treatment process but also indicate the level of water purity.

The Living Machine is dependent on electricity to pump air through the bases of some of the aerobic tanks and may be a bit heavy-duty for most private homes, but for hotels, farms, or factories it represents a very practical option. Of the twenty or so examples around the world, the smallest to date processes 3,000 gallons a day — being the output from about eighteen people — and the largest processes about 300,000 gallons a day — the output from around 1,820 people. After its passage through the machine, the water is claimed to be clean enough to be discharged safely into the sea, or used for irrigation.

One of the systems more suitable for domestic use, although also applicable to far larger units, is the reed-bed method of sewage disposal. This is an open-air system, not requiring any electricity to run, but it does need a fairly large area of land. The same 'ecological engineering' principles apply to the reed-bed as to the Living Machine and the purified water at the end of the process is suitable for irrigation purposes. In the absence of a naturally occurring wet site, an artificial pond is made, but in this instance, the 'pond' is planted with the common reed, whose Latin name is *Phragmites australis*. A variety of other water-loving plants is recommended to be planted as well.

The domestic effluent, as it flows through the root systems of the plants, encounters both aerobic and anaerobic areas. So the water-borne substances that demand oxygen for their decomposition are dealt with and the substances that contain ammonia — urine — break down to create nitrogen gas, among other things; the ammonia is thus rendered harmless and the nitrogen can be taken up by life forms that can use it.

Also on the domestic scale, there is the Flow Greenhouse, a system similar in inspiration to the Living Machine, but on a scale suited to one household. The Flow Greenhouse deals with all the washing water from people, dishes and laundry by allowing this grey water to flow into a waterproof tank with an outlet pipe. The water descends through four layers of material: first topsoil mixed with sand, then sand mixed with straw, then sand mixed with broken shell and finally, gravel. The water flows out of the bottom of the tank and out of the greenhouse to a percolation bed — a trench, or a series of trenches — filled with gravel containing porous land-drainage pipes. The gravel has a covering of topsoil mixed with sawdust, into which vegetables can be planted. The greenhouse can be a lean-to against the house wall, minimising the distance the waste water has to travel. If this system was used for a house that also employed a compact composting toilet, such as the one called The Throne, from which after one year a compost that has been described as 'pleasing, black, open and sweet' can be removed, there would be no need for sewers and no excuse not to have a magnificent garden!

In many parts of the world, there is no choice to be made about mains sewers, mains water supplies, or any other regular supply, because they simply don't exist. In 1980, an Indian called Lucas Babu gave up his practice as a homeopathic doctor to return to his home state of Tamil Nadu. His dream was to raise the quality of life for his fellow Tamils and other minority tribes in the state. He founded the Rural Integrated Development Organisation (RIDO). Very few people in the rural parts of the state had access to clean water on a regular basis, despite years of lobbying, until Babu organised a peaceful march called the Walk for Water.

Hundreds of thousands of people joined the Walk for Water, and this time the local government was sufficiently impressed to sink a bore hole and fit a pump with a circular concrete sink around it in every hamlet and village. Through his organisation, Lucas Babu has done many things to change the quality of life for the people of his state, but it is likely that the Walk for Water is one for which he will be best remembered.

Water Aid is an international NGO based in London, but working in Asia and Africa to help communities find drinking water in their own localities, without depending on expensive distribution schemes from far away. Water Aid's aim is by

> working through partner organisations, to help poor people in developing countries achieve sustainable improvements in the quality of their lives by improvements to domestic water supplies, sanitation and hygienic practices.

Since 1982, 1.4 billion people have been identified as lacking access to safe supplies of water and 2 billion as lacking any effective sanitation; 25,000 children die every day from water-related diseases. Like most NGOs, Water Aid was created under the auspices of government, as a result of a conference organised by the British water industry. The conference was attended by representatives from government departments and leaders of businesses and charities who were brought together to discuss how the UK could respond to the United Nations declaration of 1981–91 as the decade of International Drinking Water and Sanitation. With the United Nations, the World Bank and the International Monetary Fund, any of whom one would expect to be the prime movers in the supply of such facilities, it seems an affront that it is left to NGOs to provide for the needy. Politicians, financiers, economists and industrialists seem to conserve their

energies for larger, more prestigious projects than to provide for
the world's thirst.

For long periods during four winters in the late 1990s, we lived
in rented houses in Tozeur, an old, oasis, market town on the
northern edge of the Sahara. We got to know a lot of local people
and learned about their history and traditions. In an oasis, the
sourcing, use and conservation of water would, you might
expect, be uppermost in everybody's mind. The bleak, beige
desert under the bleached, beige skies surrounds forty square
kilometres of date orchards, whose tall palm trees — every part
of which is used — have been the source of sustenance to the
town for over a thousand years.

The distribution of water through the rows of trees is fair and
even-handed, following a system that was first mapped 800 years
ago. The Berka is marked by a modern café now, but it is still
used as the gathering place for the men who use the date
palmery's water supply. Here, the charges for water and the
repair and maintenance of the interconnecting waterways are
discussed and decisions made at intervals over the year. The
meetings are informal, with no bureaucratic structure, unlike the
affairs in the modern municipal buildings 100 yards away.

Both hot and cold springs pour out of the ground. In some
places, ancient, split-palm logs with their centres gouged out are
still used to channel the finer runnels, but most of the channels
are now through pipes or concrete canals. Tiny fish, like min-
nows, dart about in the hard, clear waters. Mules and donkeys are
led to drink in the shallow canals between journeys as freight
carriers for the oasis. The palmery area has not always been as
large as it is today, but as it has been extended by prising more
land from the desert, the ancient water supply system has also
been extended.

The palm trees stand about thirty to forty feet high and are
planted in rows, beneath which other fruit trees have been
planted in a more random manner. These include vines that
support themselves on the palms, or on pear, apricot, peach, fig
or olive trees and beneath these are neat, rectilinear plots, in

which vegetables and animal fodder are cultivated. Each plot is edged by an earthen bank about a foot high. The men employed in the water distribution use mattocks (short-handled, heavy hoes used for breaking up soil) to make narrow breaks in these banks at a specific time every day for each landowner. Exactly one hour later, the men return and use the mattocks to close the gap. During that hour, the day's water supply has flowed across the porous soil and nurtured all the plants within the plot.

It is on this basis of one hour's water a day that the rate is charged to the palmery owners. Although there are cars and trucks in the town itself, the oasis roads are narrow and the transport, like the water distribution system, is ancient and traditional. Asses and mules, some with panniers, some drawing small, flat carts, carry dry stable sweepings on the outward journey and crops on the return. In the town itself, the French colonialists, who departed about forty years ago, left behind a well-plumbed domestic water distribution system, as well as a mains sewage disposal system that has recently been updated with larger pipes.

There is an idyllic quality about the oasis gardens. They are peaceful, abundant and beautiful, with men working quietly at traditional hand skills to maintain that abundance. But the end may be nigh. On the hilly south western edge of the town, building was underway from our first visit. This is the Zone Touristique. One of the earliest buildings to be erected was the Dar Chreiat Museum, with its restaurants and Aladdin's Palace, a very elegant and stylish place, attractive to locals and tourists alike. Around it now is an ever-increasing choice of expensive hotels, each one individually elegant and all equally beautiful architecturally.

The development of tourism is a high priority for the Tunisian government and these hotels represent a high standard of amenity: but at a price. The cascade of water outside one hotel is matched by a lovely indoor water garden in another. They all have rooms *en suite* with flush toilets and showers. There are jacuzzis and swimming pools. None of this water usage is discussed at the Berka and none of it comes from the water channels that serve the oasis gardens. Each hotel has its own bore hole that has been sunk below the level of the water table that serves the oasis. Parts of the oasis are dying as a result. Its quiet beauty and vibrancy, the result of centuries of continual hand work, is in sharp contrast to the opulent profligacy of the hotels in the Zone Touristique.

Travelling across the desert during my last visit, I passed through a number of towns on the journey. In every one, a street has recently been renamed Avenue Environmentale. What a golden opportunity the Tunisian government has passed up to apply up-to-date, environmental criteria to the design of the new hotels, not only in Tozeur, but in all the other towns that are being developed for tourism.

By contrast, we carry our water in flagons from a well a quarter of a mile down hill from our house. It is delicious and the well never runs dry, but as it takes time and effort to bring the water home, we don't use it for washing. Instead, our corrugated roof has guttering which is plumbed into four barrels, two of which stand at the front of the house and two at the back. We also have two free-standing ones, which are not plumbed. All six hold forty gallons and they all have a spigot tapped into the base for drawing off the contents. The free-standing barrels are our reserve, only to be used when the plumbed ones are empty due to lack of rainfall; we refill them by hand as soon as rain occurs. Each barrel contains one week's supply, so, in all, we have six weeks' water in the event of drought. Ireland is not subject to frequent drought! We wash ourselves all over every day and conserve the grey water to use for slopping out.

Our system is not unique. Houses in isolated places, not served by a mains supply, often have far larger storage facilities than ours. In India, for example, communities are served by huge stone or concrete tanks that hold thousands of gallons of water conserved during the heavy rains of the monsoon, for use throughout the rest of the year. In country areas, you often see simple wooden tackle for lifting buckets full of water from the bottom of these deep tanks.

Whatever hand work is involved in a domestic water supply, awareness and care are also involved. People with piped water usually keep the tap running while they scrub their teeth and may allow as much as half a gallon to flow down the drain unnecessarily; but when I clean my teeth, I use only a cup full of water. Jeremiah calls our way of living the Bucket Economy, because we carry so many elements of our domestic needs through our front door in a bucket. Few people choose to live this way and it would be inappropriate for many more, but it has the virtue of focusing our minds on conservation.

How can this focus be brought to people whose effort is not employed in supplying their own basic needs, such as water? Maybe a simple, camping holiday experience would be enough. Water shortages impose awareness which usually disappears once supplies are restored, but, if awareness were constant, perhaps those shortages would be less frequent. I hope that improved knowledge of water's abilities and character may contribute to more respect for its use.

Ten

SUBTLE ENERGIES

*The upholder of the cycles which sustain all Life is water.
In every drop of water dwells a deity whom indeed we
all serve. There also dwells Life, the soul of the primal
substance — water — whose boundaries and banks are
the capillaries that guide it and in which it circulates.
Every pulse beat arising through the interaction of will
and resistance is indicative of creative work and
urges us to care for those vessels, those primary and
most vital structures, in which throbs the product
of a dualistic power — Life.*

Viktor Schauberger

About fifteen years ago, a friend with whom I was staying in North Wales took me to hear a talk given by a GP who was also a qualified homeopath. Dr Paul Nickson's audience was a group interested in human health, few of whom had professional interest in medicine, but who met monthly to listen to an invited speaker. By a process that seems to contradict most current orthodox scientific thinking, a substance can be diluted and shaken repeatedly; not only will all molecular trace of the original substance disappear, but as the dilution increases, so does the potency. Dr Nickson described the result beautifully and I have never forgotten it: 'A homeopathically potentised remedy is like a beach washed clean by the tide,' he said. 'Someone walks across the clean washed sand — nothing has been added and nothing has been taken away, but the beach is different.'

There are two ways to achieve a homeopathic potency, but in each the method is the same. One part of a substance is mixed with nine parts of pure water and shaken (a process called 'succussion'). Then one part of this mixture is taken and mixed with nine parts of pure water and succussed. For the third time, one part of this mixture is then mixed with pure water and succussed. The result is the 'third potency' and is expressed by the name of the original substance followed by the numeral 3 and an 'x' (signifying 10), hence Aconite 3x, for the third potency of the herb Aconite.

The dilution and succussion process can be repeated indefinitely, the number of times being indicated by the numeral written between the name of the substance and the 'x'. (If a homeopathic remedy is labelled with the name of the substance followed by a number and the letter 'c', the dilution has been one part to ninety-nine parts of pure water, the second way to make a potency.)

Symptoms mimicking those that may be caused by a substance can, in broad terms, be remedied by a homeopathic potency of that substance. The skill of the practitioner is needed to define the exact potency that will suit the symptoms. As the toxic side-effects that often occur after orthodox medicines have been taken do not occur when homeopathy is used, many homeopathic remedies can be safely chosen by the lay person for themselves or their families. The worst that can happen is that the remedy won't work owing to incorrect choice!

Homeopathy's greatest critics are the pharmaceutical companies who make the drugs used by orthodox medical practitioners. They complain that it contravenes mainstream medical paradigms and that it is open to lay use. Most of all they are challenged by the fact that large quantities of any remedy can be produced from only minute amounts of a substance — and therefore very cheaply. The medical establishment often condemn homeopathy as 'quackery', or 'auto-suggestion', without having experienced its use in practice. They are perhaps angered most because it offers 'medicine' — usually in the form of tablets or drops — and therefore *seems* similar to orthodox medical practices, although the process of diagnosis is very different. Despite its honourable, 200-year-old history, homeopathy continues to be demonised by some sections of the scientific medical orthodoxy.

Jacques Benveniste upset the medical orthodoxy's apple cart when his experiments on water appeared to confirm that homeopathy works. Benveniste was a research scientist employed by Inserm, the French National Institute for Health and Medical Research. His job was to test scientific theories using practical experiments. In 1983, he was asked by a research worker with an interest in homeopathy if he would explore the biological effects of some homeopathic dilutions. Although sceptical, Benveniste agreed and designed experiments using a cell called a 'basophil', which is a type of white blood cell the body employs in the immune defence system. Because basophils have a transparent, colourless, jelly-like appearance, in order to study them they have to be stained; a specific dye has been developed to do this. However, there is a molecule which, if it is present, can inhibit the ability of the basophil to retain the dye. The molecule is called anti-immunoglobulin E, usually abbreviated to 'aIgE'. Benveniste and his team of assistants used every homeopathic dilution from 1x to 30x, examining each diminishing dilution to see if the same results of dye eradication could be detected on the basophils as was detected when undiluted aIgE was used.

During 1985, Benveniste's two assistants, Elisabeth Davenas and Francis Beauvais were working on this experiment when they observed a phenomenon that they later called 'the second curve'. The eradication of the dye occurred up to the use of aIgE 3x, after which less and less of the dye was eradicated as each successive dilution was used — something any non-homeopath would expect. The experimenters were astonished, however, to discover that after the ninth dilution — aIgE 9x — the dye eradication ability of the dilution began to increase and it increased with each successive dilution. There followed a variety of other experiments to validate the results, until Benveniste was satisfied that they were correct.

When he announced his results in 1990, it was after four years of having conducted 250 further repetitions of the initial experiment, using the 'double blind' control that conventional science recognises as a technique for precluding faulty or fraudulent results. He was ridiculed by his scientific peers. A few days after Beneveniste's announcement, the chief editor of *Nature*, a prestigious, professional periodical, brought a physicist who specialised in uncovering scientific fraud and a professional magician to Benveniste's laboratory. There they spent five days witnessing successful repetitions of the experiment, only to go away and announce, '"High dilution" experiments a delusion'.

Michel Schiff is another scientist who became involved in observing Benveniste's experiment with high dilutions. Schiff is also a keen observer of the way scientists think, how they respond to new theories and the practical verifications of theories that appear not to conform with accepted scientific parameters. In the introduction to his book, *The Memory of Water*, Schiff makes an important point:

> The lay person may not worry too much about the consequences of academic prejudice on nineteenth-century chemistry or on astrophysics. In the case of the memory of water, however, the issues are less academic; they bear directly on medical research, on human health and on the experts' monopoly on medical knowledge.

Elsewhere in the same book, he writes,

> I hope that my testimony will be useful to those who want to know more about the scientific status of homeopathic dilutions and about what happens when scientific orthodoxy appears to be threatened [because] the history and sociology of science suggest that, when an environment is hostile to or unready for radical discoveries, the chances of these discoveries ever emerging in public are very slim.

The same limiting attitudes, the mental constraint on the horizon of the scientific mind, were applied to the work of Wilhelm Reich and Viktor Schauberger, just two of the very many, few of whom we will ever hear about.

Benveniste's work on this sequence made him famous among homeopaths because his experiment inevitably gave scientific validity to homeopathy; but it has made his working life difficult among his scientific peer group who are traditionally prejudiced against it because it appears not to conform to accepted scientific paradigms. In this instance, scientists acted to protect the scientific status quo. The Askeaton/Ballysteen Animal Health Committee were thwarted by a combination of industrial interest (to protect profits) and political interests (to protect the history of high employment and therefore the votes that would return the politicians to power).

What both issues have in common is the lay person's recognition of experiential truth: those who have used homeopathy know that it works, for both humans and animals. People living in the Askeaton/Ballysteen area are aware of the animal deaths and ill health caused by industrial pollution. Scientific experimentation, industrial production and political management of a population's life remain acceptable to that population for as long as they can all be perceived to be beneficial. Once they are revealed to belong to another agenda, on which the interests of the population rank low, then that population must act before matters worsen, as they have done in Askeaton/Ballysteen, Camelford and Tamil Nadu, for example.

The well from which we collect our drinking water is a shallow basin of rock that fills to a depth of eight to ten inches with the spring water that seeps from the rock at the back of the basin. The depth never varies by more than an inch or so, even in the driest weather. Viktor Schauberger claimed that a spring that remains permanently protected from the sun maintains its level; he illustrated this claim by an experience he had as a forester. It was his responsibility to supervise the preparation of the route when his aristocratic employer wished to go hunting. On one such occasion, he and his workmen came across a small stone building housing a spring. As it looked dilapidated and unstable, he told the men to demolish it. One of them remarked that if they did, the spring would stop flowing. Despite this, it was pulled down.

A week or so later, Schauberger passed that way again and found the workman's assertion correct — the spring was dry. Out of curiosity, he ordered the housing to be rebuilt. As soon as it was completed, the spring, once more shaded from the sun, flowed again. The spring we use conforms to this theory. The steep-sided ravine in which it rises protects it from exposure to the sun throughout the day, every day of the year.

On the other hand, I know of springs that do not conform, but which nonetheless flow consistently. One of these is the huge and magnificent well at Millstreet in Co. Cork, which provides the town with its domestic water supply. The edges of the forty-foot wide pool have been defined by a neat, circular wall, with a chain around in the form of a rosary, not surprising given that it must have been sacred for millennia. Despite its width, the pool is only a couple of feet deep and it is hypnotic to watch the water bubbling up through the gravel floor with a living urgency. Another spring where the water bubbles through the gravel bottom is a smaller, but no less beautiful one at Cerne Abbas in Dorset. This is sheltered by a grove of trees, but not completely shaded from the sun. Similar in depth to Millstreet's, it is about eight feet across and enclosed within a stone-built square of walling. A narrow outflow channels the water to a pond out of which a stream runs below the doorsteps of all the houses in the street.

Traditionally, these waters, like many others, have healing attributes, especially the power to heal afflictions of the eyes. I realised why this might be when I visited the Cerne Abbas well in winter, when the seasonal rain makes the force of the rising water greater than in summer time. Instead of bubbling through the gravel in the corner of the pool, the water rises with such force that it raises the surface into a pair of churning domes, each about fifteen inches in diameter, for all the world like a pair of eyes.

In spite of some wells that apparently contradict Schauberger's theory, on the whole water does show a preference for dark and lowly places. This characteristic lends much to its traditional identification with the feminine, Yin polarity. Hamish Miller and Paul Broadhurst, in their book, *The Sun and the Serpent*, detect a pair of parallel lines they call the 'Michael' line and the 'Mary' line. From St Michael's Mount in Cornwall to The Wash in Norfolk, the former links sacred sites on high ground (most of which are now marked by Christian churches, dedicated either to St Michael or to St George), places of male energy, fire rites and the Death of the Serpent (or Dragon). The latter traces a line via low, sometimes subterranean, places. In these places are wells dedicated to St Mary, or St Bride, Brigid, or Bridget — in either case a Mother Goddess figure, if a bit neutered by the Christian take-over. The sites on the Mary Line confirm the nurturing, healing, succouring nature of water which caused the dedication of the wells to female figures with the same attributes. Much of the detective work to find these wells was done by dowsing, or water divining.

Before we took the road to Wales for good, we used to go there once a year during Jeremiah's summer holidays from teaching. On one occasion, he found a short, fibreglass fishing rod in the house where we were staying. He decided he would try his hand at fishing in a nearby stream, something he had never done before. Having made his way to the single-plank bridge spanning the narrow, fast-flowing stream, Jeremiah spent half an hour trying to cast the hook into the water. Several times he thought it had caught in the branches of the overhanging bushes, but each time he could trace the line its full length. At a junction a foot or so from the hook, the line also bent each time, so that the last part always lay parallel to but above the surface of the water. Whilst he couldn't understand this phenomenon, he could feel every movement of the water, although the hook never entered it.

Eventually, frustrated by his inability to fish and puzzled by the sensation he had felt, Jeremiah returned to the house thinking that, perhaps, he might be a water diviner. Out of the hedge he carefully cut himself a hazel twig, the cut about three inches below a junction of two long, straight twigs, both of which he trimmed to about a foot and a half in length. By trial and error, he learned to balance the tip of each branch between the fingers of each hand, to give the tension that reacts over underground water. Over the years, he has perfected this skill and although he cannot explain it, he can say how deep the source is that he can feel and whether or not it is pure and suitable for drinking — and he is always right.

Some years after Jerry discovered his dowsing ability, I took our son, Tito, then about thirteen years old, out of school every Wednesday afternoon for the summer term, so that we could spend a few hours with an elderly dowser. John Strand Jones had retired and although lame from arthritis, he was still an active dowser and a member of the British Society of Dowsers. He had learned water divining from his mother in the early years of the twentieth century, for she demanded his youthful company whenever she went on any expedition to find water. At some stage, she would step behind a hedge to remove her corsets, from which she took two of the whalebone stiffeners. It was John's job to carry the corsets! She tied one end of each whalebone together to form a 'v', which she then held by the open ends, in the same way that Jerry holds his hazel rods.

Although the general view has relaxed in recent years, it is still widely held that water divining, or dowsing for lost property or missing people is the work of the devil! During the last 200 years in some European countries, dowsing was prohibited and practitioners severely punished if they were caught. Threats of punishment, however, have not prevented women from determining the gender of hen eggs by suspending a ring, threaded into a cord to act as a pendulum, over each egg. And the sappers, the builders and field workers for the British army, have always used diviners to find water for regiments stationed in unknown territory. Equally, the police forces of many countries, including Ireland and the UK are known to employ psychics — frequently dowsers — to help discover the whereabouts of missing persons, although they do not broadcast the fact.

Pendulums, corset stiffeners, reshaped clothes hangers or hazel rods are only amplifiers of what our subconscious selves are already aware. Provided we can clear our minds of intrusive thoughts to keep an empty clarity while we are dowsing, any one of us has this skill. I equate it with telepathy. Instead of making mental contact with another person, we can make mental contact with something else, because I think all things have an electro-magnetic field, or aura, in which all sorts of information which can become accessible to the dowser is held. Dowsing, telepathy, or any other 'occult' skill, can only be learned (or, as I prefer to think, 'recovered'), when we also·learn to trust instincts and intuition. Our scientific, rationalistic culture has stolen away our natural ability to do this. Repeated propaganda maintains that, because these are skills that science and rationalism have failed to explain, they therefore don't exist. Or, calling conveniently on the corroboration of organised religion, they ascribe such skills to the devil and therefore too dangerous for 'ordinary' people to practise. If anyone wishes to recover their natural skills, I think it is first necessary to discard the strictures of the Materialist Superstition, science, rationalism, religion and the devil, all in one go!

Wilhelm Reich was, like Schauberger, an Austrian, and although the two men were contemporary, I don't think they ever met. Reich made an interesting discovery that was replicated by other scientists. He noticed that when hay was soaked in water and began to soften, particles he described as 'vesicles' began to detach from the edges of the blades of hay. These particles then formed little colonies, with movements and behaviour patterns that resembled simple life forms. He tried a variety of methods to eliminate the possibility that some air-borne pollutant was causing what he was seeing. Finally, Reich decided to boil the medium in which he had detected the formation of the vesicles. When he placed the boiled medium under his microscope, he was amazed to discover that the process had started almost immediately the medium had been removed from the heat. In addition, the formation of the phe-nomena he had observed was happening even more strongly. He re-named these entities 'bions', because of their resemblance to life forms. Reich's experiments were replicated by other scientists and the phenomena recorded in great detail.

If, as seems probable — judging by such work with bions — there is something specially different about water, then the work of Dr Bernard Grad of Magill University in Montreal may hold the key. During the 1960s, Dr Grad did a series of experiments of the orthodox, double-blind variety to discover whether any emanation from a person handling water could have any effect on the water. In his first experiment, he used two groups of seeds. Each was first watered with saline, then dried and thereafter watered with equal amounts of tap water. The difference between the treatment of the two groups of seeds was that the saline used to water one of them had been held for fifteen minutes by psychic healer, Mr Estebany. The growth rate, development and chlorophyll content in the group of seeds that the healer had held was greater than the control group. In a further experiment, Dr Grad used two people and three groups of seeds. One of the people had 'green fingers' and the other had been diagnosed as 'psychotically depressed'; each of them held the water for a group of seeds for fifteen minutes. The green-fingered gardener had charged the water with an influence that resulted in growth rates superior to the control group. The clinically depressed person had influenced the water so that the growth rate of the seeds in that group was much poorer than the control group.

In a follow-up to this series of experiments, Dr Grad examined the water itself. Using infrared absorption spectrometry, he found that the water that had been held by the healer displayed the bonding angle of the water molecule to have shifted, subtly, but detectably. This change caused two other effects: (a) the bonding difference reduced the tightness of the meniscus, or surface tension of the water — a feature that lasted for twenty-four hours; (b) the bonding between molecules of water having changed, a change also occurred in the bonding between the hydrogen atoms and the oxygen atom within the molecule. Could this be the key to water's ability to memorise substances with which it comes into contact? It seems so. This applies not only to substances, but to forms and intentions as well. Just as we all have the ability to dowse, to find water and other things, so we all have the ability to create blessing. It is not necessary to have been initiated into some arcane order, or to be a priest, in order to give blessing. After all, if you think about how cursing has been effective, even when done by non-initiates and lay people, blessing is simply the opposite. Try pouring some water into a small earthenware or glass vessel and hold it in the palm of one hand, while directing blessings into the water via the other hand. Hold this hand over the top of the vessel for fifteen minutes and then use the water to nourish plants, animals, or people; I am sure you will see a difference from using unblessed water for the same purpose.

Dr Robert Miller of Atlanta, Georgia is a research chemist who has confirmed Dr Grad's experiments with those of his own. He has also gone on to find that water that has been subjected to a magnetic field has the same qualities as water that has been blessed. Perhaps it is enough for the vessel of water to be in your aura, not even touched by you and for that electro-magnetic field to be charged with your thought-forms of blessing, for the 'magic' to work?

Dr Miller also found something else that confirmed claims made over 200 years ago by Franz Anton Mesmer — yet another Austrian. The energy charge transmitted to the water, by either the healer or the magnetic field, takes approximately twenty-four hours to seep out of the water into the surrounding atmosphere; if a metal rod touches the surface of the water, however, the discharge is instant. (By the same token, it is ineffective to use a metal container for the water you wish to charge with blessing, because the metal will discharge that energy, not retain it as the earthenware or glass would do.) Mesmer used this feature with groups of people seeking healing, when he connected them to such a rod and to one another by cotton cords, forming a natural fibre 'circuit', when the rod touched the water.

Viktor Schauberger also magnetised water and examined it under a microscope. He observed that the character of magnetically-charged water has an amorphous structure with the content of free oxygen largely bound, unlike non-magnetised water and he photographed what he observed. Also recognising that temperature plays an important role in the behaviour of water, Schauberger found that when it was subjected to centrifugal motion — as in the standard hydro-electric scheme — water becomes warmer, more strongly crystalline in structure and a haven for harmful bacteria. This was revealed under the microscope and, again, photographed by him.

Water that is subjected to centripetal motion, however, is thereby encouraged to move in its natural way, its character and abilities are enhanced, and it takes *ten times* less of it to produce electricity and water that is vitalised emerges from the turbines of the centripetal generator he invented. Water emerging from the turbines of the generally used centrifugal electricity generators is so denatured that it behaves as though it was poisoned, causing the higher forms of aquatic life inhabiting the water below the outfall to die.

If the 'potency' of blessing that has entered water from the thought form emanating from the hands or the aura of an individual can dissipate back into the atmosphere over twenty-four hours, maybe there is a way to 'fix' that blessing for a much longer period, if not indefinitely. Perhaps this is what happens when flower essences are made by the sun method (or crystal, or gem essences made by the sun or the moon methods, or the making of elemental essences by exposure to the appropriate element). The 'potency' being fixed in this instance would be the combination of the virtue of the flower, gem, or other entity and the energy of the sun or the moon, or some other cosmic energy. Probably the most well known of these essences is Dr Edward Bach's Rescue Remedy, which is a combination of the essences of five flowers. There are thousands of others, all of which derive their means of processing directly, or indirectly, from Dr Bach's techniques. And they work. Julian Barnard, in his book, *The Healing Herbs of Edward Bach*, estimates that the potentised water from a glass dish the size of a cereal bowl represents a potential three million individual doses of remedy.

Dr Bach, who intuitively pioneered the making of flower remedies during the 1920s and 1930s, was very clear that it does not take an initiation, or a doctorate, to qualify an individual to make these remedies, only a mindful attention for good and a dedicated focus during the process. Water potentised by the life-giving energy of the sun can have its molecular bonding permanently altered to the benefit of all living things.

The fact that water is virtually everywhere and in virtually everything should make us realise that it carries a whole science and a spirituality glimpsed by Dr Grad, Viktor Schauberger, Dr Miller, Wilhelm Reich and those of us who work with water and with the energies it can absorb. All of these energies can be reliably accessed by dowsing.

In a report following the International Conference on Flower Essences held in Scotland during October 1997, Sabina Pettitt of Pacific Essences, wrote:

> Vasudeva Barnao from Living Essences in Western Australia, showed us a video of patients being treated with flower essences while in hospital. Living Essences are being used in sixteen hospitals in Western Australia for pain control and for drug and anaesthesia detox. This is great news, because as you know we are committed to demonstrating how easily these vibrational remedies work with physical as well as attitudinal healing.

In Nebraska, USA and in Leicester, England, there are specialist institutes dedicated to the exploration and promotion of flower, gem and other essences, where enquirers can gain help in the choice and use of these remedies.

Slowly, the orthodoxy is coming to accept that vibrational medicine, such as homeopathy and flower essences, have a meaningful role to play in the healing process. In the British Isles, we are very fortunate that increasing numbers of GPs, like Dr Paul Nickson, are seeking qualifications in homeopathy and other alternative and complementary disciplines. In Australia, the hospitals that have started to use flower essences for pain control and for detoxification protocols are leading the way that many other western hospitals soon will surely follow. The Royal Surrey County Hospital in Guildford, England has built a new cancer unit with a wing dedicated to St Luke. The intention is to offer complementary health services through information and guidance toward relevant practices for cancer patients and their carers to augment the chemotherapy and radiotherapy also offered as standard treatments. The age of co-operation is quietly coming in.

Eleven

HEALTHY WATER, HEALTHY LAND

And the merchant said, 'Speak to us of Buying and Selling.'
And he answered and said:
To you the earth yields her fruit and you shall
not want if you but know how to fill your hands.
It is in exchanging the gifts of the earth that you
shall find abundance and be satisfied.
Yet unless the exchange be in love and kindly justice it
will but lead some to greed and others to hunger.

Kahlil Gibran

I am not an ecologist. I have no experience in that calling, beyond a lay person's interest and my own experiences of trying to live a simple life in harmony with nature. I fail my own targets quite as often as I reach them, but I keep on trying. Sometimes, when I'm talking to someone about carrying water from the well, they are incredulous that we don't fit a pump, or try to find another source that would require less labour. Without bringing them to the well, it's difficult to explain that it's a delight to do such work.

The walk is invigorating, whatever the weather, and it is always different. We meet hawks, chaffinches, blackbirds, robins and ravens, amongst other birds. A rare joy is the sight of hares playing in the spring, or a lone fox on the way home after a night's hunting. In March, there are violets, primroses and wind-flowers stitching the banks with the sequins of spring. In July, there are rare butterfly orchids — so rare we count them —

which may show only six or seven blooms in low years, but in good years we have counted as many as fifty. From June to the end of August, rubies lie in the hedgerow — incredibly delicious wild strawberries. No pump could offer all of that.

To us, it is a matter of course that we clean seasonal debris from the bottom of the well, or out of the gutters of the house. It is part of our lives to husband our six barrels of washing water and the eight flagons of drinking water. The water of the well is kept pure by the freshwater shrimps that live in it. On one occasion when I made a quick visit to Wales, taking a flagon of water with me, I discovered I had inadvertently collected a shrimp in it. It was a matter of honour to bring it home and restore it to the well, unharmed. We fantasised the stories he would have to tell his mates, but that was just the fun — bringing him home unharmed was the ecology.

Conserving water is part of our way of life. We made the choice that it would be when we chose to live without plumbing. For years, we pooped in the garden, in a fresh-cut divot every day. More recently, we began to use a variant on the earth closet, a seamless, stainless-steel pan primed with sawdust in the shelter of the house. Each deposit is also covered with sawdust and our combined efforts are buried in the garden, in a fresh-cut divot every day and the pan is scoured — no smells, no germs, no wasted water. But I can still remember the first departure from using a 'flusher'. We built a strong, weather-proof outbuilding, comprised of two compartments each containing a primed 'chemical toilet'. The chemical was dilute Lysol. How I squirm as I remember the 'splash-back'! The transition to the hole in the garden was an improvement. Of course, having a garden that is not overlooked is a prerequisite for this facility and happily ours is like that. On one occasion, however, I heard a sound and turned towards it to see our cat, busy at the same occupation a few yards away and looking as startled at me as I was at him. It made me laugh, but I think he just blinked!

With the decision made so many years ago, our conservation methods are entirely habitual and no longer self-conscious. For anyone wishing to embark on a similar lifestyle now, there is so much help available that was absent in 1967, when we began. Even so, when I look at the mainstream habits of my friends and neighbours, it sets up a stream of thought. All animals are inherently lazy, once their bellies are full. The human animal is no exception. We all prefer to 'take time out' than to work hard, all the time. In general, if there is an opportunity to hand over a job, as a species, we take it.

Over the centuries we have surrendered responsibility for more and more of our basic needs by following this lazy instinct. This is a generalisation about our modern way of life, but the challenge is to find anyone who does not fit into it. In our laziness, we pride ourselves on the numbers of young people in schools and colleges in our society, but they are only acquiring knowledge for use in a job, not knowledge they need for living. Their general knowledge and local wisdom score very low points in the formal educators' sense of achievement. Far from increasing knowledge, the Western paradigm is destroying it.

During the twentieth century, there has been a grave loss of languages through the extermination and displacement of indigenous peoples, who have had no choice but to learn the language of the displacer. Gross losses in skills and wisdoms have taken place as well. If, for example, the rain forest is felled and no longer exists, all the local knowledge and skills that enabled people to live there are worthless. This loss is as serious to human consciousness as the loss of the species cleared away by the felling is to the environment.

Similarly, in Western society we no longer grow all our own food, or know the person who grows anything we don't grow that we eat; we no longer carry fuel for our cooking or heating; many of us no longer cook; we no longer draw water for washing, drinking, or cooking; we no longer make our own clothes, or cause them to be made; few of us wash our own clothes; we have handed over care of our health; we no longer build our own houses, or create our own furniture.

As we relinquish each responsibility, we lose all the wisdoms and skills that go with it. If you grew grain, could you grind flour from it? If you collected fuel for your fire, could you distinguish the woods that burn hottest, the ones that spit, how to make a faggot? Could you cook a meal over a handful of sticks? Could you spin or weave and can you darn a sock or make a skirt? Do you know how to make soap? Are you aware of simple hygienic habits, or seasonal dietary additions or omissions that maintain good health? Can you mix mortar, or build with stone, create a plumb-line or mark out a site?

Many people believe that there is no need to know these skills, they are obsolete, we've neither need for them, nor time to do them. Yet why is it that the labour-saving devices that replaced our independence have not given us 'time to take out'? The food-processor is far more complicated to wash than a bowl, a knife and a spoon; the washing machine may save our muscles and our knuckles, but it also denies us the company of others at the wash-hole, or the communal wash-house. There are many more examples, but they all reveal the same fact: we now go to work to earn money to buy, replace and maintain these gadgets and to pay for the energy they consume when they are used.

By relinquishing responsibility for our own livelihood, we have not only lost the wisdoms and the skills, but we have convinced ourselves that we no longer have the ability to choose — this is not the choice of the brand of appliance, but whether or not to have the appliance in the first place. The received myth is that not-to-have is to admit poverty and in a society that reveres wealth and its outward and visible signs, this is to sin.

Now that the supply of water and the disposal of it are no longer the responsibility of individual families, they have become instead occult — meaning unknown, mysterious. And because the guardians and practitioners of the skills involved in that supply and disposal have not been elevated to the status of priest, or something similar, they, their skills and the water they bring and remove have no status either. The axiom, 'easy come, easy go' is applicable here. Because care and conservation have not been seen to have any part in the on-tap, flush-it-away attitude prevalent among the Europeanised populations, it comes as a shock when hose-bans and water-rationing are introduced as shortages occur.

Water usage may be profligate in the home, but both usage and waste are even greater in industry. The big question is how can change be brought about in either? Here are some suggestions for domestic savings. If you have a garden, use washing-up water and pee, mixed together at one part urine to five parts of washing-up water, to water plants. Use a bowl or a potty to pee in at night and keep it in the lavatory. Even in a town garden it is possible to make a compostable toilet in the garden and use that during the day. This immediately conserves the two gallons of water lost every time the lavatory is flushed. In a family of four, that could be as much as forty gallons of water every day. Use a pint of warm water to soap the body all over and turn on the shower only to wash off the soap. Only have a bath as a treat, or for some therapeutic reason.

Plumb the guttering into a conservation tank, or a series of tanks, so that a supply of washing water is available if the mains supply fails. Mend all leaks as they occur. Sell the dishwasher and wipe dishes clean of food residues as soon as a meal is finished. Wash them then or later, using a small amount of very hot water — develop the skill not to scald your fingers as you do so — and stop using washing-up liquid.

If you work in an industry that uses water, supply simple savings tactics, for example, always turning off supplies that aren't in use, report, or mend leaks as they occur, examine ways of using less. This may be much harder to do at work than at home, because the boss or the union representative may feel the feathers being ruffled. Sometimes it may be necessary to use devious means via a social club, or union meeting, or by some imaginative method occurring as the need arises. Taking the initiative in the workplace has a notorious history of provoking disaster for those who do so.

Water has such tremendous importance in our lives at so many levels that conserving it in any way is bound to have a profound effect. Those who attempt to do so are most likely to be those who are also attempting to apply care and conservation to other aspects of life. The good news is, there's a lot of it about! In the US, a periodical called *Plain* is produced by people who have chosen to lead plain lives. They have brought back handwork and domestic and horticultural skills into their lives, with some having stopped driving cars and driving horses and carts instead. They are developing their minds along with their muscles, and accounts of the difficulties and the successes they meet with as they adapt to new/old ways make both entertaining and instructive reading.

A high proportion of the contributors to and the readers of *Plain*, which carries no advertising, are people who represent a phenomenon that US economists and journalists have coined a word for: 'downshifting'. Many of those who have been earning a large income to pay for the mortgage, the car, or cars, the domestic gadgets, education for their children and an annual holiday, have found that in order to earn enough, they hardly have any time with their families. As a move to freedom, they are making decisions that involve resigning from the high-paid job, moving house, often from the city to the country, taking a less demanding, lower-paid job and becoming self-reliant, in order to enjoy life with the family.

This movement is sufficiently impressive for several books to have been written about it and for US economists to have estimated that five per cent of well-paid executives have already downshifted. If a further five per cent follow suit, their defection from the ranks of the high-taxation bracket will have a marked effect on the US economy.

This assessment makes a breakthrough, proving that the individual choices so many people have believed denied to them — though, in fact, denied *by* them — when made, create change. This is 'people power' and these are the people who, fifty or one hundred years from now, will be regarded as pioneers, heroes and heroines. Many of them will make their chosen homes in existing communities of traditional streets or hamlets, but growing numbers are joining together and building new homes from natural materials that include few factory processes. The amenities they build into these homes do not depend on mains utilities. Their homes are likely to include many conservation features, such as solar, or photovoltaic energy, wind power, non-pollutant insulation (not for them the polystyrene insulation boards that, when heated in an accidental fire, kill by the gas they emit), and water storage and sewage disposal methods that waste not nor pollute. They are probably deep into permaculture and cyclic renewal. They may plant a tree to mark each family celebration, find time to make music with their neighbours and read aloud to their children. If I write about a simplified lifestyle as though it is idyllic, I'm not doing so to make it extra attractive, or to sell the idea. It really is idyllic, but the idyllic interludes are usually separated by periods of hard work, often harder than one has ever known before.

There are other sorts of water conservation outside the house. Most of them are handwork and are as easily applied to the domestic garden as they are to a commercial enterprise. For example, weeding between the rows of cultivated plants exposes the soil and permits ready evaporation, but if weeds are pulled before they go to seed, they can be left where they grew to provide ground cover. The traditional growing practices of Central American tribes were designed to provide ground cover, naturally. Corn (maize) was their staple grain and they planted two or three on each of a series of low mounds. Around the small cluster of maize were sown beans, which require support as they grow, which was provided by the maize. Between each mound, giving the water-preserving ground-cover, peppers or pumpkins (squash) were sown, whose creeping habit not only conserved the moisture, but choked out the weeds once the creeping plants became established.

In Europe, chickweed is often sown for the same purpose and it provides green manure if it's dug in before it seeds. Whole gardening techniques have been developed around mulching, as this ground cover technique is called. There is even a no-dig method for growing potatoes that depends on a heavy mulch. If the seed potatoes are laid on the ground, regardless of any plants already grown there and covered with thick slabs of hay or straw unsuitable for feeding animals, they can be harvested clean, because there is no soil to adhere to them.

The amalgamation of small fields by the destruction of quick hedges and stone or earthen banks, also exposes the soil to more wind and sun and therefore to dehydration and erosion. When Schauberger turned his attention to farming, he recommended that furrows in ploughed land should follow a serpentine course, rather than the conventional straight course. The variety of shade provided both before and after noon by the serpentine furrows protects the soil better, causing less evaporation.

Recycling has become a trendy, 'green' thing to do, but there is a way of thinking that is totally cyclic and leaves no room for *re*cycling. This is the permaculture way. It has been applied most frequently to gardening, but to work properly, it needs to be applied to the whole environment and to all living things. The word was coined by Bill Mollison, an Australian architect, from *perma*nent and agri*culture*. The rain forest is an example of naturally occurring conditions that permaculture tries to emulate. Tall trees provide shelter and attract moisture for shade-loving plants, a habitat for birds and tree-climbing animals and insects, as well as support for vines and other climbing plants.

Shorter trees can flourish beneath them, and below the shorter trees annual herbs or perennial plants, very like the date palmery in Tozeur. Within this layered pattern of life, water is attracted from both above and below and has a cyclic existence while sustaining the plants and their inhabitants at all levels. A permaculture garden is a self-consciously created imitation of the multi-layered environments of the rain forest, open to variation depending on the prevailing climatic conditions.

Once the permaculture way of thinking has become a habit and multi-layered possibilities can be seen in everything, 'weeds' becomes an inapplicable word, because the value of *all* that grows in the garden becomes apparent. It's the cult of monoculture that has made enemies of self-seeded plants and uninvited animals and insects and that has named them 'weeds' and 'pests'. There really is no such thing as a weed or a pest, except that we humans have invented a scenario in which these creatures play these roles. The ways we have invented to kill them and our exaggerated enmity toward them is rapidly turning round and damaging us, possibly terminally.

Monoculture is a side-effect of the materialist superstition. Wealth, it is believed, is generated when goods can be sold from one country to another and paid for in the (quite artificially nominated 'stable', 'international' currencies) deutschmarks, sterling or US dollars. This monetary wealth is not 'wealth', but an illusion. The true wealth existed in the rain forests that have been clear-felled and in the small, multi-cropping, subsistence farms, that have been ploughed under and often forcibly taken from the original farmers to provide land for monoculture cash-crops. The reversal of incredible abundance to imminent desert caused by this short-sighted monoculture is also happening in countries that have no rain forest, but a tradition of arable farming and grazing.

Within these areas, the encroachment of desertification is also a worrying problem, brought about by the use of inappropriate chemical fertilisers, herbicides, pesticides and fungicides. The policy of monocultural, chemical farming works on the principle that many must die for a few to grow, a policy, incidentally, that also applies to the lives of people who 'get in the way' of potentially cash-creating developments. That many must die for a few to grow is anathema to the co-creative gardener. Imelda Carroll was a co-creative gardener who, with the help of her husband, turned a derelict acre of treeless ground, exposed on a narrow peninsula to all the storms the North Atlantic has to offer, into an acre of rampaging life that provided many of their needs as a family — and the cats, the dog and the ducks.

Co-creativity, like permaculture, can be applied to all aspects of life, not just the garden. It requires the practitioner to open the mind to emanations — 'spirits', if you like — from all the forms of life in the garden (or whatever), whether already established, or intended. The dowser's mind is needed, open and non-judgmental, for the answers to the questions asked by dowsing, or its kindred skill, kinesiology. Some of the lettuces and brassicas in Imelda's garden were called the 'tenements', because these were the ones the lettuce and brassica-loving slugs, snails and caterpillars chose to inhabit. Imelda communicated telepathically with the spirits of these creatures and 'discussed', for want of any other word, at the outset of the year, the whole sequence of annual growth and eating patterns.

There were no conventional rows in her garden. Curious, how the spirits, 'devas' or the *sidhe* as Imelda referred to them in Irish, guided her to make serpentine and spiral 'rows', before she'd ever heard of Schauberger. In the four years after Imelda began to work with the other inhabitants of the acre on which she and her family lived, abundance took over. The variety of plant life increased, not just because Imelda introduced different plants; they came because they chose to. She also observed that the breeding patterns of the voracious eaters, the slugs, the snails and the caterpillars, changed. There were fewer of them! They no longer reproduced so fast once they were aware that no-one was going to kill them. All life forms in *Ard na Naentog* — Irish, meaning 'Nettle Height' — live in their own cycles of birth, growth, death and renewal, at whatever measure that may be.

Co-creativity in a garden context is better known in Findhorn, Scotland, or Perelandra in Virginia, USA, but those are much larger ventures taking the energies of many people to maintain them. Imelda's single family garden was an example of what can be done on a small scale.

There is a yawning gap between the small-scale, locally effective, harmonious use and conservation of water and the huge, man-made reservoirs and irrigation schemes that have been built in the last half of the twentieth century. In her book, *Masters of Illusion — The World Bank and the Poverty of Nations*, Catherine Caufield tells the story of the Bhumipol dam in Thailand. This was designed primarily to provide hydroelectricity for a growing industrialisation. Irrigation of an already productive agricultural area that would permit two or even three crops of rice a year in the place of the tradition one, was also part of the planned use of the dam. The flood waters engulfed farms and villages in the valleys behind the dam. The long-established, socially and culturally satisfying life of the inhabitants was brought to an abrupt end, with enforced evacuation to an area pre-selected by the Thai government. There the soil was poor, the housing inadequate and there was no drinking water, sanitation, or schools. Their quality of life was degraded and remained degraded.

When the irrigation scheme got under way there proved to be a serious shortfall in the quantity of water it could provide, owing to the need for water levels to remain high to run the turbines. This, in turn, led to serious losses for the farmers downstream, who had been persuaded by the Thai government to prepare and sow a second rice crop. The Chao Phraya Basin, the area intended for irrigation, was the fertile agricultural area of Thailand, but this, too, was degraded by the irrigation scheme. The area that received water via the irrigation scheme was much smaller in the end than had been projected. Also, when a second dam was built to make good the shortfall, the flow of the river was so restricted that sea water encroached from the estuary, destroying fishing grounds and causing salination of previously fertile land.

This pattern is repeated *ad nauseam* for most of the dams that have been built. The largest yet built will be across the Yangtse in China. It will displace 1.2 million people and, probably, result in many unplanned for, unexpected ecological hazards. This is part of the pattern. The benefits that accrue from these projects have never yet benefited any of the people who have been dispossessed to make room for them. Catherine Caufield puts it succinctly,

> Dam building is the world's most popular form of development. The popularity of dams stems from their dual function. They regulate water and they exalt the rulers who build them. The steel and turbines of a single dam declare far more spectacularly that a country has entered the modern age than do any number of one-room schools or village water pumps.

Or, as a memo Caufield quotes from the World Bank records,

> '. . . pure water [has] many valuable side-effects, but . . . one could not measure their contribution to production.'

The World Bank celebrated its fiftieth anniversary in 1994. In a nutshell, its creation was based on the belief that wars would end if everyone in the world had plenty of material possessions. To this end, money was lent to poorer countries where there was little or no industry, or commercial farming, in order for both to be developed. When these borrower countries encountered difficulties in making repayments, the Bank lent more money, so that they could do so. All the conventions that restrict the borrowing power of individuals who visit their high-street bank looking for a loan were flouted to keep money flowing; money, it was claimed, flowed when countries produced goods to trade with one another. Little check was made on how the loans were spent. Some of them were spent genuinely on the projects out-lined for the loan, others were not. In either event, greater or lesser sums enriched politicians, industrialists and the larger landowners of the borrower countries. That any of the projects, dams, roads, railways, factories, or monoculture crops, benefited any of the country's ordinary citizens was a peripheral accident. More of them were deprived than ever benefited.

As Catherine Caufield remarks of the twenty-one projects with the highest profile that the World Bank funded in its first twenty-five years of existence,

> Despite their size and importance, the Bank did not study any of them once they were completed. Thus it did not see — or learn from — many of its own mistakes. Instead, it financed their replications around the world. Now, years later, it is clear that during the Bank's glory years many of its most important projects did more harm than good.

It did more harm than good by being concerned with quantity rather than quality — the quantity of money flowing between countries and not the quality of life of ordinary people. In fact, the callous manipulation of these ordinary people is revealed in a cynical internal document quotation about so-called development in Papua New Guinea,

> A characteristic of PNG's subsistence agriculture is its relative richness: over much of the country nature's bounty produces enough to eat with relatively little expenditure of effort . . . Until enough subsistence farmers have their traditional lifestyles changed by the growth of new consumption wants, this labour constraint may make it difficult to introduce new crops.

At the same time as the World Bank has brought increased 'liquidity' to world markets, it has made damaging and irrevocable inroads into ancient cultures and ecologies. It is the wealthy, Europeanised countries that prime the pump for the World Bank's lending programme. Once enough of the population of these countries downshift, the tax harvest will be reduced and so will the market for consumer goods, for downshifters are aware of how unnecessary most consumer goods are. This will have two results: (a) there will be less tax income for these states to contribute to the World Bank; and (b) the reduction in demand for consumer goods and chemically produced food will reduce the market for the borrower nations.

In the contributory states, the population has long enjoyed the right to choose how they live and how they spend their income. A powerful coercion would need to be invented to prevent the downshifting, home-based food production, local exchange trading systems and so on that so many members of these populations are adopting. Resistance to any coercion would surely be very strong.

Competitiveness is an integral part of the education systems in the above-mentioned wealthy countries and competitiveness, whether between nation-states or neighbouring householders, is driven by greed. Greed for power, for wealth, or just for *more*, is a force that always causes loss to others. Conservation, on the other hand, is driven by need and works well by small-scale efforts that, when combined, can create big results. If we conserve our resources and enjoy our chosen lifestyles while at the same time refusing to contribute to the ethos in which such a damaging force as the World Bank can exist, it must change its ways, or close. Until the education systems exchange the teaching of competitiveness for instruction in forms of enquiry and instil in our offspring a right-to-know mindset, let us homeschool ourselves and them. Let us teach ourselves to ask basic questions about the activities of the World Bank, or the local authority, or whoever and to persist until we get answers.

Twelve

AT SEA AND ASHORE

They call me deranged. The hope is that they are right!
It is of no greater or lesser import for yet another fool to
wander this earth. But if I am right and science is wrong,
then may the Lord God have mercy on mankind!

Viktor Shauberger

———————

The only accessible beach on St John's Point in Co. Donegal is composed of tiny fragments of coral and, if one looks carefully, a multitude of minute sea shells. Shelving gradually and safely, it used to be a favourite place for a swim among people who knew it. There's a scattering of houses and cottages along the Point's seven miles of single-track road, which are largely occupied by small farmers and fishermen. The fishermen's fathers had punts and half-deckers that they used to catch herring, mackerel, sprat, lobster, crab and shrimp in their respective seasons, until about 1980.

Today, many of the fishermen travel off the Point and a further five miles to the west to join one of the trawlers that berth in Killybegs, a natural harbour (and most important in Ireland in terms of the tonnage of fishing vessels). These men may be away from home for stints of several weeks, or even a few months; some may actually fly out to join their boats after shore leave. Even though the boats are registered in Killybegs, they fish so far from home that the catch is brought ashore to ports anywhere in Europe. No longer does a man walk from his house on the Point to his boat on the shore, when the tide is right, knowing he'll be home again for his next meal.

Ten years of land reclamation and factory development have altered the shoreline of Killybegs dramatically. It is a small but very wealthy town; but it is also a working town where many of the men and women who live there, although they don't go to sea, nonetheless work with the fish in the factories — filleting, freezing, cleaning, salting, 'smoking', packaging and processing fish into fish meal. The fish meal factory is one of the oldest factories on the harbour shore and the least savoury. Sometimes, in a strong south westerly wind, when it is working full-out, we can even smell it at our house, ten crow-flown miles away! There, fish offal from the filleters, fish in excess of demand, under-sized or damaged, are reduced to oil and meal, by methods that resemble cooking, baking and pressing. The products from this factory are used in cosmetics, margarine, pet food, fertiliser, cattle feed and as pellets (processed in France, from meal derived in Killybegs). These are fed to caged fish, back here in Donegal, among other places — and to anything else into which they can be subsumed.

As with farming, the art of fishing has been converted into an 'industry'. In the days when boats still went out after dark to find herring off the Point, it was a man's skill and wisdom that took him to a spot where, when he flashed a lamp, he would see the silver bellies of the fish flash back at him as they dived to avoid the light and he would know to cast his net. Today, the skippers of the big boats use sonar to plot the site, depth, density, volume and species of a shoal from quite a distance, without leaving the comfort of the bridge. On board are maybe two crews, each of up to thirty men, one crew on- and one crew off-duty — a third crew being on shore-leave in rotation with those at sea. Many of these boats have freezer holds to preserve the catch, some even house factory units for processing at sea. The Auction Hall on the New Pier in Killybegs sells the catches that dock there, tuna to the Japanese, mackerel to the Nigerians, turbot, plaice, cod, gurnet, John Dory, haddock, monkfish and many more to buyers from other distant parts of the globe. The foreign buyers stay in a modern, featureless hotel built on the site of an older one, fondly remembered by locals for its idiosyncratic landlord.

When the punts and half-deckers were in use off the Point, the 'big' boats of that time were mostly timber boats manned by crews of four or five at most. The crew would be home most nights and only occasionally fished so far from the harbour that they slept on board. When the Common Market embraced Ireland in 1973, this began to change. In the early 1980s more than one steel-hulled boat sailed to Norway to be 'stretched'. They were sawn in half from port to starboard and a new section inserted to provide a larger hold. People thought them big when they returned, but bigger boats have been built since then — big boats with big crews and big holds that bring in hundreds of tons of fish from a single trip. Of course, they're not fishing off the Point. Few fish get a chance to come in far enough for any boat to catch them there anymore. These modern boats have to be equipped for deep sea voyages in virtually any kind of weather — although they can't fish in bad weather, they may have to return to port in poor conditions. The fish of the continental shelf, for centuries abundant, are now so depleted as to be unfishable by the standards of today, so the boats have to sail further from land and to harvest species often hitherto unknown.

To me, fishermen have always seemed to be the last of the genuine hunters, who risk their lives to bring home food. Now, I'm changing my view. They still take risks with their lives, but now the way they fish is more like plundering than hunting — even the fishermen themselves can be heard comparing their techniques to 'vacuuming' the seabed. And just as the land-based hunters eventually turned to farming plants and animals, the fishermen-hunters have turned to fish-farming. Mollusc farmers place the seed shellfish in convenient places to grow mussels and oysters on ropes, scallops in lantern cages and clams in perforated envelopes. They feed naturally as the tide comes in and out and the farmer harvests them when they grow large enough.

The migratory salmon is also now caged and farmed in a way that can be compared with the farming of hens in batteries. They are overcrowded, denied space to swim freely, denied their natural, migratory instincts and force-fed on artificial foods. The latter include a chemical dye to make the flesh pink (a pigmentation that occurs normally when the fish eat their natural food, shrimps, in the wild). Their fins become frayed from the constant abrasion of other fish and the walls of the cage, by which they are easy to identify on the fishmonger's slab — if they have not been cut off to hide the give-away damage. Local people will not buy such fish, because the flavour ranges from negligible to unpleasant and the texture of the flesh is soft and slimy owing to the fish's lack of exercise.

In the late 1990s, fish caged in the sea near Killybegs contracted a virus which killed them faster than they could be caught and filleted, so the carcasses were deposited at the local refuse dump. After a short time, the authorities regarded the thousands of salmon corpses as excessive and barred the fish farmers from dumping any more. The result was that many more thousands of dead fish were dumped out at sea, even though they were infected. Just as hens crowded into battery cages are prone to parasitic infestation, so are fish in cages, the sea louse being the commonest parasite. The fish farmers routinely dose the fish with Ivermectin, which descends through the caged creatures to settle on the sea bed amongst the accumulated salmon poop. Like the manure of Ivermectin-dosed cattle, the salmon poop is thus rendered inaccessible to the creatures that cause its decomposition and the sea bed is sterile for several hundred yards beyond the cage area.

Angling associations on rivers that historically contained seasonal migrations of another salmonid fish, the sea trout, have campaigned vigorously against fish farming in estuaries. They argue that the sea trout is being exterminated by the pollution and by the explosion in the sea louse population. Nevertheless, the Irish government has legislated to permit the licensing of fish farms for the whole of the Republic's seaboard, which could be as much as 3,000 miles of shoreline. It will, undoubtedly, be the most accessible parts that will be farmed — the same places that are popular for leisure use.

The Norwegians, among the first to farm salmon in cages, now also concentrate on farming non-migratory white fish. The

Chinese have been fish farming for centuries using cages made from bamboo in stacks of four or five, each containing a different species, always one that could thrive on the effluent from the one above. This organic process has not been followed up by European experimenters, no doubt because the use of chemicals and artificial feed is an integral part of fish farming in Europe (mollusc farming depends on natural feeding so that mussels, oysters, scallops etc. are organic food).

Another scourge to fish farmers is known as 'red tide'. This is an algae that floats on the surface of the sea, colouring it red. It is poisonous to humans and other mammals, as well as to many fish. It multiplies and thrives as a direct result of the run-off into rivers and the sea of the chemical cocktails and excess animal effluent from farmed land. Sea farming has been established simultaneously with an increase in knowledge and understanding of the effects of the use of chemicals in all aspects of farming. Just as the fishermen of Ireland refuse to eat farmed salmon, what farmer would eat beef that has been given either polluted food or growth promoters — even the legal ones? Most farmers when rearing a beast for their own use will admit to avoiding many of the suspect substances, while using them on the beasts to be sent to market.

It was pesticides — DDT in particular — and their detrimental effects on wildlife, that preoccupied Rachel Carson when she wrote her book *Silent Spring* in the 1960s. Forty years later we identify these same substances in new ways, indicating their common chemical base, such as organophosphates. When these terms are used, they refer to synthesised, non-naturally occurring chemicals. The prefix, 'organo' has been adopted because it acknowledges the presence of carbon in the compound and carbon is a basic element in all forms of life. Coal and fossil oils were, millions of years ago, living creatures and the carbon-containing chemicals derived from them are in the 'organo' prefixed range. This prefix has no relationship with the term 'organic' used to describe foods that have been grown without any use of chemicals. It is the presence of the carbon in the synthesised chemicals, however, that has caused our health problems. Their carbon is to our bodies what the Trojan Horse was to the city of Troy — an innocent vehicle for a horde of dangerous invaders; where the carbon (which the body recognises) can go, the other components of the chemical can follow. And where do they go but to the power centres that maintain our patterns of life — the brain and the endocrine glands? On the way, they can and do cause cancer.

Because of its intractable character and the difficulties in curing it, cancer is feared in the twentieth century like the plague was feared 500 years before. It invades the body secretly, with no obvious source of 'infection' and is often so advanced once detected that remedial action is very invasive and return to normal life is often improbable. Expensive laboratory tests are conducted on a continual basis to explore DNA for carcinogenic genes — to which only five to ten per cent of cancers can be attributed — and to determine if some of the chemicals so common in our environment are also carcinogenic. The fear of carcinogenicity has focused most scientific exploration in that single direction. This may be why it took so long for the brain and endocrine damage caused by organophosphates to be recognised — and that it was discovered accidentally.

There are some startling statistics about the chemicals in our environment. Tens of thousands have been released since World War Two, many of them developed during that war for military purposes. The killing ethos that spawned them has followed them, as Sandra Steingraber says, 'into civilian life', where we have nominated 'pests' and 'weeds' to use for target practice. War continues against nature, using, worldwide, 600 different forms of pesticides alone. Of these, 4.1 million lbs of them are exported annually from the US to 'underdeveloped' countries, all pesticides that have been banned on their continent of manufacture. DDT, which is included in this deadly cargo, can be found in diminishing residues since its abolition in the US in the 1960s, but residues are rapidly increasing in the uninformed countries to which it is exported. Especially ironic is the claim that a mere one per cent of any one of these poisons reach the target, while 99 per cent disperses into the air, the soil and, sooner or later, into water, whether wells, streams, lakes, or rivers. The poisons finally reach the ocean, where this deadly soup is more concentrated by the year.

Fifteen thousand chlorine-based compounds used in different types of solvent and bleach, amongst other things, are also exported in volume to 'underdeveloped' countries. Yet they too are banned for use in 'developed' countries. What an arrogant disdain we show for our fellow beings in this commercial deceit. What disregard for all other creatures, who, like human beings, become the inadvertent recipients of cumulative deposits of several hundreds of persistent chemicals, because none of us have bodies adapted to breaking them down.

Sandra Steingraber, in her book, *Living Downstream: An Ecologist Looks at Cancer and the Environment,* explores the toxic chemical contamination of her home state of Illinois. She felt urged to make this study as a result of her bladder cancer, diagnosed when she was a young woman and which she learned is a form of cancer profoundly influenced by environmental contamination. Out of her explorations, Steingraber has identified many significant facts: women born in the US between 1947 and 1958 — a mere eleven years —are three times more likely to develop cancer than their great grandmothers were at the same age. Organophosphates were originally synthesised for use in the gas chambers of Europe to 'exterminate' what a fascist culture saw as 'undesirable' races. Between the 1930s and the 1970s, the production of synthesised chemicals for all purposes, including the manufacture of plastics — once thought inert, but now proven to be anything but — increased one hundred times.

We do well to inform ourselves about these compounds and we can do so without taking a degree in chemistry. Sandra Steingraber lists three facts in particular that anyone can absorb and act upon,

> . . . many . . . compounds are themselves synthesised from synthetic chemicals that are highly reactive. By accident, or on purpose, these industrial feedstocks are routinely released, dumped or spilled

in the general environment. While PVC plastic is, biochemically speaking, quite lethargic, the vinyl chloride from which it is manufactured, exerts striking effects on the human liver. Second, inactive synthetic substances can shed or off-gas the smaller, more reactive molecules from which they are made. Third, brand new reactive chemicals can be created if these substances are subsequently burned — as when perfectly benign piles of vinyl siding are shovelled into a garbage incinerator and poisonous dioxin rises from the stack. The incinerator itself, in this case, acts as a *de facto* chemical laboratory — synthesising new organic compounds from feedstocks of discarded consumer products.

The development of consumer products from synthesised materials has been going on for nearly 200 years. Apart from during the last half century, however, this was concentrated on plant sources, of which hemp is one currently enjoying a small revival. Wood pulp and other plant material were superseded in the desire to develop a chemistry centred on the oil-extraction industry, to which an all-out effort was devoted after World War Two. Prior to this, there had been plenty of oils in use from plant sources — castor beans, rice, olives, grapeseeds, almonds, palm and corn, to name a few — all of which are renewable and organically benign. It is the developments from fossil oils that have brought the problems, that and the killer instinct.

Steingraber offers a considered rebuttal of the scientists' arguments which place the 'blame' for cancer firmly on those who experience it, by emphasising the need to avoid smoking and to eat diets that exclude suspect components, such as animal fats. She shows that, while an individual's habits can have some input (such as smokers who develop lung cancer) the 'blame' for the increase in other forms of cancer such as childhood leukaemias, bladder, stomach, oesophagal, colonic, liver and brain cancers, lies squarely with an adulterated environment. Sufficient work has been done on examining just a few of the chemicals by which we are surrounded to conclude that many disorders, not alone life-threatening cancers, have environmental causes.

Where does all this depressing information lead? Sandra Steingraber is clear, 'From the right to know flows the duty to enquire — and the obligation to act.' How? In as many ways as we can individually imagine. There is no great loss without some small gain: we have petroleum-based fuel oils, but their development has led to international transport and widespread travel which has made it possible for ordinary people to see for themselves what is happening in other countries. There is a multiplicity of frequencies in the air because we have the telephone, fax machines, Citizen's Band and the Internet, which have made it possible for those of us who can't travel to talk to people anywhere on the globe and to learn what is happening in their locality.

We have to live with what's around us, but we don't have to permit its continuance. If, individually, we conduct an ecological audit in our own homes, we can surely find ways to limit our use of damaging chemicals and to curtail our use of plastics. For example, using pencils and fountain or dip pens instead of ball-points, carrying cloth shopping bags and refusing plastic wrappers. It is impossible to destroy the expanded polystyrene 'beans' with which some firms pack parcels, without creating dioxins. I send them back to the firms who send them to me, with a note about my difficulties in getting rid of them. Some companies have started to use packaging that looks like the expanded polystyrene, but is actually cereal-based and dissolves very quickly in water. By making such apparently trivial changes, your awareness is sharpened and other necessary alterations in usage can become evident.

The oceans of the world are not only becoming a sump for human wastes, they are also highways. Ironically, the largest ocean-going vessels carry oil and petroleum products. In some parts of the world, such as the Pacific, the sea brings vessels carrying the goods that islanders cannot produce for themselves. When the cost of fuel oils rose rapidly in the 1970s, many of the vessels that supply the islander's needs reverted to sails, retaining an engine solely for when there was no wind.

Experiments on sea water, reported during the mid-1990s, confirmed Schauberger's claim that +4° Celsius is the optimum temperature for healthy, lively water. Research is also underway to harness wave or tidal power to convert into electricity. Desalination of sea water is fairly common in some parts of Asia where fresh water is very scarce. Apart from these uses and as a source of food, the ocean is largely disregarded. The manipulation of rivers is a greater preoccupation for governments and international businesses such as the World Bank, which has funded many projects that dammed rivers to generate hydroelectricity or to irrigate land. Many of these have proved illconceived and damaging to the populations living at the sites and to the ecology above and below the dams, because of interference with the natural flow of water. The World Bank's alleged lack of supervision of any aspect of the projects, lack of feedback and lack of follow-up studies has, it has been argued, led to abominable abuses and corruption, ranging from misuse of the loans to the murder of complainants.

Jacques Delors spoke with conviction in his departure speech from the post of Commissioner of the EU about the 'resource wars' of the twenty-first century. Far from finding a way to avoid wars, the lack of accountability within the World Bank's activities is going a long way to fulfil Delors' prophecy. By becoming informed and acting on our information, we can close the World Bank and its allied institutions, just as we demolished the Berlin Wall. By making greed unacceptable, there will be no resource wars. Banking, like medicine, education, industry and religion, is part of an authoritarian system which can only remain authoritarian if we continue to be subservient and unquestioning. Each time we ask a question, we make a chink in that authoritarianism, because those in authority have to give us answers; each answer reduces the secrecy and the mystique which maintains their authority. As we gain information we also gain confidence and strengthen our abilities to make decisions for ourselves.

Part Three

FOOD

Thirteen

FOOD AND CULTURE

The will only is required, without that it is
useless to think of the attempt.

William Cobbett

I think it was in 1956 I took the City and Guilds Cookery exam. I have a hazy memory of being constrained all day in white overalls, a white apron and a white hat, of the anxiety about whether the spuds and the brussels sprouts would reach the point of being perfectly cooked simultaneously — and the panic when I mislaid the vanilla pod for the custard. But I remember clearly what I did after my boyfriend brought me and the meal back to my one-room flat and left me there. As soon as the door was shut, I picked up the small leg of lamb that I'd so carefully roasted and bedecked with a ruff of white paper around the bone. I sat down in the middle of the floor with the apron draped over my knees. My fingers stuck to the paper ruff as I realised how hungry I was. The meat was still warm enough not to have congealed — unlike the unappetising chill that had overtaken the vegetables — and the juices ran down my chin as I chewed it to the bone. I relished the thought that this informal meal was giving me back the sense of fun with food that the formality of the examination room had denied me.

During the war years of my childhood, I never knew the taste of tropical fruit. When my mother came to my bedside shortly after eight o'clock one summer evening in 1945 to tell me, with tears in her eyes, that the war was over, my response was to ask, 'Does that mean we'll have bananas again?'

In the years between the Armistice and the City and Guilds, I had developed a liking for all sorts of tropical fruit. I must have passed the examination, because a few months later I was asked by some friendly neighbours to cook a meal for them. They invited me to join them and their guests at the meal — cook, waitress and guest all at once. I was a cut above roast lamb by this stage, so I suggested pork and pineapple to the hostess, preceded by melon for *hors d'œuvres*. For me, that meal actually ended at the melon. I thought nothing of lifting the new-moon of melon to chew its succulence out of the skin. The table became totally silent and I realised I was being stared at from all sides. As I remember the glee of the juice of the leg of lamb on my chin, so I remember the shame of the juice of the melon! I'd never eaten a melon in public before.

By learning to observe before I ate, I never made that sort of mistake again and, by eating with friends from many cultures over the years, I learned to value the eating customs from different places. It really is a good idea not to eat your melon with your fingers at a meal in a European home, because there's no finger bowl of water, as in a Chinese home, nor a warm, damp towel, as in many Indian homes, to remove the juices when you have finished. Using the cutlery on offer is preferable — when in doubt, I always work from the outside of the battery of weapons ranged each side toward the plate in the middle.

As a childhood treat, we went as a family to London and my father took us to Ley-On's, a Chinese restaurant in Soho. The glamour of the brocaded walls, the tasselled hanging lamps, the tiny, pretty dishes and the subtle flavours of water chestnut, crispy noodles and bean sprouts beguiled me. Eager to fit in where I already felt at home, I soon became a dab hand with the chopsticks. I was lucky: I learned later that Chinese children, to protect them from the shame of maladroitness when they grow up, are taught first to eat with the skinniest, most difficult chopsticks; only when they've mastered them are they allowed to graduate to the thicker ones that we're familiar with.

In Arab countries, all restaurants have a washbasin and soap for washing the hands before eating, although spoons, not fingers, are usually used. What I enjoy about a meal with an Arab family is sitting on the floor round a low circular table, on the centre of which is one large bowl of food. Dipping into the cous-cous, or rice, or spaghetti, you are spared from, 'mind you clear your plate', or 'why don't you eat all your vegetables?'

A steamboat meal is really a versatile party time, or family meal. Every eater cooks her or his own meal and it takes ages! The steam-boat is a trough, a bit like a rum-baba tin, that encircles a chimney under which is a small charcoal fire. In the trough is water or stock and on the table, arranged round the steamboat, are dishes of mari-nading fish, meat and prepared vegetables and piles of neat, indi-vidually rolled bundles of rice noodles. This is a Chinese invention, so with chopsticks you put the foods of your choice into the boiling liquid in the trough. There are delicate, brass filigree wire ladles to remove the parts of your meal as they're cooked. Eating, cooking, dipping into the sauces that also stand around the steamboat, talking and enjoying, this is a way of eating to relax anyone.

However, I still enjoy eating with my fingers, so I'm completely at home in India. Even the most rustic village restaurant has a supply of clean water and a washbowl for use before and after eating — and food really *is* served on pieces of banana leaf. One deftly scoops a ball of rice and sauce into the mouth. Even here there are hazards, however: it is only permitted to do this with the right hand, for it is considered customary to wash your bottom with the left hand after defecating and so, wisely, the same hand must not be used for eating.

'Food is here to stay' became a catchphrase round our table when our children were young. It was said by someone when-ever a favourite meal was being consumed. Our son used to lick his plate on such occasions and had to be persuaded that, like eating melon with the fingers, it was all right at home but not when eating out! The first time I met an eminent Tibetan Buddhist lama, I saw him lick his plate at the end of a meal. Commenting on it afterwards, I was told, 'That man wastes nothing, he's known starvation', and heard of his capture and escape from the Chinese with another young monk and of their hungry trek of many months across Tibet to India and freedom.

The young lamas' journey led them to safe houses, where they were fed and sent on their way with a small supply of tsampa. This is roasted barley ground into flour which is mixed with tea laced with yak butter — very sustaining in that cold, dry climate. They were able to glean wild foods along the way to eke out the small amounts of food their hosts could spare for them. As they travelled for many months, the choice of wild foods available changed from one season to the next.

Food, like incense, is an integral part of all great celebrations, where it is usually the staple grain that is revered. For example, wheat for the Christian Eucharist, for which it is ground and made into crisp biscuits; or rice grain, which is thrown as a sanctifying shower at some Buddhist ceremonies; or bananas at Hindu funerals. Unleavened bread, made from wheat, is the ritual meal for Jews in memory of the Passover. For First Nations people of the Americas, corn was the holy being which sacrificed itself that humanity might survive. Unlike the materialist urge to improve on nature by hybridising seeds, among the Hopi tribe each family in a village was charged with the responsibility of keeping pure one of the many strains of corn: red, orange, blue, black, white or any one of the other colours and sizes that grew. This was because their tradition recognised the variety of the many aspects of the one. To its shame, the practice of hybridisation has mixed and, in some cases, discarded strains not regarded as having commercial potential in order to produce a 'standard product'.

In many traditions, on all continents, travellers were entitled to help themselves to grain growing by the wayside — a sort of absent hospitality. And hospitality itself is always inclusive of food sharing. Until this century, in Wales, a visiting family brought with them a loaf to avoid undue strain on the resources of the host household. Within living memory in the British Isles the front door was always left open to indicate a welcome to travellers or visitors. This is still the case in Mongolia where the visitor will be greeted with a cup of horse milk and later be offered a spoonful from a disk of thick fresh cream passed round on a plate.

Many other customs associated with food are linked to planting and harvesting, not just with eating. Festivals to mark the sowing of grain are common in many parts of the world, although some no longer have any religious or spiritual significance. They are marked instead by some other celebration that has grown out of the work of sowing, such as the Horse Show that marks Dydd Sadwrn Barlys — Barley Saturday — in the town of Cardigan in Wales.

Humankind has woven reverence, prayer and ritual among the trinity that maintains life: air, water and food symbolised by the winds, the springs, rivers, lakes and oceans and by the life-supporting grains. As the materialist philosophy has taken over, reverence for this trinity has diminished. As a simple example, once all participants in a meal would have given thanks before consuming it, now very few do this. Of those I have heard, I like best and use a version of a Hindu prayer,

> A Blessing on the creatures who have given themselves for this meal (as appropriate), the water, the plants, fish and animals;
> a Blessing on those who cared for and nurtured them;
> a Blessing on the tools they used; and
> a Blessing on the tool-makers;
> a Blessing on those who sell and those who buy;
> a Blessing on the cook and a Blessing on those of us who eat this food, that we may bring this Blessing to all living creatures.

Such a cyclic thought, oft repeated, would surely make us more mindful of how we treat the creatures that we eat.

The word 'pagan' is derived from the Latin *paganus*. It was used to define a country person whose life was non-military, and therefore was the opposite from a soldier's, someone whose work produced the harvest shared with the town dweller. As religious life has become more intellectual, 'pagan' has come to be used to deride people whose beliefs and practices still centre on the spirit inherent in each living thing and who celebrate natural cycles. 'Heathen' is derived from words of old high German and Scandinavian origin, with a similar meaning to 'pagan' — someone who lives in open country and (with derision), who does not follow any of the Abrahamic religions, Judaism, Christianity or Islam, but who are regarded as polytheist, because of their reverence for the Many.

The organisations that we call 'religions' can truly be termed the 'bureaucracy of spirituality', because of the way they classify, deride, protect and proselytise. Spirituality, on the other hand, implies a liberty from the mediation of priests, a direct contact with the non-physical and self-responsibility for belief and practice that is, by its nature, tolerant, all-encompassing and finding no need to proselytise. Materialism and secularism have removed our thoughts from consideration of spirit, bureaucratised by religion or not, most people now associate spirit only with isolated ritual, such as the Eucharist and no longer with daily events, such as breakfast or a snack in a café.

The people of industrialised Western countries have not only lost any sense of spirit in association with food, but also any sense of its seasonality. Now that we have the means to preserve and transport food from almost all parts of the planet, seasonality seems no longer important. However, in the temperate regions, where there is a wide range of temperature and climate difference between summer and winter, the seasonal variety of food remains important. This is because the presence or absence of natural daylight has an effect on our metabolic rate, on how our bodies use what we eat. While central heating may give the illusion of summer temperatures, the absence of daylight informs our bodies otherwise. Relearning how and what to eat can bring a greater sense of well-being, as well as the return of the thrill of seasonal variety.

It can also give the body foods appropriate for the pace at which it needs to function. Acidic fruits such as strawberries and raspberries, eaten in winter time when the weather is cold and damp, can contribute to disorders common in such climates — rheumatism and arthritis. Too much of the sugary preserves made from these fruits can also create an internal environment in which such disorders can gain a hold, whereas stews and pies made from root vegetables and grains, natural fats and proteins are ideal for winter eating. The fruits and salads of summer time keep the body cool and metabolising at a more appropriate rate for the heat and longer hours of daylight.

In the past, before freezing and cold storage became readily available and enticed us into inappropriate eating, other means of preservation had to be used (ice houses have existed as long as recorded history, but were only accessible to the wealthy). Smoking and salting were the commonest ways to preserve flesh. These techniques were used primarily for the winter months, for which it was virtually impossible to make and store sufficient food for the animals reared during the summer. The older animals were culled and killed and those not eaten in the harvest festivities were salted and smoked, or simply salted, to be eaten in the dead of winter and up into the spring.

The seasonal feast varied from the equinox, when day and night are of the same length, to the winter solstice, which is the longest night of the year. The further north, the earlier the killing, feasting and preserving took place, because the cold came sooner. Pig meat was salted and some of it was smoked to make bacon. Fatty beef was also salted, as were oily fish such as herring, mackerel and salmon. The fat in the meat kept the flesh tender and moist. Today's husbandry techniques, however, ensure much leaner meat which requires additional moisture, which is why bacon may have an element of salt in its preservation, but it is also — legally — pumped with water to ensure it doesn't shrink in storage. It is this artificially introduced moisture that makes the modern rasher exude liquid and shrink as it's cooked. Similarly, many fish sold as 'smoked' are not smoked at all, but dipped into a smoke-flavoured chemical dye that gives an illusion of smoked food.

The grains in any family food cupboard today will come from many parts of the world. The average range of breakfast cereals illustrates this: rice crispies (rice from India, America or Italy); puffed wheat or Weetabix (wheat from Canada, the USA or Europe); cornflakes (maize from the USA); porridge (oats from Scotland or the wetter parts of England); muesli (a variety of grains, rolled into flakes, such as wheat and oats as above and rye, usually from some part of northern Europe). Grain crops vary according to altitude, climate and temperature range and, formerly the one that was dominant — usually only one — was the staple for that area. Oats can be cultivated on small plots in hilly country even in areas of high rainfall, because of their unique ability to ripen after harvesting, even in the barn, if a particularly wet season demands this. Barley and rye are also grains well suited to highland cultivation, but in areas more assured of a sunny ripening and harvesting time. From the staple grain, breads of enormous variety have been made, such as: biscuity oatcakes; fluffy-fleshed baguettes of white wheat flour; pumpernickel from nutty, semi-fermented rye grain and flour; golden tortillas from maize meal.

Vegetables and fruit grow mainly in the summer and these too were subject to a range of preservation processes, many of which have been superseded by cold-storage, gas-storage, or industrialised versions of the old means. Roots, such as potatoes, carrots and swedes, can be protected from frost and hungry animals by heaping them into piles and covering them with straw and earth to form a 'clamp'. Onions and garlic like dry, dark conditions and can be hung, their stalks braided into cords to keep them in skeins. All the bean and pea family can be dried; both were, and are, although no longer in the traditional wooden barrels or earthenware crocks. The brassica range of leafy vegetables, such as cabbage, broccoli and brussels sprouts, mostly store well in dry, cold conditions for a few weeks; those that don't can be pickled.

Apples and pears keep for varying lengths of time according to type, or breed, usually nowadays, in gas or at low temperatures, whereas soft fruit can be made into conserves using either honey or sugar to preserve them, or they can be 'canned' or bottled. The arbitrary rules of the EU trading community have denied fruit growers many of the old varieties of apples and pears but, thanks to the efforts and foresight of a small group of people, old varieties, often of far superior flavour and juiciness, have been retained and nurtured and can be found in preservation orchards. These fruit are not allowed onto the commercial market, but may be obtained for home cultivation from the preservation groups.

As important as sourcing and storing of food, is the sourcing and storage of fuel. Solar power is a popular source of energy among ecologically-conscious people. To me, it signifies something else, which has given me a very real and practical way to understand Einstein's idea that energy is matter that has not coalesced and matter is energy that has coalesced. I came to this as a result of not having modern amenities in my home, from the need to light fires using paper, twigs, turf, or sometimes coal. Lighting the paper under the dry twigs gives very little heat and it burns for very little time, although long and hot enough to ignite the twigs that burn a bit hotter and for a bit longer. Thus the turf or coal, both of which burn longer and hotter than either the paper or the twigs, is ignited. Each of these components gives out an amount of heat for a duration of time relative to the degree of sunshine — solar power — that it has absorbed. The denser the fuel, the longer it has been exposed to sunshine. Turf and coal are compressed, so the sun-energy has been compressed along with the original plant material, of which both turf and coal are comprised.

Solar energy is not only about heat and light, it is about movement, healthy bodily functions and good cheer. Ripe fruits, for example, need to be sun-ripened to impart this benefit to the full. Imported fruits are often artificially ripened, after having had their ripening process artificially retarded so that they survive a journey of perhaps many thousands of miles. This is one of the reasons why it is important to eat locally grown foods, in season. If foods are at least grown in your own country, they are therefore not subjected to this artificial control of their evolution into ripe fruit, with the resultant loss of nutritional value.

Two major developments resulting from the industrial revolution had a profound effect on the growing, storing and eating of food. First, fewer people were left in the countryside to produce the surpluses to feed those who had gone to the towns. Secondly, the new town dwellers, because of the long hours they spent working in the factories, had a growing need for mass-produced, ready-to-eat food. Fish and chip shops date from the beginning of the industrial revolution, as do some other forms of eating house and take-away restaurant.

It has been during the twentieth century that an exponential increase in fast-food outlets has done more than any other commercial enterprise to alter ancient eating habits. Little value is now set on the tantalising smells coming from domestic kitchens that whet the appetite, nor is there a savouring of colours, textures, flavours and the company of the family to share a meal and exchange news. The fast-food ethos has invaded the domestic kitchen as well as the high street; families are more likely to eat meals prepared in factories and sold requiring only to be heated than for any family member to prepare food from the raw state and cook it by conventional methods.

During the 'McLibel' case, when McDonald's, the burger empire, sued environmental activists Helen Steel and Dave Morris, it was revealed that fifty per cent of US citizens habitually eat fast food from commercial outlets. McDonald's have been major contributors to this fundamental change in eating habits. Their libel case against Steel and Morris lasted for 313 days stretched over four years and was the longest case in British legal history. During the trial many facts emerged that revealed the seamy, uncaring aspects of this mega-business. One of the challenges to McDonald's was that the food they prepare is not nourishing and balanced, but sourced for low price and highest possible profit.

Morris is quoted as saying that the trial has shown 'just how strong ordinary people can be if they're determined to achieve something and they stick by it whatever the consequences'. The determination he and Helen Steel showed is an example to us all, while the attitude of McDonald's was also a public lesson in the uncaring, profits-are-all outlook of much of transnational commerce. While McDonald's won seven of the twelve legal points in their claims and Steel and Morris's counter-claims, the adverse attention that the case brought raised the general awareness towards some of the practices engaged in by McDonald's. Steel and Morris were unique in bringing counter-claims instead of promising to be 'bound over to keep the peace', as people had previously done in similar circumstances. Barristers familiar with the case couldn't understand how two people, with no legal training, could decide to defend themselves and to do it so well for so long — that, too, was without precedent.

John Vidal in his book *McLibel*, about this case, also reveals that this is only one among many such cases brought by McDonald's against its critics. It has also trademarked names and phrases, such as 'McFamily', 'McKids', 'McNuggets', 'McCycle USA', 'You're the One' and many others. Its willingness to sue almost any food shop using the term 'Mc' seems to be borne out by the story, told in *McLibel*, of Mrs Mary Blair's small sandwich bar in Fenny Stratford, Buckinghamshire, England.

A Scotswoman, she thought that naming her shop McMunchies and mounting that name on a replica of the Scottish flag — the blue Cross of St Andrew — would imply both her Scottishness and the edibility of her menu of sandwiches, which was entirely burger and chips free. In September 1996, three months before the close of the marathon McLibel case, Mc Donald's wrote to Mrs Blair demanding that she remove her sign within fourteen days or the Corporation would sue her. Mrs Blair apologised simply because she could not afford to fight the case, although, like many others, it seems improbable that an action such as hers could seriously be considered a threat to the McDonald's Corporation with its $30 billion a year turnover. It would appear that McDonald's uses libel litigation very much as the medieval Christian church used its self-created laws of blasphemy during the years of the Inquisition. Just as ignorance of God was no excuse for transgression, all had to be punished, so it is with McDonald's.

Steel and Morris are not alone in their desire for fair dealing and good food to be available to everyone. Many others have been behind movements such as CAMRA (the Campaign for Real Ale). Men in England, who spend so much of their time relaxing in one another's company in pubs, finally recognised that factory-made beer with chemical ingredients, despite the hops and yeast mixed in, tasted inferior. The success of their protest has resulted in thousands of new small breweries, which sometimes serve just the one pub where the brewery is situated. It is now possible to drink a beer with a flavour and a quality peculiar to that one brewery — as it was in the centuries before factory production of beer took over. Beer from these small, natural breweries is nourishing and chemical free.

How much more important to our health and survival would be a Campaign for Real Food? Without a campaign as such, maybe CAMRA was the inspiration for other movements and businesses which concentrate on locating foods that are wholesome, nourishing and tasty. There has also been a resurgence in local markets, where growers sell direct to consumers. Farmers' Markets, as they are called in America, are flourishing, not only in most small towns, but even in large cities. Farmers' Markets and Farm Shops, especially organic ones, are common in Canada, Australia, US and England.

In Ireland, Country Markets, an off-shoot of the Irish Countrywomen's Association (ICA), have been for fifty years in many towns a source of fresh eggs, home-made jams and cakes as well as garden fruit and vegetables. The Dublin Food Co-op runs an organic market on Saturdays in Pearse Street to which organic growers bring their produce from counties outside Dublin.

The Box System of supply is another that is on the increase. Here, organic producers offer, often for a fixed, weekly price, or sometimes for a seasonal or annual fee, to provide a container of seasonal vegetables each week. The containers are delivered or collected according to prior arrangement. The quality and price are better and cheaper than most shops can provide, because the food doesn't travel so far, nor is it bought and sold more than once.

Businesses such as the Better Food Company in South West England also offer a delivery service of boxes of food. Here the selection is broader and is unlikely to include direct trading between producer and consumer, although their catalogue defines which organic foods they offer. The company is obviously con-cerned to supply that higher quality of food.

Richard Guy's Real Meat Company Limited offers a similar delivery service for their meats in cool boxes, anywhere in the UK. They also have retail shops in some towns, but their real claims to fame are listed on the front of the education manual they send free of charge to enquirers:

Choice: The opportunity for discerning consumers to make an active choice against intensive farming.

Committed: Dedicated not just to quality, but also to purity and welfare.

Unique: Fully independent random welfare/diet checks on participating farmers.

Independent: National free-range/alternative meat supplier that is independent from intensive farming interests.

Standards: Highest welfare standards — covering not just the farms but transport and slaughter.

Accountable: We are able to trace all stock back from shop to farm. You can meet the farmer!

Accessible: We allow access to all supplier farms to journalists and public alike.

With both these companies, it is possible to learn their sources, not something you could do with ease at McDonald's. The Soil Association can supply a frequently updated directory of Organic Farm Shops and Box Schemes.

I am comforted that events such as the McLibel case expose the inorganic, non-nourishing and inhumane products and attitudes of the mega-businesses that assume we will succumb to their advertising — and that we will remain ignorant of their lack of care for us. I find it consoling also that through the multiple efforts of interested people, it is possible to buy organic food, from flour, beans, or porridge to packaged snacks, jams, or wines, and to obtain seeds or cuttings of food plants banned by ignorant bureaucrats.

Fourteen

NOT JUST THE DODO

Let those who come with arms in hands,
meet with flowers.

Anon.

The only truly indispensable human occupation is the growing and harvesting of food. Yet I remember the awe of a young, city-bred boy who visited us and was goggle-eyed at the streams of warm milk our own children could coax from the goats' udders and at the wonder of collecting hen and duck eggs from the nests in the poultry houses. The strawberries, peapods or blackcurrants in our garden were, to him, untold treasures. He also enjoyed tending the goats as they grazed the 'long acre' — the verges of the quiet road we lived by. His parents might have taken part in the human chain we used to muck out the goats' shed annually, so that their manure would feed the soil our vegetables grew in.

In the summer, we reserved as many gallons of our goats' milk as we could from which to make cheese. One gallon of milk converts into one lb of cheese and the whey that parts from the curds during the process needn't be wasted either. We learned from a Norwegian friend to make 'Ge-tost' by simmering the whey (which precipitates the residual proteins), in a lid-less pot on the back of the range. Once the liquid had almost all evaporated, the pan was removed from the heat and the paste in the bottom beaten with a wooden spoon until it was cold, to impart a soft, creamy consistency, rather than allow the formation of gritty-textured crystals. The creamy paste sets into a consistency resembling cheese, with a flavour both sweet and salty. Norwegians slice it thin and serve it at breakfast, but in our family it was eaten at any opportunity for as long as the harvest time lasted. Industrially derived whey and substances abstracted from it are used in margarines, paints, plastics and very many other, apparently unrelated products.

On the quarter acre sloping site which incorporated our house, goat shed, barn, studio and garden, we found much of our livelihood: milk and cheese from the goats, meat (until we became vegetarian), vegetables for much of the year and eggs from the truly free-range hens and ducks. All these gave us a proportion of what we needed that we therefore did not need to buy, although we did buy hay and grain to feed the animals. Had we had even five acres of that mountainy land, we could have grown both grain and hay.

The myth has grown that it is impossible to 'make a living' on a handful of acres; even ten is thought to be far too few acres. This is to ignore that many people in other parts of the world do make a living from much less than five acres.

The assumption in countries where farming is an industry is that what is grown on the land is to be sold, so that the income from the crop will provide the grower with whatever is required for a livelihood. No more the rich variety of foods that can be made at home in joyful company with family and neighbours, but only mass-produced, industrially processed, commercial foods, bought in a franchised outlet indistinguishable from any of its lookalikes, worldwide.

In the introduction to his book, *Short Circuit: Strengthening Local Economies for Security in an Unstable World*, Richard Douthwaite describes a visit he made to Inishbofin, an island off the west coast of Ireland. He writes of helping to unload the passenger ferry, of the goods destined, first, for Day's shop, the only shop on the island. He itemises, 'sugar, biscuits, jam, flour, margarine, toiletries and disposable nappies . . . (and) . . . non-returnable bottles of Coca Cola'. The one hotel on the island is forbidden by law to serve unpasteurised local milk to the guests; the advent of electricity in the 1980s means a fridge-freezer that will house the long-life milk cartons in every home. The headage payment for cows is less than that for sheep, so who would keep a cow, now?

Similar reasoning is behind the absence of hens and, therefore, of eggs, of fields of potatoes, or oats, or any of the other produce that the islanders not only used to create, but also supplied to the mainland, within living memory. Even fish is brought to the island from Donegal, over one hundred miles away! Money and legislation based on its control has taken the place of true livelihood, so that islanders, like mainlanders, can claim the dole and only a mere handful of them do not.

Dwellers in rural areas have always found some way, as we did, to supplement their livelihood and to minimise the need for money. The further from the towns and cities, the longer lasting and the more ingenious these ways have been. For example, until the final evacuation in the 1950s, the inhabitants of Inishmurray, an island that lies a nine-mile boat journey out in Donegal Bay, augmented their home-grown potato crop, oats, mutton, eggs, etc. by making and selling poitín, illicit spirit. They remained uncaught, although it was common knowledge that they did this, because they could see the revenue men's boat approaching and were able to hide all the evidence long before the arms of the law could embrace them!

Twenty-five years ago, our neighbours Gwyn and Ann fattened a pig every year. It was fascinating to be present on the day the pig was killed, to see and learn skills handed down for generations. Once dead, the animal had to have the stiff hairs removed from its hide. Hot water and a sharp knife were necessary, and Gwyn quoted his father as he insisted that the water used must have only just reached boiling point and not have lost any of its oxygen. Hams and flitches (the sides with the ribs) were pared and cleaned and set aside to be salted, with the reminder that a menstruating woman must not touch this meat, because it would go bad. This might sound like an old wives' tale, but some years before, I had learned that women, who constituted the majority of the workforce in the chromium-plating part of car production, were required to keep a record of their menstrual cycle. They were not allowed to work on the days they were menstruating; at that time, the skin secretes an acid not normally present which can leave permanent discoloration on the chromium. Recently, a colleague who lives in Warwickshire discussed this with an elderly acquaintance who remembered that, when he worked in the sewing needle factories of Redditch, post-menopausal women were employed as packers of the plated needles, just for this reason. No doubt this secretion was also the one that could cause the meat to refuse the salt.

No part of Gwyn and Ann's pig was ever wasted. Head cheese — a sort of brawn — was made, the intestines stripped, turned inside out and washed clean of all they contained to make the casing for the sausages. The latter were made from the minced trimmings and some of the offal, most of which, however, was minced and wrapped in the membrane that holds the intestine in place to make faggots. Herbs from the farmhouse garden, thyme, sage, onion and garlic all went into these delicacies. The big kitchen of the old, stone farmhouse was redolent with the chat and laughter of busy women using skills and knowledge that they had absorbed since childhood, in their preparation of food that would help to feed their families for many months. No pig was killed or processed in a month without an 'R' in it, because, of course, May, June, July and August are the hottest months of the year, when the meat would be most likely to go off quickly and when flies would be about, eager to lay their eggs in cosy, meaty crevices.

Although we are no longer meat eaters, I remember with warmth the work of the day, the companionship and the sharing. The perishable, unpreserved parts of this pig harvest, the sausages, brawn, faggots, were shared among those of us who came to the house to take part. I recall the flavours of those dishes, made from the pig who ate only domestic scraps and potatoes and grain grown on the farm.

One day, Gwyn learned of a pig-producer's grant. He converted unused cow stalls into pig quarters and brought in seventy weaners for fattening. The food for this multitude came from the corn merchant in bags which contained all sorts of concentrates, only some of which were grain. The work was so great bringing in the food and the water to the pigs and mucking out their manure that Ann and Gwyn no longer had any time to rear, kill and process their own pig for the house. In their larder lay plastic-packed rashers that had come from a Danish bacon factory: the days of home-made sausages, brawn, faggots and bacon were gone forever.

Thus, only one generation ago, factory farming arrived in the mountains of West Wales. It has come only slightly more recently to the West of Ireland. It does nobody any good —and I include the animals. Juliet Gelattley, in her book, *Silent Ark*, describes with great poignancy the conditions she witnessed as a teenager on her first visit to a pig farm some twenty years ago. The pig that was killed on Gwyn and Ann's farm was familiar to us. We had scratched its head, wondered at its tidiness when we saw how it made its bed in the darkest corner of the sty from the straw it was given. It didn't defecate there — its manure lay in another corner of the outer, open, sunlit part of the sty. It was a clean animal and it was a character.

Pigs in an intensive pig-rearing unit don't have styes with a sheltered part, or straw for bedding, or an exercise yard open to the sky. They are chained into sectioned stalls, where they are unable to turn round. They stand, with difficulty, on slatted floors through which, in theory, their manure will drain. They never see the sky. If they're female, they are kept constantly pregnant until their fertility begins to fail and the numbers in their litters decrease — a fertile sow can bear fourteen piglets in one litter — when she is killed. They are never given straw, or any other kind of litter material to snuffle through and to arrange a nest for their young. These intelligent animals are kept in Belsen-like conditions as baby-pig-machines, or, if they're being reared for meat, force-fed in immobility and with growth-promoting hormones to hasten the process.

Our small area of self-sufficiency, like Gwyn and Ann's pre-industrialised farming, was dependent on a variety of creatures. These were domesticated animals and birds, a variety of vegetables, bushes and trees that, in turn, required not only our help in housing, feeding and nurturing them, but also the presence of undomesticated life. The latter — insects, micro-organisms and non-cultivated plants — were necessary for food, for fertilisation and for decomposition, to continue the resurgence of the cycle of decay and regeneration. The small-holding represented a micro-cosmic pool of bio-diversity. 'Biodiversity' refers to a range of species in a geographical area, (not necessarily including humans, but not excluding them, either), whose living and eating habits constantly contribute to healthy living, healthy reproduction, healthy decomposition and regeneration within the entire mixed population, because of the self-regulation inherent in its variety. It is a natural feature of the environment which some cultures recognise and honour, as do the native African, American and Australian traditions, while some ignore and marginalise it. Biodiversity in the rain forest is frequently quoted by environ-mentalists (perhaps because it is there that it still exists in its most natural and abundant forms), who also emphasise that one acre of the rain forest's biodiversity may be different from the next acre and that this variety, too, is of value. But biodiversity is not to be found exclusively in any one part of the planet. It is probable that the most diverse number of species exists in any acre of rain forest, but it exists also in your back garden, window-box, or the local park — it simply may not be so diverse there.

The Old Testament insists that God gave humankind — or rather, mankind — domination over all other forms of life on earth. There was never any mention of partnership or interde-pendence, or of the Many facets of the One. The Age of Reason, born after the Renaissance, while it discarded many of the religious beliefs and practices of former centuries, retained many of the attitudes, including mankind's perceived right to dominate.

It is only a short step from 'dominate' to 'exploit'. The empires that began 400 to 500 years ago were led by countries strongly imbued with the Christian culture that was already beginning to fragment into sects. The French, Spanish and Portuguese empires were predominantly Roman Catholic in ethos and the Dutch, German and British empires largely of a Protestant ethos. What they had in common was the urge to dominate by proselytisation and to exploit the lands they conquered. Thus those who would not accept the religion of the conqueror were, on many continents, tortured and sometimes killed for their intransigence; any goods or resources of gold, silver, timbers or precious gems, were stolen or plundered.

Industrialisation grew out of the same ethos, which is why corporations — in this materialist age they have supplanted the churches — see nothing wrong in forcibly removing or allowing indigenous people to be killed. This is in order to clear land, such as the rain forest, so that the trees can be cut to create grazing, or roads made to access gold mines, or rivers poisoned by the chemical smelting of the gold. One specific example is the application of chemicals to the grazing land, as happened to the Yanomani people in Brazil.

Domination and exploitation have been accelerated by industrialisation which has caused enormous movements of people from rural to expanding urban areas over the last 200 years. Inevitably, this has led to alienation. If you don't live in a biologically diverse environment, you are unlikely to recognise its value. This is especially the case where the dominator culture has us all imprisoned in its claw and we are all active in continuing the process of destruction by designating so many life forms as 'pests', 'weeds', or 'germs' and destroying them.

Subjects of this millennia-long culture, we are all dominators and this is most clearly reflected in the language that we use, in which lies a subliminal expression of that culture. When I hear myself use phrases like, 'I'll stick to my guns', or, 'It's going like a bomb', or, 'I'm only killing time', it makes me feel ashamed, because I am contributing to the dominator ethos. On a rare occasion when I revealed this personal idiosyncrasy, apropos the use of the expression, 'killing two birds with one stone', a friend volunteered, 'feeding two birds with one loaf', as an alternative. I was overjoyed by this and have tried harder ever since to convert the swords in my vocabulary into ploughshares. To me, it's a very short step from 'Onward Christian soldiers, marching as to war,' to making justifications for any actual war; 'Onward Christian ploughmen, planting love for life,' as a potential alternative has a completely different ring to it. Military metaphor and terminology proliferates both in medicine and in agriculture: the 'battle against bacteria'; the 'conquest of cancer'; the 'war against weeds'; the 'cohorts of cattle' and so on. When you say 'I could kill for a Coke', the day is not far off when someone will do just that.

The extreme of domination is the perceived right to kill the subjugated, or those we wish to dominate. At the top of the pile there are corporations and governments. The government of the USA thought it appropriate to bomb Tripoli in 1986, in the hope of killing Colonel Gadafi. In this failed attempt they killed 101 people, including Colonel Gadafi's four-year-old daughter.

In the McLibel trial, McDonald's claimed that it was not their responsibility that their subcontractors and suppliers displace indigenous peoples and destroy the South American rainforest in order to supply beef for the burger craze that McDonald's have helped to create. The law of cause and effect, however, is clearer to those who are affected by these activities. Every burger, by this definition, contains an essence of all the micro-organisms, the flowering forest floor cover, the butterflies, spiders, stick insects, snakes, jaguars, bats, scorpions, creepers, fruits, nuts, trees, fungi and bushes that once grew on a piece of land the size of your kitchen floor. Each burger represents the amount of the biodiversity destroyed to accommodate the passion for profits that is the essence of all the discussions in every major food corporation. At the bottom of the pile are millions of ordinary people. We can refuse to buy burgers, use pesticides in our garden, or utter expressions that incorporate thoughtforms about killing. Our individual efforts are small, but multiplied by millions, they can prove overwhelming.

The inevitable result of the dominator ethos is our present state: a few huge, impersonal corporations, controlled by a few people, who are alienated by lack of contact with the peoples and other life forms displaced or destroyed by the result of their decisions. They are also alienated from the attitudes that perceive their behaviour as reprehensible. However, simultaneously — but on a local rather than a global scale — there are movements

afoot that start from a point, central to which is the importance
of the needs of ordinary people.

Ordinary people, whose lives never benefit from the activities of
trans-national corporations, are creating their own community enterprises. These all have a common aim: to make life more secure,
more meaningful, more healthy and more enjoyable. Many of these
enterprises include gardening or farming. Local Exchange Trading
Systems (LETS) subvert the national currency by providing a rate
of exchange with which people who trade by the LETS method
can identify. This form of trade is immune from theft, usury, inflation, or speculation and, integral to its ethos, also creates community interaction — people meeting people and making friends.

Community Land Trusts (CLT) function in urban and rural
environments, in both of which is a desire to make land accessible and meaningful to the lives of the people in the locality.
These trusts use lease systems under common ownership (usually
achieved through fund-raising) and 'sweat-equity'. The latter is
accumulated by the efforts of the people involved, who give their
time and labour in land clearance, building, renovating of housing,
forest and field. The land and housing are being prised away
from speculative landlords and protectionist industrialists to give
people of low income a stake and a pride in their home area.

With security of tenure and a financial basis that excludes a
future rise in prices or rents through speculation, populations are
stabilising. Their jobs are often self-created, in ways appropriate
to the neighbourhood, such as harvesting sustainable wood for
fuel in established woodland; the work serves the needs of the
CLT members and then beyond. In CLTs, as in LETS, people work
together and make friends. The individual needs of the elderly
and the very young are learned and provided for. Through group
self-help, through successfully negotiating with town and county
government and through achieving results, self-esteem, knowledge, trust, companionship, hope and livelihood — all components
of community — are created. The lives of ordinary people are
enhanced by their own efforts.

Woven through these enterprises is food production by organic
gardening and farming, a technique that encourages bio-diversity

and eschews death-dealing chemicals. When as a girl I sat the City and Guilds Cookery examination, none of the ingredients I had bought had been marked 'organic' and I had never heard the term 'biodiversity'. In the 1930s, virtually all food was 'organic' because it was grown without any chemical intervention. 'Organic' has only become used in the last twenty years to discriminate between food that has been grown with chemical intervention and food that has been grown without.

'Biodiversity' was seldom heard even in the 1980s, although it's heard almost daily now to describe habitats that have not been interfered with by humans, usually humans using chemicals, or some other means of killing. The influences that brought about the needs to use these terms are many and deeply interwoven, but at no level do I believe that anyone deliberately set out to do harm.

Until World War Two, most farms were family owned and much smaller than they are today. The Enclosures Act, that had deprived so many peasants of their livelihood, had created hedges; many of these were live and became home to a wealth of animals, birds, insects and small plants, not to mention micro-organisms, for countless generations. Many of these farms still produced a diverse number of crops, often in relatively small amounts. Farms that kept cows were also likely to make butter and/or cheese; the buttermilk or whey would be fed to a pig or two; hens would scratch for food around the haybarn and grain stacks; the manure would be used on the land annually and the seed swept off the haybarn floor to be re-sown on the hay field after the harvest.

Farmers and most non-farmers — at least in the countryside — tilled gardens where they grew a range of vegetables, herbs, flowers and fruit in ground also manured annually by muck from their own animals or from a neighbour's. There was a tremendous variety of livestock and crops. Local breeds of cattle, sheep, pigs, hens and ducks are just some of the creatures that were proudly bred. These creatures were renowned variously for their flesh, the cream content of their milk, their hardiness, the quality of their fleeces, length of lay, firmness of shell. Likewise the fruit and vegetables all had local varieties with great ranges of characteristics, including local names. Not only were these crops organically reared, there existed — albeit in a landscape of habitats largely dominated by humans — a biodiversity that has been severely damaged by the developments that have come in the wake of agribusiness and the industrialisation of farming.

Wars create enormous social upheaval and uncertainty. They also offer opportunities that might not have occurred under other circumstances. Many men returning home when peace was declared after World War Two came with new ideas, fresh contacts, awakened ambitions, less subservience — and started their own businesses. Government saw the opportunities to adapt new technologies and substances that had been developed in the war effort in a civilian context. For instance, polytetrafluoroethylene had been developed in government laboratories in an effort to discover a substance with a very low friction ratio, ideal to coat bearings, or to make moulds, among other things. We know it better as Teflon, when it is used to coat the insides of cooking utensils. Another example is the chemical so widely used in insecticides, called 'organophosphate' because it contains phosphorus, which was first developed to kill people in gas chambers. There are many other examples. The development of means of transport by road, sea or air meant that goods could travel further, faster and there was no longer a need for any nation to remain self-sufficient in food supplies.

More food at low cost inevitably led to a move towards monoculture, chemical fertilisers, the amalgamation of farms and the 'protection' of crops by chemical means. Only gradually did it become evident that prolonged use of chemical fertiliser instead of humus-rich manure degraded the soil; that the destruction of hedges led to wind erosion; that crops, although they grow faster, are less nutritious under these growing conditions; that residues from chemical pesticides actually damage human and animal health; that antibiotics and hormones, given to 'protect' livestock and to make them grow faster, also play havoc with their health and with that of humans.

It has taken years of trusting the system for the eating public to recognise that the plenty all around us is flawed. It is virtually impossible to detect chemical residues in foods by taste alone and quite impossible for the ordinary consumer to detect medications, legal or otherwise. Impossible, that is, until the harm is done and you discover that you have hyperactivity, candidiasis, anaphylaxis, or cancer. Organic food is not a fad. It is what we need to return to if, like the soil eroded from the monoculture fields, human health is not to be irreversibly eroded.

Just as it was by experience that it was realised organic food is the basis of healthy eating, so it is only as we are losing biodiversity that it is being recognised as a vital component in the interdependence of species that guarantees the continuation of all. In our garden, there are two classifications of plants: cultivars and volunteers. The former we cause to grow where they grow and the latter grow where *they* have chosen. Among the volunteers is a large patch of stinging nettles from which we gather new shoots in the spring, because they make a tasty, nutritious ingredient in many a dinner. Later, just before the nettles flower, I harvest some of them to dry for use as a tea. Once the flower has appeared, the patch is mobbed with butterflies. We think these are three very good reasons for maintaining this particular volunteer. And the nettles are just one among many.

Round about the time that our young city-living visitor was getting excited about the treasures of our garden, we first began to hear about organic farming. Articles appeared in periodicals, such as *Practical Self-sufficiency*, about the virtues of this technique in which not only the notion of growing without using chemicals, but of planting ranges of crops that provided protection to each other, such as carrots, which repel onion fly, being planted intermingled with onions, which repel carrot fly, were promoted. At that stage, we knew no-one using such techniques in the area of Wales where we lived, but ten years later, we were weekly visitors to a farm not ten miles away where we could buy farm-made cheese from an organically reared herd of cows. Within less than the next ten years, not only could we buy stone-ground, whole-wheat flour, but it was ground from organically grown wheat. The growth in demand for organic foods has ensured that the wholefood retail movement can be confident of constant customers who can now buy organic foods across the range of domestic requirements.

The publicising of outbreaks of BSE in British cattle and the fears, not then confirmed, that eating beef could lead to the development of CJD in people, was one of the factors that has led to a marked increase of scrutiny by domestic shoppers of the foods they buy. The forty per cent drop in sales of beef that was admitted by the Ministry of Agriculture and the fact that it was sustained over a considerable period, is a wonderful example of the effect that people's individual choices can have. Had each of those individuals not made the choice not to buy and eat beef over that period, thus causing a noticeable loss of income to farmers in particular and beef sales in general, no changes in the rearing of cattle for meat would have even been contemplated. That changes are being introduced is solely due to public demand.

The complexities of unravelling the damage caused by industrialised, chemical farming is nothing compared to the complexities of abandoning that form of farming altogether. However, the demand for organic food is ensuring the growth of organic farming. Originally started by people who themselves wished to eat organically grown foods, people with farms, small-holdings, market-gardens and non-chemical processing units are no longer considered to be on the outer fringe of commerce.

While organic food does cost more than any non-organically grown equivalent, the extra expense can be offset by the much higher expense of loss of earnings through illness, costs of medical attention or of permanent disability, which can be the result for some people of eating inorganic food. When buying organically produced foods, but not meat, organic or otherwise, the cost of groceries is less, because non-animal protein is much less expensive than meat. We are fortunate that we have alternative foods to those supplied by corporate business, whether in farming, agri-chemicals, or the retail trades and that we are able to exercise choices in how we live and what we eat.

Fifteen

SWEETS TO THE SWEET

Give up your ethics, give up your questions and you are no longer a fully functioning human being.

Beth Burrows

I have great difficulty in killing anything, even flies, or tiny irritating midges. It just makes me feel terrible. But once something is dead, it holds no fear for me, rather, I am awed and fascinated by its individuality and the way it is made. In the days when we ate road-kills and I had to skin and eviscerate rabbits or hares, because their inside parts closely resemble the inside parts of us humans, the children and I could spend hours looking at, wondering at and talking about how these body parts work. I usually kept the livers, hearts and kidneys to use along with the muscle-flesh, but I discarded the heads, intestines, lungs and reproductive parts — the cat and the dog enjoyed those bits. What remained, the flesh that I cooked for us to eat, was the protein part of that meal.

Animal sources of protein in the food humans eat also include eggs, fish and milk, or foods made from milk, such as cheese or butter. Vegetable proteins occur in all the reproductive parts of a plant. Thus, grains, pulses, seeds and nuts are the protein-rich plant sources; of these, the pulse, soya-bean — at forty per cent protein — is the most protein-rich of any food that humans or animals eat, including animal flesh.

Proteins are the building blocks of all forms of life. In mammals, birds and fish they occur as each physical component: blood, lymph, hair, feathers, skin, muscle, nails, claws, hormones, glands, blood vessels, etc. The building blocks of proteins are amino acids. There are twenty amino acids and out of these are made all proteins. If the twenty amino acids are attached in groups of three to any of the sequences of the four DNA bases, A (for Adenine), G (for Guanine), C (for Cytosine) and T (for Thymine), it is possible to derive sixty-four possible combinations of amino acids. Out of these, it is possible to make an almost endless variety of sequences. Any specific chain of sequences of the sixty-four combinations is equal to one particular protein.

Each amino acid combination within the protein chain is attached to its neighbour by a peptide bond. A peptide is a chemical that exists for this purpose — perhaps you could visualise it as the component that gives the necessary flexibility to the long chain of amino acids that make up any particular protein. The long chain that constitutes any protein is required to bend and fold, shorten or lengthen in accordance with its designated nature. In other words, the type of flexibility it displays, as well as the sequences of the component amino acids, is an integral part of a protein's character. It is one of the factors that determines to what bodily part a particular protein molecule belongs.

Around the time that we became immune-system aware because of AIDS, we also began to hear more and more about DNA (Deoxyribonucleic acid) and of RNA (Ribonucleic acid). Advances in the development of technological instruments allowed for the detection of these minute parts of living flesh. Enclosed by the nuclear membrane of every cell of every component part of every living creature is a molecule of DNA, each of which is a long flexible ladder. The uprights spiral round one another and each complete revolution of the spiral is made between each ten of the rungs of this ladder. This sort of spiral, one that involves two intertwining spirals, is called a double helix.

Each upright of the double helix is composed of a chain of deoxyriboses — a five-carbon sugar, separated from the next five-carbon sugar by a phosphate. Each rung has three components: the two ends that attach it to the uprights and a joining component in the middle, which is the only common factor to each rung; it is a weak hydrogen bond. The parts that the weak hydrogen bond connects and which form the attachments to the uprights are called bases and of these, there are only four kinds. They have names that are abbreviated for simplicity: A, for adenine; G, for guanine; C, for cytosine; T, for thymine.

While the hydrogen forms the bond, it will not bond any old pairing, only what is called complementary base pairs. The complementary base pairs are A-T and G-C — no other possible combination will work. Each of these nitrogenous bases that are the attachments of rungs to uprights can take one of four permutations: A-T, or T-A, C-G, or G-C. If these four possible attachments occur in sequences of three, then the sixty-four possible combinations can occur by which the twenty amino acids can be encoded.

Each upright of the double helix ladder, including the third-of-a-rung bases attached to it, is a chromosome. There are forty-six chromosomes and in each chromosome is embodied between three and four million genes — all due to the arrangement of the complementary base pairs and the amino acid sequences of which they are comprised.

The DNA exists in the very centre of each cell, in its nucleus. DNA in any given cell contains the 'blueprints' for the making of proteins and enzymes within that cell. The proteins and enzymes are not made in the nucleus, but in the body of the cell, outside the nuclear membrane. Proteins need enzymes in order to develop, but enzymes cannot exist without the presence of proteins — a chicken-and-egg situation, that scientists seem unable to unravel. DNA, therefore, dominates cell structure and reproduction because it contains the detailed instructions for the creation of each protein.

The protein selection by the DNA in any cell determines the sort of cell, therefore the sort of tissue and therefore the sort of creature or organism. To put it another way, each molecule of DNA is a hologram: it contains the detailed instructions for the cell in which it exists and the details of the entirety of the creature of which that cell is a part. As if that wasn't enough, it also contains the ability to reproduce itself.

Cells reproduce at different speeds in different parts of the body. Brain cells last sixty years or more. It's probable, if you're healthy, that they'll last as long as you live, even if that is more than sixty years. On the other hand, red blood cells last for four months, although white blood cells last for only two days. The cells of the intestinal wall are renewed every thirty-six hours, so the cells that absorbed your breakfast yesterday will not be the same ones that will absorb your breakfast tomorrow.

Cell reproduction is triggered by DNA, but completed by RNA, which makes the proteins for cell replacement by taking two forms, messenger RNA, or mRNA and transcript RNA, or tRNA. To carry its message, RNA has to resemble DNA, but it is also different from DNA. The uprights of DNA contain the sugar deoxyribonase, but RNA contains in its uprights the sugar ribonase, although in each instance the sugar is divided from its neighbour by a phosphate in a repetitive chain. Where DNA has rung bases A, T, C and G, RNA has rung bases where T is replaced by U, the abbreviation for uracil.

RNA has to have a template, which is formed by the DNA straightening itself and the hydrogen bonds parting. The resultant single strand, with the rung bases, is the template; the mRNA strands that form from it each contain a codon of three adjacent bases from the DNA template that will accept the appropriate anticodons of the tRNA, shamrock-shaped molecule when it joins it.

The mRNA strand takes the DNA message out through a pore in the nuclear membrane into the cytoplasm that constitutes the body of the cell between the nuclear membrane and the outer cell wall and locates with particles referred to as ribosomes. The tRNA molecules also leave the nucleus through the pores to gather together loose amino acids that have been doing nothing more than picking up energy in preparation for this moment. The reattachments between the codons and anticodons take place in the presence of an RNA polymerase enzyme. It is as though the mRNA is the choreographer who indicates the position of the dancers and the tRNA is the prompt who gathers the dancers together for the performance. Specific amino acids are led by each tRNA molecule to the appropriate ribosome where they all join hands at the instructions of the conductor — the enzyme — until, finally, they have formed the predetermined protein chain.

Meanwhile, the now separate halves of the DNA migrate out of the nucleus to the opposite sides of the cell where they redevelop their matching halves, return to the double helix form and become the core of the new nuclei of two daughter cells.

All this is understood and has been observed, but no-one has yet been able to say what prompts the prompt. Who is the director who employs the choreographer? What is it that starts the mitosis, or cell division that results in the beginnings of a whole, new being? What continues the process of division and re-division as that being grows to maturity and then continues to divide and re-divide in the maintenance process that lasts until the death of the organism?

Could the energy that coalesces into matter at the commencement of each single-cell conception, be called spirit? Could spirit be the energy that disperses when the multi-celled organism, or being, de-coalesces from matter? There are theories and beliefs, but no certainty, in the sense that Western science regards certainty. Using the same principles as those of the cinematographic editor when cutting and splicing film, the scientists who genetically 'modify', or edit, DNA, cannot discern all the frames of the film; this is because, so far, only very few of the several million genes in the chromosomes have had their purpose recognised.

The macrocosmic picture of protein is in the protein we eat, along with enzymes enfolded through it and the carbohydrates and the fats we also eat, many of them similarly endowed with enzymes. All include one or several of the vitamins and trace minerals that are important ancillary agents in the activity on the microcosmic scale within our cells. It is the amino acids in grains and pulses that make it important to eat those that are whole and unrefined. Pulses contain one set of amino acids and grains another. Together they form whole proteins in animal and human diet. At the ratio of one part of pulse to three parts of grain, protein balance is achieved; this protein derived from plant material is easier to digest than that derived from animal flesh.

In our digestive tracts, proteins are deconstructed ('digested') into their component amino acids by the activity of specific enzymes, both those created in our guts and those we ingest along with the food. As simple amino acids, this protein material can be absorbed into the blood, to be conveyed to the liver for storage and for further distribution as required. Without the proteins we eat, the DNA and RNA could not fulfil their roles satisfactorily. Too much complex protein, such as red meat, can be almost as harmful as not enough, because an excess of protein lays stress on the enzyme-producing cells and on the capacity of the liver to store the product of the digestive process. Ill-health can ensue as a result. Of the carbohydrates we eat, some are in combination with the proteins as, for example, in whole grains, wheat, rice, rye, maize and oats.

Fats are present in grains, but not so much as they are in seeds and nuts. Of all the carbohydrates we eat, it is refined white sugar that causes the greatest problems. The carbohydrate in grains is the sort of carbohydrate our species has evolved using and from which we derive energy. A carbohydrate is a complex chain of monosaccharides, or simple sugars, which, when combined in the complete carbohydrate, are called polysaccharides. It is only after enzymes have disentangled this complex chain and reduced it to its component single sugars that these sugars become accessible to the body. Refined white sugar is a disaccharide, in other words, it is composed of two sugars, glucose and fructose, which combined as the disaccharide are called 'sucrose'.

Glucose is the sugar which is the only form of energy the brain can use. The liver converts and stores any excess glucose the body ingests and digests in the form of glycogen; because it too is a polysaccharide, glycogen has to be re-digested in order for the body to be able to use it. Too much sucrose, which provides an excess of glucose, puts strains on the liver's storage systems, on enzyme secretion and digestion. In fact, the sound operation of the human digestive system shows most clearly the value in the maxim, 'moderation in all things', ill-health resulting from over indulgence.

However, sucrose entered the human diet only in recent generations — and we like it. It has a 'more-ish' influence on our taste buds and the more refined it is, the more we like the taste. Unfortunately, the more refined it is, the less remains of the trace minerals and vitamins that exist in the plants, sugar-cane and sugar-beet, from which sucrose is derived. One of the reasons that a convenience-food diet is damaging to health is the presence of sucrose in almost every processed food from tinned garden peas to packets of crisps. When sucrose was identified as a problem, substitutes were sought, so that we could continue to get the sugar-buzz on our taste buds.

Those substitutes have brought their own problems to human health; one of them is so hazardous that US pilots have been forbidden to consume 'diet' drinks which contain the sweetener aspartame. Aspartame is the generic name for the substance that assumes other names given to it by different manufacturers, of which 'Nutrasweet' is a deceptively safe-sounding example. It contains methanol, otherwise known as wood-alcohol, which when heated is even more swiftly absorbed by the body than when it is cool. In the body it quickly separates into its component chemicals, one of which is formaldehyde, which destroys brain cells. It is not surprising, therefore that ninety different reactions documented in 1994 after a study by the US Department of Health and Human Services, ranging from muscle spasms, to headaches, epileptic-type seizures and heart disturbances have been recorded as resulting from its ingestion. The onset of chronic illnesses, including brain tumours, multiple sclerosis, Alzheimer's, diabetes and congenital birth defects have been attributed to it. In fact, aspartame is the root of seventy-five percent of all adverse reactions to food additives reported to the FDA (Food and Drugs Administration). Only by reading the list of contents on the labels of processed foods can we discover if aspartame, or any other hazard may be included.

Processed foods are a minefield for the unwary! Food labelling is an inexact guide either to the contents of the packet, jar or can or to the various 'processes' that may have been inflicted on the food. An example of this was the presence of alar — chemically, daminozide — in apples and pears. No labels ever included alar until it had been banned; then producers were happy to announce, 'Contains no alar!' on the labels of produce derived from or including apples and pears. Daminozide is a growth controller, that assures the grower that all the fruit on the trees will ripen to the same size; it is not in any way necessary as an aid to apple or pear growth. That it is absorbed into the flesh of the fruit on which it is used means that it is impossible to remove it and, as it is known to have allergic effects on some people, it is undesirable.

Parents For Safe Food was formed in Britain in 1989, at which time it added its weight to the worldwide agitation to have alar banned. The good news is that it was, despite the British government's Advisory Committee on Pesticides renewed assertion that it was safe, made in December of the same year. In 1990, this group of concerned parents joined with the London Food Commission and Geoffrey Cannon to produce the *Safe Food Handbook*. One of the founder members of Parents for Safe Food contributes the following in the section after the introduction,

> I am frustrated at the way current legislation leaves the benefit of the doubt in favour of the producer instead of the consumer. We don't know the long-term effects of these chemicals. They are loosely controlled. There is insufficient testing for residues and products should at the very least be labelled as to their content. Without this information we are deprived of choice.

That sums up how many people feel. The book describes in detail how labels can be interpreted. It also offers a wealth of advice and information about all aspects of food and its effects on us, along with all the chemicals — whether residues or additives — that it contains.

Until the industrialisation of food processing and, later, of farming, food allergies were virtually unknown. In fact, it is not the food to which the body is allergic, but the chemicals that it contains. These may be residues from chemical fertiliser, from any of the pesticides that were used as the crop was growing, from preservative sprays, waxes or dips that were used to enhance shelf-life, or from additives during any processing stage. The latter may include colourings, preservatives and, of course, sweeteners such as aspartame. The residues may include medications given to animals, birds or fish destined to be killed and eaten.

The body is not equipped to identify such chemicals, because they have never existed in nature — having being created in the laboratory — and are therefore unknown to human DNA. If a chemical causes disruptive reactions in the body's processes, as so many of them do, the only way the body can identify the chemical is through the food that was the vehicle by which the substance first entered the body. This is why someone, who has first manifested an allergy to a food that was not organically but chemically grown and who then eats the same food that has been organically grown and is free of chemicals, still has an allergic reaction: the body is playing safe.

Some allergic reactions are transitory, while others may last a lifetime, such as the permanent photo-sensitivity that accompanies an allergy to penicillin and some plants. Amongst these allergies are some that can appear quite sinister, because the disruptive reaction can have a cumulative intensity which is termed ana-phylaxic. The good news is that this only occurs within a well-defined range of foods and medications; these are: penicillin and other antibiotics, eggs, dairy products — milk and products derived from it; fish and shellfish, wasp and bee stings, all nuts, especially brazil, and, those with which anaphylaxis is most commonly associated, peanuts. The difficulties arise in the pattern of the reaction, because anaphylaxis can, but may not, occur the first time the body encounters any of the above. Or the first reaction may be so mild that it is ignored, or, equally unpre-dictably, the very first reaction may be life-threatening. If, after a reaction, the body is again 'challenged' by the same food or medicine, the next reaction will be more severe; its incremental severity can no more be predicted than can the possibility of a reaction in the first instance.

Anaphylactic shock can kill, which is why hospital personnel always ask if a person being admitted has any allergies. In order to avoid this, it is essential to avoid the allergen; only total abstinence can assure no reaction. In the event of a severe reaction, adrenaline is sometimes used as an antidote; at other times, anti-histamine is used. Bear in mind that some people are also allergic to anti-histamine. Doctors can get very touchy about this — as one who has this allergy, I have experience of this!

Non-chemical processing of food is as important as organic growing, because allergies to colouring, sweeteners and preservatives can cause other distressing reactions, even if they are not life-threatening. Hyperactivity is a reaction that can disrupt families severely. From a broken sleep-pattern, which disturbs other members of the family, to an inability to concentrate, to constant movement, to prolonged screaming and distress and digestive disturbances such as diarrhoea or constipation, hyperactivity can manifest in a variety of ways. It is said that it affects more blond, blue-eyed boys than it does girls. In either, dramatic changes in behaviour can result from the withdrawal of commercial drinks with artificial colouring, especially tartrazine and from sweets of all sorts, including cakes. Other foods can also be implicated.

If you have a child who is inattentive, disruptive, impatient and aggressive, try withdrawal, but also find someone who can do an allergy test and a hair test for mineral and vitamin deficiency, which may also be present. You can also contact the Hyperactive Children's Support Group, for which the address is in Resources. Following dietary adjustments, you may not recognise the intelligent and charming child who was once so different!

Preservatives, colourings, sugars and sweeteners present a complicated obstacle course, not only in the life of a young child, but also in the life of a breeding adult. The mother's diet before and during pregnancy will have the most profound effects on the development of new life, through egg, embryo and foetus to baby. However, the diet of the father during at least the year before his semen fertilises the mother's ovum will have a significant bearing on the quality of that semen and the factors it can transmit to the future child. Especially critical are the first three months of pregnancy, but the no-go areas for a mother at this time are the same as they should be for the father during the vital previous year: inappropriate diet, drinking alcohol (even in moderation); smoking; exposure to radiation from televisions, computers, microwave cookers and mobile phones; medications, especially antibiotics and steroids of all sorts and exposure to a variety of chemicals. These can all seriously prejudice normal foetal development.

Tiny amounts of the wrong material, or brief exposure to other influences during those early months, can disrupt the minute and scarcely defined endocrine system, especially the hypothalamus. This can cause a range of abnormalities, from the barely detectable to a life-threatening deformity. Nature often steps in to dispose of a foetus that is unlikely to sustain a normal life and it is 'miscarried', or aborted. Women who experience a series of miscarriages sometimes carry normal babies full term after making radical changes in their diet and lifestyle. Foresight, the Association for the Promotion of Preconceptual Care, has a feast of books, videos and seminars to help parents wishing to give their children the best start in life. Plainly, DNA is affected by what we eat, as such women's experiences illustrate.

Do you remember how hard it used to be to find shops selling grapes? Not only were they expensive, but they were packed carefully in fragments of cork to minimise bruising and thus delay the rotting process. Grapes are cheap and available all year round now, probably because they have been irradiated. The effect of radiation is to destroy the enzymes, bacteria and fungi in food — naturally occurring and otherwise — and to slow down decomposition to stalling point.

Remember that not only is there biodiversity of large organisms, such as mice, oaks, elephants, herrings and people, but within each of these there is another biodiversity at the microbial level. When its habitat is the food of another species, this helps in the digestive process. Not all of this microbial population is destroyed by irradiation, but it is sufficiently impaired to say that the life-force that existed in the food before it was irradiated has gone; virtually all that remains is flavour, fluid and fibre.

Some years ago, a friend gave us a punnet of glossy, red straw-berries in the middle of January. My naturally suspicious nature made me explore the transparent plastic container for a label: 'Produce of Bogota, Colombia', I read. The fruit had already travelled halfway round the world, yet remained as though it had been picked within the hour. We left the strawberries in the punnet and put them in the larder. A fortnight later, when I brought them out, they still looked pristine fresh — not natural strawberry behaviour — but, undoubtedly, irradiated. We didn't eat them.

Irradiation is promoted by the nuclear industry as a clean, efficient method of destroying dangerous germs and 'infestations' in foods, although the fact that not all are killed can cause the food to become more rather than less hazardous. As there are no tests that can prove a food has been irradiated, one can only be suspicious, especially of anything from Holland, the only country in Europe where any food can be irradiated at the discretion of the wholesaler. The wholesaler and the retailer are the true beneficiaries of irradiation of food, because of the extended shelf-life and the increased opportunities for sales, especially in items that are out of season, like our glossy strawberries. Fortunately, Holland is unique in its liberality toward irradiation as few governments, worldwide, have permitted its use. Unfortunately, despite the growing resistance from the buying public to any food it regards as having been tampered with — and irradiation constitutes 'tampering' — the nuclear industry has prevailed and no government has made labelling mandatory.

For over a year, I was in correspondence with the Irish Department of Agriculture, during which I had incomprehensible and uninformative replies to my letters. Finally, after I had sent a letter itemising the inadequacies in the Department's replies and reiterating my request for information about the government's intentions toward the labelling of irradiated and genetically modified foods, the reply told me to direct my questions to the Department of the Environment . . . Within a week a general election was called. Trying to extract information is often a tedious and frustrating occupation.

While commercial interests in the nuclear industry continue trying to establish general use of irradiation for foods and medicines, they have achieved a remarkable influence on industrial production in Europe. The European Commission has issued a directive permitting the use of radioactive nuclear waste in recycled glass, plastics and metals destined for use in the manufacture of consumer goods. Dr John Gofman has called this 'the same as issuing permits to commit random murder'; as Dr Alice Stewart said about the same directive, it will 'necessarily add to the number of mutant cells in living organisms'. Furthermore, there would be no way to trace this recycled health hazard, because companies using it will not be required to report this activity, nor to obtain a licence. Both these scientists have been recipients of the Right Livelihood Award for their work; thank goodness such an award exists to highlight the existence of experts whose ethics are not distorted by inappropriate, self-serving allegiance to a commercial company, as so many 'experts' are.

So much of this information may seem at first glance to be a cause for alarm, but the fact that it has been gleaned from publications that are readily available is a cause for relief, although not a reason for relaxing vigilance. Our knowledge of how the body works is not totally comprehensive, but the knowledge we have is thanks to scientists. It is thanks to vigilant support groups that counter-action to practices perceived as dangerous so often comes about. Ordinary people are, in general, honest and even-handed and we are astonished to find that so many government representatives and spokespersons for commercial enterprises are not. Constant pressure, however, can bring about change, as the history of so many support groups can show.

Sixteen

THE KING IS IN THE ALTOGETHER

Scientific theories can never provide a complete and definitive description of reality. They will always be approximations to the true nature of things. To put it bluntly, scientists do not deal with truth; they deal with limited and approximate descriptions of reality.

Uncommon Wisdom by Fritjof Capra

If I was a judge awarding marks to the entertainer who deserved to be thought of with the greatest frequency, my vote would go to Danny Kaye. He might be recalled by some for his light-hearted gate-crashing of the studio where BBC's ponderous weekly forum of intellectuals were broadcasting on The Brains Trust. He comes to my mind, though, singing a refrain from one of the songs in the musical based on the life of the Danish story-teller, Hans Christian Andersen, in which he starred. I hear this refrain at some point during nearly every news bulletin I hear or read and during any discussion of current affairs: 'The King is in the altogether . . . it's altogether . . . he's altogether as naked as the day that he was born!' This tale survives because, like all such tales, it reminds us of our human frailty and gullibility. However, by relegating it to a child audience, adults try to reject an inference that any event so patently fraudulent as the King's New Clothes could occur in the adult world. And yet . . .

Over the past few years, a succession of trade agreements have been negotiated between the nations of the world. Each new one has been broader in scope, has changed practices in greater numbers of the world's nations and had more far-reaching implications for more of the ordinary people of the planet. One that covers Canada, USA and Mexico is the North American Free Trade Association (NAFTA), or Now Another Freedom Taken Away! The purpose of NAFTA is not related to the improvement of nutrition among the populations of the participating nations, nor to improved working conditions, to fair pay, or anything else that might enhance their lives. This it has in common with all other trade agreements, the purpose of which is to make increasingly large profits for the transnational corporations that control industry. How can an agreement between governments benefit transnational corporations, while it fails to benefit each government's population? The answer lies in the collusion between governments and corporations.

There is a constant migration between the seats of authority in national governments, including government-sponsored bodies and the seats of authority on the boards of corporations. The momentum for this migration is the personal accumulation of wealth and power which these positions bestow. The fear of the loss of wealth or power is as strong as the wish for more of either or both. The existence of these human characteristics is enough, even without a hint of bribery or corruption, to impel trade agreements. Elected representatives may talk about increasing the number of jobs — failing to mention either their quality or duration — while corporations will talk about profits and stock exchange ratings. Each is referring to a source of power, however, the job-holders voting the politicians back in and the same workers' productivity providing the profits for the corporation. The 'middle-man' in the relationship between the decision makers in government and the decision makers in business is the lobbyist. The purpose of lobbying is to explain the needs of business to legislators and to influence their decisions.

Trade agreements in recent years have dealt with many different types of products from many industries. Agriculture always features in such agreements, as a major consumer of the products of both the petro-chemical industry and the pharmaceutical industry, between whom it is increasingly hard to distinguish, owing to so many company amalgamations. Grains, the staple food of any nation, are produced in greater quantity than any other type of crop, with the exception of animal food and the sources of sugar, cane and beet. These receive attention and regulation under trade agreements.

NAFTA was no exception. It opened the Mexican borders to cheap corn grown in the USA by industrialised, mechanical and chemical methods far more cheaply than the small-scale, hand-worked farms of the natives of Chiapas, the resource-richest district of Mexico, could achieve. Whatever benefit the Mexican government hoped to receive as a result of joining NAFTA, it was sufficient for it to take heavy, punitive measures against its own farmers who were resistant to the agreement. Villages have been razed, crops destroyed and people massacred — all, it would appear, with government connivance. Especially vulnerable have been those who have organised themselves under the banner of the Zapatistas, who see the corn agreement under NAFTA as just another series of moves designed to destroy the remnants of their ancient culture as the race that predates Columbus and his marauding hordes.

In India, a similarly strong resistance has occurred, but without such disastrous government response. This time the resistance is not to grain crossing national boundaries for sale, but to the imposition, under GATT, of new practices with regard to wheat and rice. The ancient custom among Indian grain farmers is to exchange seed with their neighbours after each harvest. New legislation has been designed to halt this practice. In future, the farmers have been told, they will have to buy patented, hybridised seed annually and also the chemical fertilisers and pesticides that the seed has been genetically modified to accept. Most of the farmers in India are women and the full implications of this plan were evident to them. Half a million grain farmers marched peacefully in Bangalore in 1994 in protest at this move, only one of many similar actions throughout India. The farmers will not accept it.

The Uraguay Round of the General Agreement on Tariffs and Trade — the 'Ultimate Reinforcement of the Global Attack on

Traditional Trading' — was negotiated by an Irish lawyer called Peter Sutherland. A total of 132 governments ratified this agreement, including the wealthiest and most industrially productive ones. GATT was unique in that, for the first time, under a chapter called Trade Related Intellectual Properties (TRIPS), or 'Take Your Rights for Profitable Sales', it concerned itself with patenting what were termed 'intellectual property'. This means any information or technology that can generate income to the patent holder, thus introducing the concept of the patenting of all or part of any lifeform. TRIPS comes up for review in 1999, after which governments party to it would be forced to adopt laws that patent life.

In 1997, the EU turned its back on appeals from citizens groups for a moratorium on life patents by reversing its decision of two years earlier, when it refused such rights. In theory, these patents can only be granted for new discoveries and cannot be applied to knowledge or information which has been in common circulation, or vested in tradition. In practice, no such strictures are applied. In India, for example, as explained in a petition to the US Patent and Trademark Office, 'Few organisms have as long a history of widespread human use as the neem tree. Ancient texts refer to the neem as the "blessed tree" and the "cure for all ailments".' The tree plays a particularly important role within Indian culture. Several centuries of Indian learning, creativity and experimentation with the neem tree have resulted in a wealth of information on how to harness the tree's potential for use in medicine, fuel and agriculture. With this long history of use, it is no surprise that there is at least one growing in every community.

The W. R. Grace Company, a transnational chemical corporation, has patented rights to exclusive use of a pesticidal extract from neem seeds, which means Indians — who have used this extract without hindrance since time immemorial — are required to pay a royalty to W. R. Grace for using it in the future. The petition against this is global and unprecedented: 200 organisations and prominent individuals from thirty-five countries have initiated a legal challenge against this act of bio-piracy, for

W. R. Grace's application flies in the face of the stipulation that such patents should not be of traditional knowledge or practices.

Companies submitting for patents are often economical with the truth. Serle, owned by Monsanto, omitted to say that the rats that had survived the trials of aspartame included those which had undergone surgery to remove brain tumours induced by the experiment, when it sought approval for this product in US. Searches by the patenting authority for verification of statements in submissions appear not to have been made.

The curious, symbiotic collusion that exists between elected, non-profit-making governments and non-elected, profit-making corporations may be explained by the following quotation from GATT Briefing Number Seven of March 1992. It was published by Rongead Lyon, a European NGO network on agriculture and development,

> Perhaps the most advanced university-government-industry con-
> sortium to focus on agricultural applications of biotechnology is
> the Midwest Plant Biotechnology consortium, which involves
> fifteen mid-western universities, three federal laboratories, thirty-
> seven agribusiness corporations with headquarters in the midwest
> and research institutes from eight states. The consortium's purpose
> is to conduct basic research in plant biotechnology to foster the
> economic competitiveness of US agriculture and agribusiness.

How the entanglements of the symbiosis actually come about, this quote from the same source illustrates:

> The relationship between universities and industries depends on
> the goal and institutional characteristics of the partners and
> consequently encompass diverse approaches. These biotechnology
> arrangements — between firms, universities, faculty members and
> student/trainees — include large grants and contracts between
> companies and universities in exchange for patent rights and
> exclusive licences to discoveries; programmes and centres at major
> universities, funded by industries, that give private firms privileged
> access to university resources and a role in shaping research
> agendas; professors, particularly in biomedical sciences, who are
> consultants in scientific advisory boards or are managers in

biotechnology firms; faculties who receive research funds from private corporations in which they hold significant equity; faculties who set up their own biotechnology firms; public universities that establish for-profit corporations (e.g. Neogen at Michigan State University) to develop and market innovations arising from research; and universities that establish alumni panels with venture capital to evaluate new university technologies for possible commercialisation.

Once the ratification of GATT was completed, the signatories became the World Trade Organisation (WTO) — or, 'We're Taking Over', which they set out to do. On 16 February 1998, the Organisation of Economic Co-operation and Development, OECD, countries' political delegates, met to consider the details of the Multilateral Agreement on Investment (MAI, also known as 'Monstrous Agency for Injustice'). Amongst the clauses in this document are legal entitlement to rights of many sorts for transnational corporations, but none for ordinary people.

Among the rights the corporations will assume is one to sue any sovereign government. This has already taken place in Canada under a similar clause in NAFTA, where the US-based Ethyl Corporation is suing the Canadian government for 367 million dollars for trying to ban the use of MMT, which it manufactures in Ottawa and around which is controversial argument over its use as an additive to motor fuels. The Corporation is demanding, 'Immediate compensation for imposing legislation which hinders its operations'. This is where I begin to see the King's gooseflesh starting to twitch! Instead of enacting legislation demanded by the electing population, governments will henceforth be obliged to enact legislation only in the interests of transnational commerce.

In the UK, an unwillingness on the part of parents to have a child vaccinated, is sometimes 'punished' by the whole family being removed from their GP's list. Legislation concerning other forms of social medication, eating habits or building regulations, for example, could come into force and resistors would face the legal consequences. But this trade agreement is not yet finalised and the People's Global Action group is mobilising worldwide co-ordination of resistance to MAI and all that it implies, starting with an international conference in Geneva in February 1998.

Even under the permissiveness allowed by GATT, any experimentation with medicines or foods, or anything that might affect them, has first, in most countries, to pass the scrutiny of the Environmental Protection Agency of that country (I wonder will it continue to under MAI?). The agencies are, of course, dependent on the information supplied by the companies making application to them. One of the largest agri-chemical companies in the world is Monsanto, the risks of whose products have been underestimated more than once by their submission of flawed data.

Monsanto is a long-established company and its track record is not notable for acts in the public interest. With and for the US army, it produced Agent Orange, the defoliant used during the Vietnam War, which caused horrific health problems for much of the population living where it was sprayed, as well as for US army personnel involved in its use. Many of Monsanto's manufacturing bases have also been responsible for extensive incidents of environmental pollution. This corporation is at the forefront of the genetic modification of major plant crops: soya beans, maize and sugar-beet. It is estimated that in 1997 alone, fifteen per cent of the soya beans grown in the US — the world's largest grower of this pulse — had been genetically modified with genes added from viruses, bacteria and the petunia flower. The reason is the same as for experimentation with other plants: so that the crop will be resistant to Roundup, the herbicide they manufacture, the active ingredient of which is glyphosate.

Quite apart from the risks inherent in chemical residues remaining in food crops, the laboratory technician, no matter how highly qualified, has not yet the ability to float the piece of DNA with the desired characteristic from an alien source into the receptor DNA with any precision. No-one can predict where the additional fragment of DNA will land, nor what its influence may be on any other aspect of the entire DNA chain. Nor can there be any certainty about how the new organism may influence other life forms.

In their endeavour to insert characteristics deemed desirable, some geneticists claim that the genetic modification of plants has resulted in no accidents. In this they are uninformed and their claim reveals an urgent need for some authority with an overview, because there have been accidents and mistakes. A very serious one was only discovered inadvertently. Michael Holmes, under the tutorship of Elaine Ingham at Oregon State University, found during his doctoral research of a genetically engineered micro-organism, Klebsiella planticola, that the microrhizal fungi in the soil — essential for plant growth — were so severely reduced by its presence that the wheat plants sown in that soil all died. Klebsiella planticola was designed to produce ethanol from plant waste, such as wheat straw, but the soil-related effects of its use, or that of any other laboratory designed micro-organism, or plant, are not part of an environmental protection agency test prior to assessment.

Another unexpected side-effect from a genetically modified plant caused an increased milk yield in cattle who were subjects of a cattle-feed test using genetically modified soya (which had *not* been sprayed with Roundup). The unpredicted increase in plant oestrogens stimulated milk secretion, but such an increase in this hormone could have serious consequences for humans, for example in the increased risk of genetically related cancers. There is no way of knowing what other effects there may be, for the cow, for her future offspring, or for humans who consume her milk and its products, or her meat.

The latter example makes the choice of crops for Monsanto's initial experiments very interesting, not only because they are among the largest volume crops, but maize and soya provide components for more than half of all processed foods. This is a staggering total, demanding a labelling strategy of great clarity, if consumer choice is to have any real meaning. However, the British Food Industry Federation has plans to label all food containing soya as having been genetically modified, whether it has or not, which makes a nonsense of labelling.

After World War Two, politicians felt they needed a 'nuclear deterrent' — more atom bombs; industrialists saw an opportunity to make a profit from a civilian nuclear industry; scientists developed nuclear-powered electricity generation. In Britain, Windscale — a bleak place on the north west coast of England — was chosen as a site for a factory where fuel rods, once their ability to generate electricity was passed, could be recycled to extract the plutonium needed to make atom bombs. Japan legislated against the stock piling of spent fuel rods on Japanese soil, although it saw nothing against their use to generate electricity. So their spent fuel rods arrive in England, along with those from an increasing number of other countries; all of which increases the accident risk from these dangerously radioactive rods as they are transported around the world.

Windscale earned itself a bad reputation for accidental emissions of radioactive material, so its name was changed to Sellafield. The reputation hasn't changed, however, and accidents continue. Chernobyl was an accident greater only in its single magnitude of emission than any one from Windscale/Sellafield and we are well-informed that Chernobyl is an accident waiting to happen again. Between civilian nuclear accidents and the experimental atom/hydrogen bomb explosions, there are some contaminants whose 'life' as a danger to all life-forms coming near them has been estimated to be as long as the Grand Cycle of the planet itself, 25,000 years.

The promoters of nuclear power lied to us when they said this was a 'clean' way to produce electricity. The ventures went ahead, regardless of the limited knowledge and the lack of certainty, because 'commercial interests' might have been thwarted had they not. Surely, living memory is to be relied upon for this mistake to be accepted and acted on? Genetic engineering is far too inexact at this stage of its development; the lack of certainty about the results not yet foreseen makes it too dangerous for genetically modified organisms to be liberated, like fairies from Pandora's Box, never to be recaptured.

Dr Vyvyan Howard of the University of Liverpool, who is head of Research for the Foetal and Infant Toxico-Pathology Department, said in the summer of 1997,

> Political decision-makers should learn from the historical evidence
> that we have of problems with pervasive technologies and lean
> towards scepticism about the claims of those who stand to profit
> directly from the 'gene revolution'.

Further evidence of the inappropriate haste being applied to the commercialisation of genetic manipulation in agriculture is that no single plant or animal has had a study of its entire genome completed. A genome is all the information encoded in the DNA of a cell of an organism. In the simplest plant being studied, there are 120 million base pairs in the DNA, all of which require scrutiny for their purpose and their interrelationships before there can be any question of human intervention in the plant's evolution. It is predicted that this one study will not be complete until 2002 — and that is one, simple plant, not any of the plants currently being manipulated and their seed released for commercial use.

There is comfort to be gained from knowing that not every government has been suborned by the pressures of commerce. While there is no internationally binding agreement to control the use and assess the safety of GMOs (Genetically Manipulated Organisms), some sovereign governments are maintaining a ban. In Europe, this includes Austria and Luxembourg. These states are members of the EU and as such subject to its Commission's rules, which clearly shows that they are out of line with other member states. However, Sweden, Denmark, UK and Ireland have made it clear that they would not support the arbitrary removal of the ban, so it remains, although it will come under regular review within the Commission.

Austria's resistance is to Ciba Geigy's mutant maize, as is Luxembourg's. Ireland, however, allowed the EPA to grant permission to Monsanto to conduct a four-year trial of mutant sugar-beet which was planted in 1997. Originally, it had been intended by Monsanto to plant in three sites, but eventually the first planting was limited to a site in Carlow on land controlled by Teagasc, the government-sponsored agricultural advisory board.

Although Ireland has a population of only approximately four million people, there is a considerable interest in wholefoods and healthy eating. This can be seen by the number of small towns as well as cities that maintain flourishing whole/healthfood shops. Close attention is paid by suppliers and retailers to food quality and availability, with a rapidly growing emphasis on organically, naturally grown foods. It is not, therefore, surprising that the activities of Monsanto and the EPA were closely followed.

An umbrella group was created as soon as the news broke that Monsanto intended to hold seed trials in Ireland. Called Genetic Concern!, it is supported by An Taisce (a heritage trust, like the National Trust in the UK); Community Action Network; Cork Environmental Alliance; CRANN (an organisation concerned with re-afforestation with native broad-leafed trees and the appropriate use of woodland); Dublin Food Co-Op; Earthwatch; Green Party; Irish Association of Health Stores; IOFGA (Irish Organic Farmers and Growers Association); Irish Seedsavers; Irish Women's Environmental Network; Macrobiotics Ireland; Sisters of Mercy (a religious order); Natural Law Party; Organic Trust; Quay Co-Op; Trinity College Dublin Environmental Society; United Farmers Association and the Vegetarian Society. Such support is a significant indicator of the lively interest taken by Irish society in environmental concerns.

Clare Watson, a member of Genetic Concern! applied to the High Court for an injunction to prevent, or at worst delay, the sowing of the mutant sugar-beet seed. After the injunction, a Judicial Review was sought, again by Clare Watson. It was set for hearing on 10 December 1997, but was adjourned until early in 1998, when it was adjourned yet again. It is worthy of comment on the arrogant attitude Monsanto has toward the concerns of so many responsible citizens in Ireland, that they went ahead and sowed the seed without waiting for the outcome of the Judicial Review. This would appear to be the sort of attitude generally adopted by such companies.

In early 1998, with the Judicial Review hearing still to take place, Monsanto applied to the EPA for permission to sow mutant beet seed at ten sites around Ireland. After receiving nearly 3,500 letters of protest, the number of sites was reduced to five, on the grounds that 'anonymity' could not be guaranteed to farmers.

Letter writing is important and relatively easy to fit into one's daily existence, but Non-Violent Direct Action (NVDA) is growing, worldwide. Before the 1997 harvest could be taken by Monsanto's employees from the site in Carlow, it was hoed up by the Gaelic Earth Liberation Front (GELF). Similar action has been reported from Australia, where a group calling itself Mothers Against Genetic Engineering is reported to have uprooted a crop of mutant canola seed on an experimental site at the University of Queensland's Gatton campus. This plant is used for cattle feed, after its oil content has been extracted. In this instance, it was planted by AgrEvo, another huge agri-chemical company, who had mutated the DNA of the canola seed to accept Basta, one of its herbicides. No doubt NVDA groups will attend to the crops of future trials — no doubt the companies conducting the trials will make every attempt to prevent them.

The most compelling action that can be taken is to abstain from buying goods that can be considered as faulty. The action of a woman on the Isle of Wight is instructive. She sent Monsanto a bill for the costs of researching foods she felt acceptable for her family, making her own bread and in preparing other dishes she might previously have bought; she also added in the time she spent travelling to shops where she was able to buy the foods that were acceptable. Extrapolated for one year, her bill amounted to £6,418.82, sterling.

More overt Non-Violent Direct Action has been begun by Greenpeace, who in Rotterdam used their boat, *Sirius*, to occupy the berth of the MV *Istanbul*. The *Istanbul* was about to enter the terminal to off-load a cargo of genetically manipulated soya beans — part of that fifteen per cent of the 1997 US crop of soya that was genetically manipulated — as well as some suspect corn gluten pellets, not approved for admission to Europe. (Incidentally, Archers Daniels Midlands (ADM), the shippers, maintained that segregation of genetically manipulated soya from non-manipulated soya was impossible. Monsanto, the growers, insisted that farmers keep them segregated so that seed could be collected for resowing. The US grows sixty per cent of the world soya crop, of which Europe buys fourteen million tonnes per year.) Greenpeace's action included painting 'Genetic X' on the side of the *Istanbul* under cover of darkness and occupying the berth for long enough to draw media attention — but not long enough to incur fines imposed by Dutch law after legal action instigated by ADM. It is Greenpeace's intention to continue drawing attention to such imports for so long as is necessary, so that public awareness is maintained.

Pioneer Hi-Bred International Inc — a very large seed company — has refused, after two years' discussion, to carry Monsanto's mutated maize seed on the grounds that Monsanto wanted too much control of farmers' prices and that a single herbicide resistance was of limited value. This decision is phrased to take into account only commercial arguments against the use of such seed, nothing on moral or health grounds. Nonetheless, organised protest groups, such as Greenpeace and lesser known ones, such as the Peasants Revolt Against Genetics, among many others, are taking actions based on moral, ethical, health and commonsense grounds.

John Vidal, in his book *McLibel*, pinpointed the polarisation of opinion and activity as the transnational corporations make themselves more powerful through their policy of globalisation, power they intend to extend through the MAI agreement. He writes, 'For corporations the trend should be very worrying; what it means is that their own globalism is being turned against them by the emerging global civil society.'

Thanks to the Internet and other means of telecommunication, the Peasants Revolt Against Genetics can share tactics and encouragement with Mothers Against Genetic Engineering at the drop of a computer key. It is regrettable that life at the end of the twentieth century requires such vigilance to maintain a healthy diet. What is interesting about the protest ethos this situation has engendered is the active promotion by protesters of sustainable, natural alternatives to the damaging routes the corporations are hastening down in their drive for more profit. It is fair to claim the development of two distinct, major groups in society: the at-any-cost-profiteers and the sustainable-futurists.

Yet, even without environmentalists, human rights groups, mothers and peasants practising NVDA, letters or judicial reviews to haunt and to attempt to daunt them, the dinosaurs of corporate business are doomed. It is their practice, each time an amalgamation takes place, to 'rationalise' the combined businesses, which always involves getting rid of a proportion of the workforce. This activity is self-defeating, because for the goods to make profits, they must be bought; to be bought, each buyer has to have sufficient income. So the corporations, by divesting themselves of workers, at the same time divest themselves of customers. Global gargantuanism is non-sustainable.

Seventeen

LET YOUR FOOD BE YOUR MEDICINE

You can no more make a silk purse from a sow's ear
than you can construct healthy tissue from unhealthy
food, unless you have become a Tantric adept. Ideally
your food should be grown in your own field or garden
so that you have full control over what physical and
mental inputs it imbibes, but since this is impossible
for most of us nowadays, the role of the food
preparer becomes paramount.

Ayurveda, Life, Health, and Longevity
by Robert E. Svoboda

In September 1990, at the beginning of my final year as a
mature student, I went to live for a couple of months on
Exmoor. The quiet roads around the house I occupied were all
bordered by beech hedgerows, making a perfect habitat for an
amazing range of mushrooms and other fungi. With no salary to
rely on and very little money, I depended on those fungi to
provide a lot of the plant protein in my diet. I fried and stewed
mauve mushrooms, brown mushrooms, white and creamy-
coloured mushrooms and a vibrant, yellow-ochre bracket fungus.

A friend had given me a book, *Wild Food*, by Roger Phillips,
so between the book and my dowsing pendulum, I garnered the
makings of many a tasty meal. (Anyone selecting fungi to eat by
dowsing should only do so if they are already experienced
dowsers. I take no responsibility for anyone's misjudgments!). At
the same time, many of the plants growing in those hedgerows

provided me with further leafy ingredients for salads and soups — and there were blackberries, too.

Gathering wild plants to eat was not a new experience for me, because for many years I have included regular harvests of wild plants in the family's diet. People who live near the sea and can find shores without pollution, have a wonderful range of sea vegetables to choose from as well. Many of these are sources of trace minerals readily accessible to the human digestive system and which also detoxify our systems of, for example, heavy metal residues. Why pay huge prices for imports from Asia of nori or kombu and so on, when a few hours spent at low tide at the appropriate season of the year can result in a harvest that, properly dried and stored in air-tight containers, could keep the family on a sea-vegetable-inclusive diet every week for many months?

The plants I gathered along the Exmoor roads were all 'weeds', but their properties are beneficial both as part of the human diet and as medication, which many generations of ordinary people were well aware of before a national medical service was inaugurated. In fact, many wild plants were used to maintain health, not just for remedial purposes. Bogbine, for example, in the marshy mountains of the Celtic countries, has been traditionally used as a blood-cleanser in springtime. The bitter decoction made by boiling the roots (as is done in Ireland), or the equally bitter tea made from the previous year's dried leaves (as in Wales), both spark up the appetite and clean the liver, bringing that surge of energy the body needs to meet the increased activity of Spring. Young stinging nettles, only a few inches out of the ground, make a welcome, fresh, green dish, with properties that augment the more medicinal bogbine by giving iron and trace elements, as well as vitamins, to further enhance the energy Spring calls forth.

Myriad pieces of traditional knowledge about the use of non-cultivated plants — some of which were once cultivated, such as dandelion, sorrel, fat hen and rocket — are being sought by the many people for whom orthodox medicine is, for one reason or another, undesirable. The volume of interest in simple remedies such as these has had two major effects. First, it has raised the fear of a loss of income in pharmaceutical companies, resulting in legislation to inhibit the use of some common, harmless and beneficial herbs. Secondly, it has made welcome inroads into the unhappy divide between orthodox and unorthodox medical practice to the extent that hospitals and clinics are introducing non-orthodox facilities to cater for the new demand. In Guildford, for example, a new wing has been added to the cancer unit of the county hospital, where patients and their carers can receive information about and treatment through a variety of therapies.

In the Wirral, Dorothy Crowther, an oncology nurse who works in St Catherine's Hospital, Birkenhead, works with Dr Al Read, a GP and a team of seventy volunteers, who include counsellors and a variety of other practitioners of non-orthodox disciplines under the title The Wirral Holistic Care Services (see Resources). There are some hospitals claiming to be homeopathic, but in which there is as much allopathic, or orthodox, medicine practised. There is also one specialised anthroposophical hospital, run on the philosophy of Rudolph Steiner, the Park Attwood Clinic, in Worcestershire.

As in pre-industrialised Europe, non-industrialised societies the world over depend on many skills for health maintenance and remedies for ill-health, amongst which herbal cures rank high. Complaints about the destruction of the rain forest are often because of the simultaneous destruction of the potentially beneficial medicinal herbs used by the non-industrialised peoples who inhabit, or who recently inhabited, the forest. Multinational pharmaceutical companies are intensely interested in the traditional uses of these medicinal plants; they employ anthropologists to research the uses and traditions associated with each plant before laboratory tests are carried out to ascertain and isolate the active ingredient.

It can take years for this research to be completed, by which time all the apparently 'non-active' parts of the plant will have been cast aside, in the tradition of the reductionist techniques of Western science as interpreted from Western analytical philosophy. This is totally to ignore the practices of the traditions from which these herbs have been derived and also the traditions of Western herbalists. In these practices, the herb, or herb part, is used in its entirety to create remedial substances, because it is empirically recognised that the 'active ingredient' works best in context with the other component parts of the plant. For example, the women of Paraguay used a plant for centuries as a contraceptive, with no side-effects. When Western scientists isolated the active ingredient and subsequently synthesised the analogue — a chemical 'look-alike' — to make the first contraceptive pill, it proved to give circulatory problems, such a thrombosis, sometimes fatal, to the women who took it.

Whilst the pharmaceutical companies are researching the plants of the rainforests of South America and Malaysia, they have an anomalous attitude towards research into the medicinal plants of the hedgerows and woodlands of Europe. The laboratory techniques used to identify and isolate the active ingredients of exotic plants are used to identify and isolate the non-active components of native plants. Herein lies the anomaly. This technique is used to demonise the native healing plants, to ban their use in an attempt to appear to be 'protecting' the European native population from the very plants that were their aid prior to industrialisation and the ability to create analogue drugs.

Comfrey was one of the first of our native plants to be examined in this way, possibly because of the high regard and the many uses it has in the medicinal herbal traditions of Europe. Its colloquial names, in English alone, include Boneset, Knitback, Knitbone, Consound and Bruisewort, although the botanical name used in all countries is *Symphytum officinalis*. Externally, as an ointment or poultice, it has a remarkable history in the setting of broken bones and the repair of damaged tissues, whether from accident or disease, because it increases the speed of mitosis, or cell division. Its internal use is encouraged at the same time as it is used externally, as a further encouragement to mitosis. Comfrey is also recommended for any sort of internal bleeding or ulceration, especially of any part of the alimentary canal, from the throat to the rectum. In addition, it is a major lung herb which, when converted into a thick syrup, proves highly beneficial in cases of hot or dry lung conditions.

Despite these traditions, which did not require anthropological research to establish, member states of the EU have published lists of banned herbs, including comfrey, 'in accordance with Article 33 of Directive 75/319 regarding herbs and herbal derivatives withdrawn in one or more member states for safety reasons' (as it reads at the top of Annex II of the Irish Food Safety Advisory Committee's report on *Food Supplements and Health Foods* to the Ministers for Health and for Agriculture, Food and Forestry, February 1994).

Under its listing in Annex II, comfrey leaf, its root and the whole herb is banned on the grounds that it contains, 'pyrrolizidine alkaloids with genotoxic, carcinogenic and hepatoxic properties'. 'Genotoxicity' means having a poisonous effect on genes and therefore causing birth defects — despite the traditional use to repair a bleeding placenta, when slivers of fresh root would be inserted into the vagina. 'Carcinogenic' means the ability to cause cancer — despite accounts of comfrey's use to heal such conditions. 'Hepatoxicity' means to have a poisonous effect on the liver. Patently, the widespread, self-confirming, traditional uses of comfrey prove it is *not* any of these things.

This is not to say that if its use was to be abused by excess, comfrey might prove to be damaging, as for example, where people have decided to go on a diet high in vitamin A, which involved drinking large amounts of fresh carrot juice. If this habit is prolonged for many months, the vitamin A, which is oil-soluble and therefore can be stored in the liver, becomes excessive and thereby toxic. At this point, people have been recorded as dying from using carrot juice unwisely, but no government has yet banned the use of carrots!

There are several cynical conclusions to be drawn from the activities and attitudes of pharmaceutical companies, the EU and national governments. The first is that once the analogue of any exotic medicinal herb has been developed, it will be of no interest whatsoever to the company that developed it if the plant itself ceases to exist. The second conclusion is more complicated. If the EU were genuinely concerned about genotoxicity of substances to which its population might be exposed, rather than ban the use of herbs with a history of medical benefit, they would not recycle low-level radioactive waste as raw material for a range of consumer goods made from glass, metal, or plastic. Nor would they permit any increase in the manufacture of plastics, whether containing recycled radioactive waste or not, because of the instability of plastics; the latter can transfer hormone-disrupting chemicals — another form of genotoxicity — into both the atmosphere and to whatever the plastic comes into contact with.

Further, polychlorinated biphenyls — PCBs — are still permitted in some manufacturing processes, despite their ability to invade ecosystems and create hormonal havoc — genotoxicity — in every species that has been examined for their presence. They would also be forced by overwhelming proof of their toxicity and carcinogenic risks to ban all the 600 chemical herbicides currently produced and used in orthodox agriculture, horticulture and domestic gardens. The banning of beneficial medicinal herbs is a form of commercial protectionism designed to deny people access to traditional, free — or at worst inexpensive — natural remedies and prophylactics.

The upside of this situation is the growing number of reliable books that are being published in the latter part of the twentieth century which deal with herbal remedies. There are also reliable plant identification books, as well as a number of workshops available to lay people where they can learn how to employ the qualities of the neglected and abused plant life that still exists. Also high on the list of sources of information must be the Internet, which has so far proved inviolable to censorship; there is a mass of herbal information there.

Mercifully, orthodox medical authorities are realising the hazards of chemical medication. The dangers of overuse of antibiotics and steroids implicated in damage to the immune system is being increasingly recognised. There is also a growing realisation that it is not only the medication that an individual receives from a doctor that can have implications for lowered immunity. The medication that vets give to animals and birds and the widespread use of antibiotics and steroids in the feed of intensively reared animals, poultry and fish, are also known to influence the health of humans who eat these creatures.

The most common debilitating disorder to result from the ingestion of antibiotics and also of steroids, consciously or otherwise, in contraceptive pills, or hormone replacement therapy (HRT) is Candidiasis. There is a range of possible symptoms, not all of which may manifest. These include: itchy eyes, itchy ears, sore throat, thrush (also called a 'fungal infection', still considered by some doctors to be the only admissible symptom of Candidiasis), cystitis, diarrhoea and/or constipation, loss of short-term memory, loss of concentration, lethargy, depression, constant tiredness and poor sleep-pattern. All of these may be chronic or recurrent, even if medically treated, until the sufferer's diet is adjusted.

Only in recent years has it been discovered that the adult human gut, during the course of its development from infancy, acquires a colony of assorted bacteria and fungi that would, if it were gathered into one lump, weigh between four and six lbs. This is as much as a vital organ, such as the heart, or the brain. Ingesting antibiotics or steroids creates serious imbalances in this colony, because some of the creatures in it are killed. The symbiotic relationship — the mutual interdependence — that exists between the human host and such bacteria and fungi benefits both; us by the enzymes and other subtle secretions they produce that help us to digest our food and they by the constant supply of nutrients they need that arrives in the food we eat.

Candida albicans is one fungus among many, but unlike many of its companions, it remains unaffected by antibiotics or steroids. Because the entire colony exercises restraints and is self-governing — thereby keeping a balance among its population — when part of that population is killed, other parts get out of hand; *Candida albicans* is one of these. It demands sugars and yeasts in its diet and it prevents the human host from absorbing and utilising necessary elements in *its* diet. If the situation goes undiagnosed and unchecked, it can advance to the point where this aberrant fungus begins to behave like dry rot in a house. It develops mycelia — long, fine tendrils — and can migrate out of the gut, through the intestinal walls and into other organs. The human host then becomes totally debilitated and very thin; this now seldom happens, however, because the condition can be more readily recognised and a diet begun to regulate the intestinal population. The diet has two aims: (a) to starve *Candida albicans* into submission by excluding sugars and yeasts; and (b) the re-establishment of the original flora by including items rich in those bacteria, such as acidopholus and biphidopholus. These are naturally occurring in some cultured, non-pasteurised milk yoghurts.

Whilst this diet is necessary, taking either antibiotics or steroids is to go back to square one, requiring you to start all over again. Even when the gut returns to normal, those medications will remain a no-go area. It is no good saying, 'I *had* to have antibiotics,' because that only reveals the lack of enthusiasm in yourself or your medical adviser for finding an alternative. There are, in fact, plenty of natural, wholesome, side-effect-free alternatives among herbs, both dietary and medicinal. You may also find, that by avoiding both of these modern medications, your general health remains much better than it was when you used either of them.

When as a girl of fifteen, I had an anaphylactic reaction to penicillin on receiving it for the first time, the severe rash that developed was not even acknowledged as an allergic reaction, such a condition being regarded as impossible in response to this 'magic bullet', as penicillin had been called. Forty-five years later, not only is it now acknowledged, but on admission to hospital, everyone is asked if they have any allergies. For me, being allergic to penicillin has enriched my life. Because of it, I have explored and found other ways to treat illness and infection which have proved successful and which have no side-effects; in fact, I have come to the conclusion that a medication that *does* have side-effects is not a valid form of treatment. In addition, because of my natural scepticism about the feeding of farmed animals that led me to stop eating meat, I have not received second-hand medication and am far healthier and more active than many of my contemporaries.

Anaphylaxis and Candidiasis are just two instances of iatrogenic illness: illness caused by medication or by mismedication. Various statistical estimates have appeared in the popular press, ranging from a staggering thirteen to thirty per cent of annual hospitalisations that have been attributed to iatrogenic illness. For the iatrogenic sufferer percentages are meaningless, because life can have been temporarily, sometimes permanently, altered by it. I have suggested asking questions of food suppliers, supermarkets and farmers. You also need to ask lots of questions if you have reason to attend a doctor. As the line of enquiry goes from GP to specialist consultant, let your questions get more detailed and searching. Don't be satisfied with an answer from only one person, no matter how authoritative. Ask the same questions over and over again of others, until you are satisfied that you have a clear picture of what you think is wrong with you, what they are offering you as treatment and what the known side-effects are, if any, of what they propose.

It's *your* body and *your* life and you have a perfect right to know as much about it as you wish, no matter if your enquiries are received as impertinence — as they sometimes are — by the medical authorities. Just persist. I know of people who have, on a diagnosis of cancer, refused to take either the chemotherapy or the radiotherapy offered and who frequently survive much longer than the prognosis. Life is a terminal condition, with or without illness, so take courage and take responsibility to live it to the full, up to its termination.

Early in our fourth winter stay in Tunisia, Jeremiah caught a chill in his chest and developed the fever, cough and chest pain one associates with pleurisy. Our landlord's mother-in-law, an elderly Berber woman, bent and wrinkled, heard him coughing and, unsolicited, sent me two desert herbs with instructions to boil them and to give them to him, with honey, twice a day. As Jeremiah believes that all hospitals should carry a government health warning, her advice was a boon. Within a week, all trace of the cough, the fever and the phlegm had left and, without having to recover from the debilitating effects that often remain after using antibiotics, he resumed a normal life. It was then that I began to learn how very strong the local knowledge of medicinal herbs still is in the oases and desert of Tunisia, just as it used to be in Europe.

Fortunately for all of us, what could be termed 'folk studies' is a popular pursuit among both academics and lay people. Along with the collecting of folk music, dance, social and religious customs, folk diet and medicinal knowledge come under the scrutiny of the collector's eye. Shortly after Jeremiah had recovered his health, the Economic Delegate in the local government offices lent me a book in French that listed many of the medicinal herbs of North Africa, each with interesting ancillary information.

There is another anomaly with regard to transnational corporations and the patenting of 'intellectual property'. There has been little or no attempt to patent any plant life in Europe, but there has been helter-skelter haste to patent everything that roots or seeds on the sub-continent of India, other parts of Asia and Malaysia. Could it be that the corporations expect more resistance to this practice in Europe than they expect in India? As fast as the corporations patent plants, the Research Foundation for Science, Technology and Ecology in New Delhi, founded and directed by the remarkable environmental activist, Vandana Shiva, records and details them. Vandana and her staff compile a double-sided *Biopiracy Factsheet*, each with a sequential number and the statement that it is

> aimed at creating public awareness on IPRs [Intellectual Property Rights], biodiversity and biopiracy, thereby building a people's movement for self-help by rejuvenating and promoting indigenous knowledge of biodiversity and its utilisation.

Each sheet follows the same pattern, first listing the plant by its English name, then its Latin botanical name, then the local names by which it is known throughout India. Then follows a description of the plant and its habitat, after which come its properties and actions according to indigenous medical systems. The patent number or numbers follow, the use intended for each patent, the patentee and lastly the assignee.

Each sheet has a section following the outline of the plant's properties and actions which is entitled 'Biopiracy and the Enclosure of the Commons', which goes on to state:

> IPR claims by scientists or corporations on our indigenous knowledge and biodiversity is a form of biopiracy. Biopiracy deprives us in three ways:
> 1. It creates a false claim to novelty and invention, even though the knowledge has evolved since ancient times in India.
> 2. It divests scarce biological resources to monopoly control of corporations thus depriving local communities and indigenous practitioners.
> 3. It creates market monopolies and excludes the original innovators from their rightful share to local, national and global markets.
> Since its properties have been systematically studied within our indigenous knowledge systems, the claim to novelty on which the following patent is based is false.

Last of all each sheet, under the banner, 'Recovery of the Commons: Self-Help Movement to Rejuvenate our Biodiversity Knowledge' announces the challenge,

> Does the epidemic of biopiracy imply we can do nothing? No — self-help and self-determination is still the viable alternative as a strategy to fight biopiracy. The following are ways you can use [whatever the herb is] in your homes and communities.

Against each use are detailed instructions on how the herb is to be applied, concluding with a list of the sources of the information.

It would appear that the corporations may have bitten off more than they can chew, in India at least. Vandana Shiva is a high profile, internationally known, articulate protagonist in the arguments against not only biopiracy, but genetic engineering. She articulates the affront to Indian people of the commandeering of plants, many of which have sacred as well as secular uses.

Effectively, the act of patenting changes the role of the traditional grower or user of seed from nurturer to thief, because, from the moment of patenting, the seed, the plant and its uses become the property of the patentee. To the latter the grower becomes only a necessary evil in the process of production. Thenceforth, any storing, use by, or gift from the grower of the seed or the plant constitutes theft. This may be legal, but it is plainly evil and rightly termed biopiracy. The laws giving corporations such control are contrary to ancient community and individual rights as well as many basic human rights, so that the sooner they are repealed, the better.

However, the road to repeal may be a long and a hard one. During the journey we do well to collect as much information about individual plants and animals as we are able. Store the knowledge among the family's documents, write it in letters to our children, compile collections with other members of organisations to whom we belong, such as the Irish Countrywomen's Association, or the Women's Institute. By recording and circulating such knowledge, we subvert monopolies sought by the corporations and we preserve valuable information for future generations that was gathered and used by countless previous generations.

Suppression of information has been a tactic among would-be monopolisers ever since domination began and it is still the practice in the field of vaccination and immunisation. The benefits of either are highly questionable. Statistical records exist verifying that the incidence of smallpox, for example, had dropped substantially before vaccination was introduced, probably due to improved diet, hygiene and living conditions. This is never mentioned in the argument for vaccination, which is curious, considering that its stated intention is to eradicate infectious disease. Contrary to the accepted myth that childhood diseases are a bad thing, they serve a purpose that fortifies the child against more serious, auto-immune disease in later life, by challenging and strengthening the infant immune system. How many times have parents noticed that a child who contracts an infant fever, such as measles, chickenpox, whooping-cough, or mumps, on recovering from it — when it hasn't been suppressed by drugs — shows a burst of new growth and energy?

The dynamics of these, mostly viral diseases have been under-stood for centuries. In some instances, it was even customary to induce, for example, measles in children with serious kidney disease because this could cure, or substantially alleviate, this condition, as the child recovered from the measles. Likewise, asthma and excema and other auto-immune diseases were seen to improve after a recovery from measles.

Viera Scheibner, in her book *Vaccination*, describes clearly the association she found when working with Leif Karlsson in Australia, between stressed breathing patterns in babies and cot deaths. She gives calendrical sequences, repeated over and over as a reliable pattern, that associate vaccination with stressed breathing incidents and, sometimes, death. The resistance these two researchers found to their work was chilling, but Viera Scheibner describes it as 'the best and most effective goad to us to continue'.

The researchers' conclusions about the implications relating vaccination to infant deaths is even more chilling and deserves more attention. When vaccinations are given to children older than two years, the incidence of stressed breathing did not result in death. Statisticians claim only a small proportion of babies die or are permanently maimed by vaccination or immunisation — the petussis (whooping cough) vaccine incorporated in the 'triple' (diphtheria and tetanus are the other two), is particularly suspect. But statisticians, like economists, use only quantitative calibrations, not qualitative ones. If your baby is killed or maimed by a medical procedure, the statistic is one hundred per cent and your grief and pain are absolute.

Medical authorities, backed by the pharmaceutical companies for whom each vaccination scheme represents huge profits, use all sorts of moral and emotional blackmail to persuade reluctant parents to have their children vaccinated. Some state bodies have refused children admission to school on the grounds that they have to have documentary evidence that they have been vaccinated, particularly against measles. This is an outrageous removal of parental responsibility and choice to which resistance, fortunately, is growing, especially due to the evidence that suggests there is a strong case to be made for the implication of a variety of vaccines in causing unpredicted breakdowns in public health.

Researchers other than Scheibner have made another association between vaccination and serious illness. The suspicion is that it was the monkey serum used as the vehicle for the vaccine that proved also to be the vehicle for the transfer of the HIV virus from the rhesus monkeys, in whom it is endemic, to humans.

A healthy body, cherished by well chosen, fresh, organic foods that constitute the most efficient and natural prophylactic in existence, will resist illness and prove the basis for a happy and a healthy life. When Gandhi challenged the British imposition of the unreasonable salt taxes, he did so in company with thousands of his fellow countrymen. Vandana Shiva is challenging further unreasonable and unjust impositions, in company with thousands of her fellow countrywomen — because most of India's farmers and growers are women.

In unified resistance against injustice, the ordinary people of the world can overcome denial of our parental responsibility, plant patenting, genetic engineering and whatever else, simply by force of numbers and persistence. The Berlin Wall fell because of the wish of the people; the monolithic communist state of the USSR crumbled, because of the wish of the people; apartheid was defeated in South Africa, because of the wish of the people.

When Kofi Annan reached an agreement with Saddam Hussein in the early part of 1998, from Baghdad he thanked the world for its prayers. When he returned to New York, he repeated his thanks. At least one radio news bulletin dwelled on the global impact a thoughtform, or prayer, shared simultaneously by millions of people, can have on any situation. When enough of us — the critical mass of us — wish for a life governed by co-operation and mutual caring, it will come about.

Eighteen

NOURISHMENT AND NURTURE

The people say they have been here for all time. Scientists
know they have inhabited Australia for at least 50,000
years. It is truly amazing that after 50,000 years they
have destroyed no forests, polluted no water, endangered
no species, caused no contamination, and all the while
they have received abundant food and shelter. They
have laughed a lot and cried very little. They live long,
productive, healthy lives and leave spiritually confident.

Mutant Message Down Under, *Marlo Morgan*

Of all the allegorical stories I have ever heard, the one I value most is about the arrival of a new soul at the Pearly Gates. Saint Peter offered a tour of the establishment and led the newcomer through the gates and down a flight of stairs. When he opened the heavy door at the bottom, a fabulous view was exposed of extensive parkland, trees, flowers, grass with large tables dotted about, all bearing vast quantities of delicious food and drinks. The newcomer was startled, however, by the appearance of the inhabitants; they were all emaciated, groaning, howling and weeping. The only tools with which to eat were spoons with handles that were ten foot long and no one could work out how to feed themselves. The newcomer turned away and Peter then led the way back to the front entrance. This he passed to ascend another flight of stairs, at the top of which he held back a gossamer-fine curtain, beyond which came into view a scene that appeared to replicate the scene in the last place they'd visited — trees, flowers, grass, tables laden with food and drinks. Here, however, the inhabitants were all well-nourished and happy, entertaining themselves and one another in conversation, by singing, making music and dancing. It was soon evident why: each time anyone approached a table, someone else hastened up and used a long-handled spoon to feed the hungry one.

Although, individually, we may lend a neighbour a cup of sugar, or feed their children when they're playing with our own, at the national, governmental level, strategies and terminologies are adopted to ensure that no-one gives a spoonful of nourishment to the hungry without exacting a price. One such strategy, with a non-specific and irrelevant name, is 'intervention'. This is what the EU calls the excess crops of grain, butter, cheese, meat, wine, oil etc. that it has encouraged its farmers to grow over and beyond the needs of the EU population. These excesses are stored in 'mountains', or 'lakes', according to their consistency, or so we are told. They are not, however, distributed to the thousands of hungry people in the rest of the world.

I remember, sometime in the early 1980s, we had a visit from a Methodist clergyman who delighted me when he said he was going soon to a meeting where the emerging famine in Ethiopia would be discussed. I expressed the hope that he and his colleagues would bring pressure to bear on the authorities to ensure that as much of this stock-piled food as needed would be transported to Ethiopia and distributed to the starving population. The clergyman got very po-faced and told me that my reaction was over-simplistic and that there were political reasons why what I hoped for could not be done.

To me, the politics of starvation are straightforward: it is the responsibility of those with an excess to make sure that it is given to those with insufficient. It is the politics of greed that prevents this from happening. Taken at the global level, it has never yet proved possible to produce food in excess of global need, but at the local level, it is the greed of farmers, spurred on by cash incentives from their greedy national governments and the trade agreements these governments have entered into, that cause excesses in production to occur.

Bob Geldof, the band-leader, did far more for the starving people of Ethiopia than any European government, or meeting of clergymen — and whatever they did was only as a result of his goading. The news coverage of the famine clutched at everyone's heart and Bob Geldof gave their feelings of compassion a focus. Metaphorically, thousands took up the spoons with the ten-foot handles, thanks to his lead.

The root causes of famine always appear to stem from natural phenomena, such as constant drought over several years, or the arrival of a blight that thrives in damp conditions. But famine in Africa, just like the famine in Ireland, is the result of greed as well. At the time of the Great Famine in Ireland, there was plenty of food. Dairy products, wheat and meat were all being exported to England whilst people were dying of famine fever and starvation, because the potato crop on which they depended had failed due to the emergence of the blight. They died because those who grew the export crops saw no need to redirect the harvests to their neighbours a few miles along the road.

Famine in the twentieth century is often due to the insistence of the World Bank that debtor countries, hastening to emulate the wealthier nations of the world, grow cash crops for export, rather than to feed their own populations. It is not the small, subsistence farmer who turns to the monoculture cash crop, it is wealthier farmers, or consortia of them or other businesses that buy up, or simply harass, the small farmers so that they abandon the small amounts of land they occupied, often for generations. The small plots are amalgamated to form huge acreages. Harassment techniques are more usual than purchase to remove indigenous people from, say, forested areas which 'developers' wish to turn into grazing, or monocrop cultivation. The dispossessed migrate to the towns, where they become ghettoised among other poor, unemployed people who need money to buy food, where, formerly, they grew their own and sold any surplus.

The story of the Enclosures in England and Wales that began in the eighteenth century and also dispossessed the peasant population, was one of the first instances of land piracy on a large scale. Today, thousands of people in each 'developing' country have suffered this dispossession — a total of many millions. The destruction of subsistence, multi-crop farming has ensured that, when mono-culture cash crops fail as a result of climatic variation, the entire population starves. It is ruling governments' decisions that contribute to famines.

Every culture on earth has, at some stage in its development, regarded the earth as mother. In English, we still refer to her as 'Mother Earth'. There can be no name more appropriate in all the pantheon of sacred names than Mother Earth. Everything we eat, drink, wear, live in, ride in, handle or work with, derives its basis from her. There is nothing in our lives that has not come from inside her, or from her surface, or from within the water she wears. She is provider for all of our need — and for all of our greed — at the moment. But, with so much abundance around us to satisfy our need, how did we become greedy? If one observes an insecure child, he or she will probably appear to be greedy, always requiring nourishment, because the nearest to the comfortable feeling of security is the comfortable feeling of a full belly.

Insecurity, in its extreme, is fear. Fear and insecurity infect the directors of transnational corporations, the politicians of national governments and each of us, but how are they engendered? They have been nurtured by the same tools earlier employed by religion — Christianity in particular — the carrot, or expectation of reward and the stick, or expectation of denial. Commerce applies the carrot in the form of advertising and the stick in the form of propaganda. For example, propaganda used by agro-chemical companies is that genetic engineering and the use of herbicides and pesticides is essential to feed the world. This ignores the fact that most of the hunger has been created by the monoculture system of farming that uses these techniques — creating the fear that food will be unobtainable without science and technology, regardless of the side-effects.

Advertising indoctrinates us with the belief that without vast amounts of material possessions and the income to buy more, one is a failure. To be a failure, to become an outcast, is to lose all comfort, all sense of self-determination, all sense of security. This fear of failure feeds disaffection, dysfunctionalism, even criminality among the poor and insensitivity, self-interest and corruption among the wealthy, who are the dominators of the poor.

If we lived in a society where it was natural to cherish our neighbours, to observe when they are in need and to nurture them and they us, we would laugh at the propaganda that feeds our present fear. It would be totally inappropriate and we would see it as such. The doctrine of materialism does not value compassion, or the urge to share; it values subservience and the urge to accumulate. Bob Geldof is a maverick who called out of us our compassion which, when we responded to its urgings, shamed those in power. In that aberration lies hope. We've done it once, we can do it over and over again, until it becomes a habit and the wheel will have turned from grasping in fear to sharing with compassion. Band-Aid was evidence of our compassion — other events are evidence of the greed generated by our fear.

In the last half of the twentieth century, governments in Europe created agricultural advisory boards to instruct farmers in the farming policies to be introduced. Under this scheme, the terms of trade agreements applying to agriculture are translated into action and new agricultural practices introduced. During this process, someone in the cattle-feed industry realised that there was an enormous amount of protein not used after butchery. Animal offal, guts, heads, feet and so on, were not used in the meat-processing industry for human consumption, but could be very 'cost-effective' if dried, pulverised and added to cattle concentrates.

This was to disregard completely that to feed flesh to animals who have evolved to eat only herbs is a failure in correct nourishment and an invitation to problems. Because it was cost-effective, the inclusion of dried flesh in the feed of cattle became a widespread practice and continued, in the UK, for some years before instances of a new disease, Bovine Spongiform Encephalopathy (BSE) began to be reported by veterinary officers to the Ministry of Agriculture.

It has been said that fourteen months elapsed between the first reports arriving and the Ministry making an official announcement about it. When it was announced, on the basis of circumstantial evidence, the animal protein in the cattle feed was blamed for the outbreak. Sheep are occasionally subject to a disease known colloquially as 'scrapie', which causes degeneration of the central nervous system. It is irreversible, has no known cure and the sheep who contract it die. BSE also causes degeneration of the central nervous system, is irreversible and has no known cure. It was suggested that sheep suffering from scrapie had been butchered, that their brains had been included in cattle-feed, that the disease had jumped species and infected cattle.

Soon after this, a similar connection was made between BSE and Creutzfeldt-Jakob Disease (CJD), a rare condition occurring in humans, which also causes degeneration of the central nervous system. CJD is irreversible and has no known cure. It was assumed that BSE had also jumped species, as more cases of CJD came to light and also that it appeared now to be occurring in much younger people than it had been detected in previously. However, doctors and scientists were puzzled by at least one CJD patient who had been a vegetarian for at least twenty years. Theories circulated about a long and unpredictable incubation period for the disease, despite the fact that some vegetarian CJD patients might never have eaten beef that had eaten flesh.

An organic farmer, who had observed the effects of organophosphate poisoning and the neurological symptoms to which this gives rise, put forward an alternative theory by suggesting that the root cause of BSE and CJD was not, in fact, the result of eating infected flesh, but the ultimate result of exposure to these chemicals. As no virus or bacteria could be detected in the flesh of those cattle or people who had died of this distressing disorder, his theory might be correct, but if it is correct, neither governments nor chemical corporations will want to know, because of the consequences. Litigation for damages against tobacco companies by people who have smoked and then developed lung cancer would appear trivial when compared with the litigation for damages that might be taken against chemical companies for the health loss resulting from exposure to so many commonly used personal, household, garden, horticultural, agricultural and veterinary substances.

Governments would need to embark on a mammoth education programme to wean people off those deodorants, floor cleaners, 'air-fresheners', de-lousers, insecticides, pot-pourris, to mention only a few of the substances containing these damaging chemicals. Might governments not then, in turn, be sued by the chemical corporations for the damage to their profits — as, indeed, they may soon be entitled to under the MAI agreement? Would it not be simpler to blame an inherently foolish feeding practice, as a damage-limitation exercise? I join the organic farmer in his hypothesis, but my suspicious nature will still prevent me from eating animal flesh because of the substances the animals are fed, including inappropriate offal. It will also keep me well clear of the petro-chemical derivatives that cause so many distressing respiratory and neurological symptoms. What an unhappy place to arrive at as a result of fear and a total lack of compassion toward the nourishment and nurturance of animals, who are, after all, our siblings on Mother Earth.

Our individual support of Bob Geldof's initiative became a mass-movement. The British public's reaction to the risks they inferred to exist in eating beef was to stop buying it. Once more, individual choice became a mass-movement! It's impossible to think of any better means of mass comment on the situation, than the with-holding of profits through loss of sales. Whatever the truth behind the BSE crisis, the ordinary people lost their trust in official announcements, especially the one that ordered the removal of bones from meat before sale, because of a risk of nerve tissue near the bone being infected. Don't nerves run through flesh as well?

Each individual choice to contribute or to withhold can be seen to have an effect, because other people make the same choices. Each challenge by evidence of the results of bad practices is a challenge that strengthens the ordinary person and helps to guide us, as a population, away from fear and greed toward a caring and co-operating society, which will, inevitably, create change also at government and at corporate levels.

A society that cares for each member of the population and which practises co-operation as a tool for nurturance and nourishment, also protects. In our society, protection is not a generally accepted, common characteristic, being practised only by some individuals or small groups. It is generally accepted that the societies for the protection of children, or for the prevention of cruelty to (domesticated) animals are there to do the job for us. No-one has charged the cattle-feed manufacturers or merchants with cruelty to cattle, but logically, that's what should happen over BSE. Humans have become accustomed to dominating other forms of life, however, so it is more acceptable to consider the profits of the cattle-feed manufacturers than it is to consider the rights of the animals to correct nourishment and protection — from exploitation, among other things.

Cattle are treated like slaves, so are sheep, pigs, poultry, horses, animals in zoos and circuses, pets and the creatures kept for vivisection. Furthermore, all those trees that are planted in rows to grow for profit, euphemistically referred to as 'forests', are also slaves. We are surrounded by slaves.

Since 1980, an organisation has existed that formally recognises and rewards people and organisations that nurture and protect. The Right Livelihood Award Foundation is sometimes called the 'Alternative Nobel Prize'. Its annual awards are made during the week preceding the Nobel Awards and also in the Swedish Parliament building. Most encouraging is the range of people and organisations to whom awards have been made — sixty-five out of 600 nominees from sixty countries, by 1996. Among these is Mordechai Vanunu, who risked his freedom to alert the world to Israel's possession of nuclear bombs. His countrymen arrested him and they kept him, cruelly, in solitary confinement for twelve years after they convicted him of treason for his action. Shalom, Mordechai.

Many recipients of the Right Livelihood Award have been 'whistle-blowers', like Mordechai Vanunu, people offering protection from dangers, mostly of human making. However, others have received the award for finding practical solutions to the human potential for damage. One of these was Bill Mollison, an Australian architect, who designed permaculture as a food-production system using low energy input, organic principles and producing high yields of whatever is included in the system.

Permaculturists are among the first to recognise that pests and weeds are in the eye of the beholder. To this end, some are introducing their students to many of the 2,000 or more edible plants that grow in the temperate parts of the planet and which are not normally part of human diet. Dominic Waldron, for example, creates what he calls an 'edible landscape' using edible perennials, such as tree onions and perpetual broccoli, as well as rocket, sorrel, plantain, dandelion and other 'wild' plants that are also edible perennials.

The multiple edible creatures of permaculture pre-supposes a degree of biodiversity absent from orthodox agriculture. In the courtyard of a neighbour's house in Tunisia was a pen of pigeons and it was only a surprise the first time to see a hedgehog amble through a doorway. Both pigeon and hedgehog would, ultimately, provide dinner — or their young would, because this was breeding stock, well cared for and content. When the time came for the creature to be killed, it was caught, quietly, taken out of the house, away from the other animals and birds, to have its throat cut. Many years before I witnessed the swift despatch of single birds or animals in the sandy desert or the courtyards of my neighbours' homes, I used to take goats we intended to eat to be killed in a abattoir in Wales.

In the Goat Society and the co-operative produce group to which I belonged, the subject of 'ritual killing' arose with a seasonal frequency. Ritual killing was referred to as if it was some cruel and evil form of torture, bound to be performed by the roadside by any stranger who asked to buy a goat, especially if he was a foreigner. That the 'ritual' might be a simple prayer and the killing swift and clean was ignored. What I saw on my visits to abattoirs, where animals waiting to be killed can smell the blood and the fear of those killed and about to be killed was far more cruel than the deaths by 'ritual killing' that I subsequently witnessed in Tunisia.

Though I no longer eat the flesh of animals or birds, obviously they have a place in the biodiversity of any permaculture project. It is the inter-relatedness of different diets, different kinds of resultant manure, different rates of decay, different varieties of life-forms that can utilise the decayed manure, or carcasses of insects, birds, animals or plants, that perpetuate such a system.

Humans are not separate from the permaculture concept, just because we seek to plan it before allowing it to become self-perpetuating. We are part of it, so our diet and our manure become an integral part of the biodiversity. Ultimately, it would make sense if our carcasses did too. When our children were young, we had a Staffordshire bull terrier, called Jack. He was much loved and cherished. As he grew older, so did the children until they left home, one by one, only to return with their children, events that Jack enjoyed.

Eventually, we were conscious of his dying process and stayed with him, talking to him, stroking him to comfort him as he died of old age. We buried him in our small orchard. We had three young plum trees that were not doing well in an exposed place which we planned to bring into the orchard. Jeremiah undertook the job and he planted one of the trees over Jack, within a few weeks of his death. None of the plum trees looked good, so he gave them all rescue remedy when he moved them. Two of them needed further care and cherishing, but the one over Jack took off, growing multiple shoots that within a year were producing luscious fruit. It took the other trees another couple of years to match this fruit.

This gave us the idea that we, too, might be buried in our own orchard. How much more appropriate it would be to provide nourishment from one's out-worn flesh to fruiting trees than to be a part of monoculture in a cemetery. Like Jack, we would each go into the ground wrapped in a blanket, not in an ecologically unacceptable box. So long as any burial, human or animal, is not likely to cause pollution to water supplies, nor drain into open water courses and is sufficiently deep, there is no law to prevent private burial in Ireland or in the UK.

It is only acculturation, habit, that makes people assume that all people have to be buried, wastefully, in a graveyard or cemetery. It is that same acculturation that is responsible for imagining that it's all right to eat cow flesh, but not all right to eat horse flesh, all right to eat rabbit flesh, but not to eat guinea-pig flesh. There is no difference — an animal is killed, dinner is cooked using its flesh.

Most people flinch and don't want to hear about animals being killed, although they'll sit down to a steak dinner, or chicken kiev, without a qualm. The same people would, often, prefer to have a pet 'put down' by a vet, rather than 'see it suffer', as it dies. The same people might deny human euthanasia, however, which is only a request to be 'put down' and released from suffering. It is as though human sensibilities should not have to deal with the real, natural death of an animal and that human life, on the other hand, is guided by a different ethic. This same mentality is inclined to deny death, to avoid funerals, hail organ transplants, hair-dye and silicone implants, none of which truly nurture self, or protect anything, except human inhibitions. Life on earth is a terminal condition. It has a beginning, a middle and an end, the experience and recognition of which can and should be fulfilling.

Apart from hoping my own carcass will be put to good use in nourishing a plant — an elderbush is my personal choice — I hope my dying will be natural, preferably in advanced years, because there's so much yet to do, but free of drugs, even if I die of a disease. Death, like birth, can be a conscious event and I want to experience all of my life, first hand and that includes my death. I can't consciously remember my own birth, but I brought our children into the world free of drugs and fully conscious. Death I hope to meet consciously, because, like the birth and the birthing, there's no action replay! By being conscious also of one another's needs, by discussing what kind of wedding, birthing, dinner party, or death one would wish for, in so far as any of that can be planned, we can offer protection to one another's rights to choose, to nourish one another's needs.

Especially in the event of funerals, there is an increasing desire for individual choice. No longer is everyone receptive to Christian dogma or dominance over funerals and the rites around them. When the baby of close friends died of a 'cot death' at four and a half months old, I was amazed to hear the clergyman who conducted the funeral refer to it as 'his'! I was equally astonished at the insensitivity he displayed when he tried to block, then edit, a prayer a friend wished to read over the grave, having consulted the parents before the funeral and having their willing consent. The reader ignored the editing and the whole prayer proved a moving completion to a sad, but unrepeatable event.

There is no requirement for the presence of a clergyman at a funeral, if the deceased has no wish for one. Equally, there is no reason why priests, priestesses, lamas or lay people from any non-Christian religion or spiritual calling should not conduct a respectful ceremony to mark the completion of a life and to bury, burn or otherwise dispose of the dead body. The *New Natural Death Handbook* produced by the Institute for Social Inventions has been compiled to help non-Christians and people with no particular religious or spiritual affiliation to plan for their disposal after death. The respect for and protection of our individual wishes, whether within the traditions prevailing in our country or region or differing from them, is part of the way we can nurture one another to strengthen the emerging fabric of a caring society.

Caring is one of the core principles of sustainability, a concept attracting many people in a variety of ways. Permaculture is the most sustainable of the organic growing techniques, be they garden or farm, but all areas of our life require the same sustainability. Housing for example, is receiving the attention of designers, both lay and professional, to make it and the services it uses entirely sustainable. Disposal systems employing natural processes, such as reed beds and solar power to provide lighting, heating — both for water and space — water pumping and the driving force for domestic tools such as refrigerators, are being designed as an integral part of houses that are built from natural materials, such as stone, timber, cob (earth), or straw bales with roofs of similarly natural materials. By avoiding processed materials such as chipboard, which contains the health-damaging chemical, formaldehyde, care for sustaining the health of industrial workers as well as that of the future occupants becomes an integral part of the design.

Sustainability is also being applied to the institutions in our lives, giving rise to interest-free banking, such as the JAK banks of Denmark, home schooling, LETS trading communities and the Eco-village movement, to name a few. Most of the protest groups forming at the end of the twentieth century arise out of the unsustainable plans for change that are thrust on individuals and communities by local or national government, or by industry — sometimes by a combination of government and industry. For example, a protest against the destruction of ancient woodland, for the extension of a road or an airfield, is usually concerned with at least two aspects of unsustainability. Firstly, the destruction of a self-sustaining amenity, the woodland; secondly, the increased health hazards resulting from more traffic, therefore more fumes and greater speed, therefore more accidents.

It is sometimes claimed by the opponents of such a protest, that the loss of, for example, 1,000 trees, to widen a road is better than the loss of one human life on the unwidened road — only if you're a self-interested human! Each tree has the same entitlement to life as each human. Furthermore, each tree lost is a loss of home and/or sustenance to many other forms of life, from the microbes among its roots, to the other plants it supports, such as ivy, or mistletoe, moss, or lichen, to the insects, animals and birds. Nurtured, as they were by ancient, non-dominator tribes, trees provide oxygen, ingest carbon dioxide, provide firewood, food and shelter for humans as well as for the other life-forms.

Being a dominator is non-sustainable, as the experience of so many developing countries proves, but being a co-operator is sustainable as the work of so many people and groups around the world is proving. Sustainable concepts include bringing into view those people and situations that have formerly been suppressed or ignored, empowering the disempowered and maintaining, with respect and care, that diversity which is our inheritance on Mother Earth. By implementing these concepts, our lives are enriched — and so is the world around us.

Nineteen

AFTERWORD

The sage does not act, so is not defeated; he
does not grasp, therefore he does not lose.

Lao Tzu

A ir. Water. Food. The sacred trinity that sustains life — a
sustenance that has been tainted, compromised in ways no
longer sustainable, not through any fault of nature, but through
the unsustainable activities of human kind. The combination of
Western philosophy, Western science and Western technology has
bullied its way into the four quarters of Mother Earth. She has
tolerated this rampage, as any mother might indulge a precocious
teenager, who has skills but scant judgment or discrimination. She
might, however, point out that the sun sets in the West.

Materialism — the Western paradigm — might claim that it is
the right of all to dress like aristocrats, live in palaces, eat, drink
and be merry — but not everyone aspires to this. Nor does
anyone aspire to being involuntarily homeless, having no more to
wear than the clothes they walk the streets in, to have to beg,
steal, or bin-pick for food. But for every ten who achieve the first
goal, thousands are forced into poverty. Materialist greed doesn't
work as a way of life that cherishes the many as one, because it
cherishes the one above the many.

When I went to England to study Shen Tao acupressure in
1989, I read a book by Diane Yahoo about her native American
traditions and beliefs. In it, I learned that her tribe maintained that
one did not leave one's youth until the age of twenty-eight; nor
did one achieve the maturity of one's life's work until the age of
fifty-one, which I was, in 1989. Since then, I have seen more of

the planet, heard more of the needs of people, witnessed more of the ways that greed deprives as it depraves. But I have also seen and heard a change that is growing from a whisper to a roar that recognises that what has been compromised, lost or killed is worth far more than materialism has given, or promises to give, because its promises are lies.

I am merely one among a multitude who have seen more of the globe than my own backyard. It is heart-warming to meet so many young people who have spent several years travelling. They take jobs to earn air fares, accommodation and food, but they have no vision of a corporate career, only a vision of a better world. Felix was eighteen years old in 1998 when she wrote an appeal — part of the whisper that's becoming a roar — after Wicklow County Council began to fell trees in the Glen of the Downs. She was part of the vigil that chose to protect this last vestige of ancient forest in Ireland. These few acres of woodland have become a symbol for something far greater, to which Felix rallies us:

> I have heard the unfathomable pain of the trees as they scream and fall under the whirr of the chainsaws . . . but we sing, chant, rant, cry, laugh much louder than the chainsaws. I have felt the physical pain of the earth. It is the pain of a mother whose children are murdering her and destroying her creation. But we can return to her side and honour her body, honour her creation, save her trees. We can recreate what has been destroyed and it is not too late. There are seeds, if there are hands willing to plant them. Brothers and sisters, enter the circle, join hands, oppose this senselessness and step into the creation.
>
> I have seen mad, crazy, biting steel monsters starting to turn the earth into an ugly, grey, sprawling, lifeless, loveless nightmare . . . but we can turn it back into a green, breathing, living, beautiful place for our children . . . our held hands and hugging bodies are stronger than their machines. Love is stronger than indifference. The Tribe is gathering and growing as more people awaken to their power and rise.
>
> Your poetry, your art, your dance, your song, your rant and yourself are invaluable at this time. Your love is your greatest weapon, because it is stronger than violence. So will you join the Tribe? The death of the forest is happening because of an indifference to and a disconnection from the earth. If we can join

hands and establish passion for and connection to the planet, if we can dance into the face of adversity, if we can combine our energies and make collective magic, our unity will empower us to fight with bows and arrows of love for one another and our beautiful earth. We can make a miracle.

Felix voices a passion felt by so many of her contemporaries, among whom negotiating skills, conflict resolution skills and community co-operation skills are valued more highly than any material status symbol. They have the youth, the vigour and the longevity that Jeremiah and I, with our generation, no longer have. As each of them reaches the age of fifty-one, they will have become a movement to be reckoned with! The critical mass will have arrived, the hundredth monkey syndrome come into being.

HOW DO YOU SCORE?

This questionnaire is designed to assist your awareness as you progress toward a more sustainable lifestyle. It is intended for your eyes only. More than ten 'yesses' in Column 1 shows you are making great progress and could go on increasing your awareness. More than ten 'yesses' in Column 2 shows the time is ripe to make a start.

Column 1

1. I buy organic food
   (a) because it keeps me healthy
   (b) because it supports organic growers

2. I do not use washing-up liquid
   (a) because it damages organic decomposition
   (b) because I don't like residues on dishes

3. I do not use a mobile phone
   (a) because of dangers from microwaves
   (b) because there are other ways to communicate

4. I do not accept plastic bags
   (a) I carry a cloth shopping bag
   (b) they're too hard to dispose of

5. I do not use my car
   (a) if I can walk or cycle
   (b) if public transport is going my way

6. I do not smoke
   (a) because I never have
   (b) because I've given up

7. I always buy recycled toilet paper
   (a) to do so uses fewer trees
   (b) unbleached biodegrades quicker

8. I always take snack wrappers home
   (a) when the litter bin is full
   (b) where I can dispose of them efficiently

9. I cultivate my vegetable garden
   (a) because I like fresh, organic food
   (b) because it's a better use of land than a lawn

10. I buy fair-traded goods if I can
    (a) because I'm concerned about workers' rights
    (b) because I know my contribution helps

Total:

Column 2

1. I do not buy organic food
   (a) because it's expensive
   (b) because I never think of it

2. I use washing-up liquid
   (a) because it smells nice
   (b) because I always have done

3. I use a mobile phone
   (a) because I can't manage without it
   (b) because I was given one/got one cheap

4. I accept plastic shopping bags
   (a) because they're available
   (b) because it's convenient

5. I use my car
   (a) whenever I go anywhere
   (b) because it's convenient

6. I smoke
    (a) because I have a right to
    (b) because I'm not worried if it harms others

7. I never buy recycled toilet paper
    (a) because I like coloured toilet paper
    (b) because I didn't know it was available

8. I don't take snack wrappers home
    (a) because my little bit won't make any difference
    (b) because I'm never beside a litter bin

9. I don't cultivate a vegetable garden
    (a) because I haven't time
    (b) because it's not worth it, I can buy

10. I don't buy fair traded goods
    (a) because I've never heard of them
    (b) because I've never thought about it

Total:

RESOURCES

Chapter One

The Green Belt Movement
Professor Wangari Maathai
P.O. Box 67545
Nairobi/Kenya
Tel.:/Fax.: *254 2 504264

Chipko
Suderial Bahaguna
Bhageerathi Valley
Uttarakhand
India

Tree Aid
28 Hobbs Lane
Bristol BS1 5ED
England
Tel.: *44 (0)117 934 9442
Fax.: *44 (0)117 934 9592

Methane Gen. Magazine from
Tooracurragh
Ballymacarbry
Co. Waterford
Ireland
Tel.: *353 (0) 52 36304

Uganda Women Tree Planting Movement
Ruth Mubiru
P.O. Box 10351
Kampala
Uganda
Tel.: *256 41 254240 or 259668
Fax.: *256 41 255288

Crann — Native Tree Conservation
Main Street
Banagher
Co. Louth
Ireland
Tel./Fax.: *353 (0)509 51718

Irish Woodworkers for Africa
Bury Quay
Tullamore
Co. Offaly
Ireland
Tel./Fax.: *353 (0)506 23557

The Tree Council
35 Belgrave Square
London SW1X 8QN
England
Tel.: *44 (0)171 235 8854
Fax.: *44 (0)171 235 2023

Chapter Two

Ogoni Solidarity Ireland
39 Upper Gardiner Street
Dublin 1
Tel.: 01 878 554

WEN Trust
Aberdeen Studios
22 Highbury Grove
London N5 2EA.
Tel.: 0171 354 8823
Fax.: 0171 354 0464

Sustrans
35 King Street
Bristol BS1 4DZ
Tel.: 0117 926 8893

The Soil Association

86 Colston Street
Bristol BS1 5BB
Tel.: 0117 929 0661
Fax.: 0117 925 2504
(Has a directory of organic farms
shops, box schemes and retailers.)

National Asthma Campaign

Providence House
Providence Place
London N1 0NT
Tel.: 0171 226 2260
(Educating and campaigning for
better health.)

Freewheelers

25 Low Friar Street
Newcastle-upon-Tyne NE1 5UE
Tel.: 0191 222 0090

AURO Organic Paints

Doon Lough
Fivemilebourne
Co. Leitrim
Ireland
Tel.: *353 (0)71 43452

Chapter Three

Cumbrians Opposed to a Radioactive Environment (CORE)

98 Church Street
Barrow-in-Furness
Cumbria LA 14 2HT
England
Tel.: 01229 833 851
Fax.: 01299 812 239

Pesticide Action and Information Network (PAIN)

Michael Leonard (Secretary)
Tuchamine
Tullow
Co. Carlow
Ireland
Tel.: 0503 61180

Stop Thorp Alliance Dundalk (STAD)

c/o McEvoys
Clanbrassil Street
Dundalk
Co. Louth
Ireland.

Askeaton/Ballysteen Animal Health Committee

Donagh O'Grady (Secretary)
Inchirourke
Askeaton
Co. Limerick
Ireland
Tel. *353 061 392112

Chapter Five

CIRCUIT

P.O. Box 1UZ
Newcastle-upon-Tyne NE99 1UZ
England

Irish Campaign Against Microwave Pollution (ICAMP)

P.O. Box 5334
Dublin 5
Fax.: *353 (0)1 831 5466

Chapter Six

National Federation of City Farms

The Green House
Hereford Street
Bedminster
Bristol BS3 4NA
Tel.: 0117 923 1800

Allotments for the Unemployed

Deda Francis
11 Mill Road
Reedham
Norwich NR13 3TL
Tel.: 01493 700 408

**An Baile Dúlra
(The West Cork Eco-hamlet
Project)**
Cullinagh
Skibbereen
Co. Cork
Ireland
Tel.: 028 22406

**School Wildlife Garden
Association
(Scoil Treasa Naofa)**
Donore Avenue
South Circular Road
Dublin 8
Ireland

Chapter Seven

**Natural Pure Water Association
Secretary**
12 Dennington Lane
Crigglestone
Wakefield WF4 3ET
England
Tel.: 01924 254 433

The Live Water Trust
School House
Brookthorpe
Gloucestershire GL4 OUJ
England
Tel.: *44 (0)1452 814 054

Chapter Eight

**Douglas Cross BSc. Med.
C.Biol. Ml Biol.**
Forensic Ecologist
Farthings
Payhembury
Honiton EX14 OHJ,
Devon
England
Tel.: *44 (0)18847 627

**Danny Brown
Chairman
Lough Neagh and Maine System
Game Angling Association**
11 Repulse Court
Antrim BT41 4HU
Northern Ireland
Tel.: *44 (0)18491 461 767

Chapter Nine

**Centre for Alternative
Technology (CAT)**
Machynlleth
Powys SY20 9AZ
Wales
UK
Tel.: *44 (0)1654 702 400
Fax.: *44 (0)1654 702 782

**Marcus McCabe
Reedbed Sewerage**
The Ark Permaculture Project
Burdautien
Clones
Co. Monaghan
Ireland
Tel.: *047 52049

**Rural Integrated Development
Organisation**
Sevagram
Morappur 635305
Dharmapuri Dt.
Tamil Nadu
India
Tel.: *04346 43 367

Living Machine
Findhorn Foundation
The Park
Forres IV36 OTZ
Scotland
Tel.: *44 (0)1309 690 311
Fax.: *44 (0)1309 691 301

Water Aid
Prince Consort House
27–29 Albert Embankment
London SE1 7UB
Tel.: 0171 793 4500
Fax.: 0171 793 4545

Chapter Ten

**The Guild of Vibrational
Medicine (Diploma Course)**
Waveney Lodge
Hoxney
Suffolk IP21 4AS
England
Tel.: *44 (0)1379 642 374
Fax.: *44 (0)1379 642 374

Healing Herbs
P.O. Box 65
Hereford HR2 OUW
England
Tel.: 44 01873 890 218

**Ainsworth's Homoeopathic
Pharmacy**
38 New Cavendish Street
London W1
England
Tel.: *44 (0)171 935 5330

**The Irish Council of
Vibrational Medicine**
c/o The Ogham Apothecary
Carlingford
Co. Louth
Ireland
Tel.: *353 (0)42 73793

British Society of Dowsers
Sycamore Barn
Hastingleigh TN25 5HW
Ashford
Kent
England
Tel.:/Fax.: *44 (0)1233 750 253

**Nelson's Homoeopathic
Pharmacy**
15 Duke Street
Dublin 2
Ireland
Tel.: *353 (0)1 6790451

PLAIN Magazine
Center for Plain Living
60805 Pigeon Point
Barnesville
OH 43713
USA

The World Bank
1818 H Street
Washington DC
USA

Chapter Thirteen

The Better Food Company
1 Hobbs Lane
Barrow Gurney BS19 3SU
England
Tel.: 01275 474545
Fax.: 01275 474783

Fresh Food Company
326 Portobello Road
London W10 5RU
England
Tel.: 0181 969 1351
Fax.: 0181 964 8050

**Genetic Resources Action
International (GRAIN)**
Jonqueres 16
08005 Barcelona
Spain
Tel.: *343 3105 909
Fax.: *343 3105 952

Irish Seed Savers' Association
Capparoe
Scariff
Co. Clare
Ireland

Richard Guy's Real Meat Company Ltd.
Warminster BA12 9AZ
England
Tel.: 01985 219020
Fax.: 01985 218950

Heal Farm (for Meats)
Kings Nympton
Umberleigh
Devon EX37 9TB
England
Tel.: 01769 574 341
Fax.: 01769 572 839

Heritage Seed Library
Genetic Resources Department
Henry Doubleday Research
Association
Ryton Organic Gardens
Ryton-on-Dunsmore
CV8 3LG
England
Tel.: 0120 330 3517
Fax.: 0120 330 3517

Seed Savers' Exchange
RFD 2
Princeton
Missouri 64673
USA

Planting Seeds Project
1045 Commercial Drive
Vancouver
British Columbia V5L 3XI
Canada
Tel.: *1 604 255 2326
Fax.: *1 604 255 1788

Organic Trust
Islands
Urlingford
Co. Kilkenny
Ireland
Tel.: *353 (0)5631411

Irish Organic Farmers' and Growers' Association (IOFGA)
56 Blessington Street
Dublin 7
Ireland
Tel.: 353 018307996

Community Supported Agriculture
c/o Robyn Van En
Indian Line Farm
Box 57
Jug End Road
Great Barrington
Massachusetts 01230
USA
Tel.:/Fax.: *1 413 528 4374

Community Land Trust Information
The Institute for Community
Economics
151 Montague City Road
Greenfield, MA 01301
USA
Tel.: *1 413 774 5933

Chapter Fifteen

The Hyperactive Children's Support Group
71 Whyke Lane
Chichester PO19 2LD
England
Tel.: 01903 725 182
Fax.: 01903 734 726

London Food Commission
88 Old Street
London EC1
England

Foresight — The Association for the Promotion of Pre-Conceptual Care
28 The Paddock
Godalming
Surrey GU7 1XD
England

Hyperactivity in Children
Stephanie Mahony
25 Lawnswood Park
Stillorgan
Co. Dublin
Ireland
Tel.: 353 01 2889766

Parents for Safe Food
Britannia House
1/11 Glenthorne Road
London W6
England

Earth Resources Research
258 Pentonville Road
London N1 9JY
England

Pesticides Trust (PEGS)
Eurolink Centre
49 Effra Road
London SW2 1BZ
England
Tel.: 0171 274 8895
Fax.: 0171 274 9084

Right Livelihood Award
P.O. Box 15072
S–10465 Stockholm
Sweden
Tel.: *46 (0)8 7020340
Fax.: *46 (0)8 7020338

Genetic Engineering Network
c/o P.O. Box 9656
London N4 4NL
England
Tel: 0181 374 9516

Greenpeace UK Press Office
Tel.: 0171 865 8255

Rural Advancement Foundation International (RAFI)
71 Bank Street
Suite 504
Ottawa K1P 5N2
Canada
Fax.: *1 613 567 6884

Peasants Revolt Against Genetics
England
Tel.: 01273556 397

South Downs Genetic Engineering Network
Tel.: 01273 556 397

Research Foundation for Science, Technology and Ecology
A–60 Hauz Khas
New Delhi – 110 016
India
Tel.: *91 (0)11 696 8077
Fax.: *91 (0)11 685 6795

Global 2000
Bd. Brand Whitlock 146
120 Brussels
Belgium
Fax.: *322 733 5708

Genetic Concern
Main Street
Scariff
Co. Clare
Tel.: *353 (0)61 921 828
Fax.: *353 (0)61 921 812

Sandro Cafolla
Design by Nature
Crettyard
Co. Carlow
Ireland
Tel.: *353 (0)56 42526

The Anaphyllaxis Campaign
P.O. Box 149
Fleet
Hampshire
England
Tel.: *44 (0)1253 318 723

Park Attwood Clinic
Trimpley
Bewdley
Worchestershire DY12 IRE
England
Tel.: *44 (0)129 986 144

John Chambers Seed Supplier
15 Westleigh Road
Barton Seagrave
Kettering NN15 5AJ
Northamptonshire
England
Tel.: *44 (0)1536 513 748

The Informed Immunisation Network
c/o 74 All Saints Road
Raheny
Dublin 5
Ireland
Tel.: *353 (0)1 832 7287

Dominic Waldron Living Landscapes
Carriglas
Glanlough West
Bantry
Co. Cork
Ireland
Tel.:/Fax.: *353 (0)27 61497

Global Eco-Village Network (GEN)
GEN Europe
Ginsterweg 5
D-31595 Steyerberg
Germany
Tel.: *49 57 64 30 40
Fax.: *49 57 64 23 68

Home-schooling
World-wide Education Service
35 Belgrave Square
London SW1X 8QB
England
Tel.: *44 (0)171 235 2880

Crystal Waters Permaculture Village
Near Maleny
Queensland
Australia

The Natural Death Centre
20 Heber Road
London NW2 6AA
England
Tel.: *44 (0)181 208 1853
Fax.: *44 (0)181 452 6434

JAK No-Interest Banking
Inger Marie Ebbesen
Thorsovej 92
Grolsted
8882 Fårvang
Denmark
Tel.: *45 86871095

Irish Eco-Village Information Network IEVIN
c/o Mieke & Stephan Wik
Streamstown
Westport
Co. Mayo
Ireland
Tel.: *353 (0)98 28423

The British Permaculture Association
P.O. Box 1
Buckfastleigh
Devon TQ11 OLH
England

**Non-Demonational Rituals
from Turning Point**
23 Crofton Road
Dun Laoghaire
Co. Dublin
Ireland
Tel.: *353 (0)1 2800626
Fax.: *353 (0)1 2800643

Plants for a Future
The Field
Penpol

Lostwithiel
Cornwall PL220NG
England
Tel.: *44 (0)1208 873 554

Chapter Seventeen

**The Wirral Holistic Care
Services**
Tel.: *44 (0)151 604 7316

SUGGESTED FURTHER READING

About Wild Food & Herbal Medicine — and Self-help and Confidence

Bartram, Thomas, *Encyclopedia of Herbal Medicine*, Dorset, England: Grace Publishers 1995

Davies, Dr Stephen & Stewart, Dr Alan, *Nutritional Medicine*, London: Pan Books 1987

Fern, Ken, *Plants for a Future*, Clanfield, Hants: Permanent Publications 1997

Hoad, Judith, *Healing with Herbs*, Dublin: Gill & Macmillan 1996

Kourik, Robert, *Designing and Maintaining Your Edible Landscape, Naturally*, Santa Rosa 1986

Mabey, Richard, *Food for Free*, Glasgow: Fontana/Collins 1972

Madden, Patrick, *Go Wild at School*, School Wildlife Garden Association, Scoil Treasa Naofa, Donore Avenue, S. Circular Road, Dublin 1995

Phillips, Roger, *Wild Food*, London: Pan Books 1983

About Appropriate Technology — and how we can redesign our homes

Norton, John, *Building with Earth*, London: Intermediate Technology Publication 1997

Winblad, Uno & Kilama, Wen *Sanitation Without Water*, London: Macmillan Education Ltd.

Yaron, Gil, Forbes Irving, Tani & Jansson, Sven, *Solar Energy for Rural Communities*, London: Intermediate Technology Publications

About Subtle Energies, Water, Crystals and Essences — sources and how-to

Barnard, Julian & Martine, *The Healing Herbs of Edward Bach*, Hereford: Bach Educational Programme 1988

Coats, Callum, *Living Energies*, Bath: Gateway Books 1996

Elliott, J. Scott, *Dowsing One Man's Way*, London: Sphere Books Ltd 1997

Gerber MD, Richard, *Vibrational Medicine*, Santa Fe, Mexico: Bear & Company 1988

Melody, *Love is in the Earth*, Colorado: Earth-Love Publishing House 1995

Titchener, Rose, Monk, Sue, Potter, Rosemary & Staines, Patricia, *New Vibrational Flower Essences of Britain and Ireland*, Suffolk, England: Waterlily Books 1997

About Subtle Energies

Edwards, Lawrence, *Vortex of Life: Nature's Patterns in Space and Time*, Edinburgh: Floris Books 1993

About Life Changes

Pilger, John, *Hidden Agendas*, Vintage/Random House 1998
About Wild Food and Herbal Medicine

Fukuoka, Masanobu, *The One Straw Revolution*, Goa, India: The Other India Press

About Appropriate Technologies

'Hemp Times' Magazine, The Hemp Company of America, PO Box 460, Mount Morris IL 61054, USA

Rowlac, John W., *Hemp Horizons*, Whiteriver, Vermont: Chelsea Green Publishing Co.

Herer, Jack and Osborne, Judy, *The Emperor Wears No Clothes: The Authoritative Historical Record of Cannabis and the Conspiracy Against Marijuana*, 11 ed., USA: AH HA Publishing Co. 1998

Fiction — to encourage us to possible futures

Hunger, Bill, *Clearcut*, Charlottesville, VA: Hampton Books Publishing Co. Inc. 1996
Miller Jr., Walter M., *A Canticle for Leibowitz*, US: Orbitt 1996
Seuss, Dr, *The Lorax*, London: William Collins & Co. Ltd 1972
Starhawk, *The Fifth Sacred Thing*, New York: HarperCollins 1993

About Different Cultures — to see life in new ways

Berry, Wendell, *What are People for?*, New York: North Point Press 1990
Drake-Terry, Joanne, *The Same as Yesterday*, Lillooet: Lillooet Tribal Council 1989
Ereira, Alan, *The Heart of the World*, London: Jonathan Cape Ltd 1990
Helena Norberg-Hodge, *Ancient Futures*, US: Rider 1991
Marll Morgan, *Mutant Message Down Under*, New York: Thorsons 1994
Peat, David F., *Blackfoot Physics*, London: Fourth Estate 1995
Somé, Malidoma Patrice, *Of Water and the Spirit*, US: Arkana 1994
Waters, Frank, *Book of the Hopi*, New York: Penguin 1963

About Life Changes — and About Changing Life

Buhner, Stephen Harrod, *Sacred Plant Medicine*, Colorado: Roberts Rinehart Publishers 1996
Callenbach, Ernest, *Living Cheaply With Style*, Berkeley, California: Ronin Publications
Cowan, Eliot, *Plant Spirit Medicine*, Swan Raven & Co. 1995

Dominguez, Joe & Currie, Ann, *Your Money or Your Life*, Penguin

Ekins, Paul, *A New World Order*, London: Routledge 1992

Institute for Community Economics, *Community Land Trusts Handbook*, Greenfield, Massachusetts: Rodale Press 1982

Pilger, John, *Hidden Agendas*, London: Vintage/Random House 1998

Seabrook, Jeremy, *Pioneers of Change Experiments in Creating a Humane Society*, London, Philadelphia: Zed Books 1993

Walsh, Mary Paula, *Living After a Death*, Dublin: Columba Press 1995

About the Politics of Meat — and the challenges to it

O'Toole, Fintan, *Meanwhile Back at the Ranch*, Dublin: Vintage 1995

Vidal, John, *McLibel*, London: Pan 1997

About Food and Medication and how to get it right

Blytham, Joanna, *The Food we Eat*, London: Michael Joseph 1996

Carson, Rachel, *Silent Spring*, US: Penguin 1962

Cook, Judith, *Dirty Water*, London: Unwin Paperbacks 1989

Hanssen, Maruice, *E is for Additives*

Juliet Gellatley, *The Silent Ark*, London: Thorsons 1996

Lang, Dr Tim & Clutterbuck, Dr Charlie, *P is for Pesticides*, London: Ebury Press 1991

Lessell, Dr Colin B., *The World Travellers' Manual of Homoeopathy*, Saffron Walden: The C. W. Daniel Co. Ltd 1993

Scheibner, Dr Viera, *Vaccination*, available from 178 Govetts Leap Road, Blackheath, New South Wales 2785, Australia 1993

Taylor, Joan & Derek ed., *Safe Food Handbook*, London: Ebury Press 1990

Visser, Margaret, *Much Depends on Dinner*, Toronto: Penguin 1986

Walker, Martin J., *Dirty Medicine*, London 1993

Webb, Tony & Lang, Dr Tim, *Food Irradiation, The Facts*, London: Thorsons 1987

About Money, Capitalism and Alternative Economics and self-help

Caufield, Catherine, *Masters of Illusion The World Bank & the Poverty of Nations* London: Macmillan 1996

Doutwaite, Richard, *Short Circuit Strengthening Local Economics for Security in an Unstable World*, Green Books and the Lilliput Press Ltd 1996

Kennedy, Margrit, *Interest and Inflation Free Money*, Steyerberg, Germany: Permakultur Publikationen 1998

About Science and Scientists, information from informed people

Colborn, Theo, Dumanoski, Dianne & Myers, John Peterson, *Our Stolen Future*, New York: Dutton/Penguin 1996

Ho, Dr Mae-Wen, *Genetic Engineering Dream or Nightmare?* Bath: Gateway Books 1998

Schiff, Michael, *The Memory of Water* London: Thorsons 1995

Steingraten, Sandra, *Living Downstream: An Ecologist Looks at Cancer and the Environment*, US: Addison-Westey 1997

INDEX